Greenlit

Developing Factual/Reality TV Ideas from Concept to Pitch

Nicola Lees

methuen | drama

Methuen Drama

1 3 5 7 9 10 8 6 4 2

First published in 2010

Methuen Drama
A & C Black Publishers Ltd
36 Soho Square
London W1D 3QY
www.methuendrama.com

A CIP catalogue record for this book is available from the British Library

ISBN: 978 1 408 12267 9

Typeset by Margaret Brain
Printed and bound in Great Britain by Martins The Printers, Berwick-upon-Tweed

Contents

Appendices

To everyone I've ever worked with in development:
you taught me all I know.

Acknowledgments

This book would not have been possible without the goodwill and co-operation of many people to whom I will be eternally grateful, in particular everyone who gave up their time to be interviewed, some on more than one occasion.

I'd also like to thank Samantha Williams, Charlie Phillips, and Hussain Currimbhoy for making introductions, and Sarah Winter and Hannah Wythe for their production management advice.

Alice Borrelli, Andrea Paterson, Natalia Quintana, Fernanda Rossi, Mike Slee, and Elle Tracy all gave extraordinarily detailed feedback on an early draft and their insights and suggestions proved invaluable.

I wouldn't have settled into writing the first draft without the use of a sofa at the Edit Center, NYC; and couldn't have continued writing without the caffeine and comfort food provided by Danny, Steve, Lou, Kerry, and Analese at Tina, we salute you, London.

The results of all this hard work would be still sitting in a drawer if it weren't for my lovely literary agent Jennifer Christie at Graham Maw Christie, copyeditor Chris Parker, and all at A&C Black, especially Jenny Ridout, Suzi Williamson, and Inderjeet Garcha.

And last, but not least, I'd like to thank Stiggy for providing the competition (and losing).

In Bed with the Commissioners

Episodes:	12x30'		
Channel:	Methuen Drama	**Delivery:**	February 2012
Executive Producer:	Nicola Lees	**Contact:**	info@tvmole.com

TV Insiders Reveal How to Get Your Factual TV Program Commissioned

This series shows you how to take an idea for a factual or reality television show such as *Supernanny, Deadliest Catch* or *The Apprentice* from **concept to commission**. Over twelve episodes, it gives you a **step-by-step guide** to **originating, developing, and pitching** your ideas to **TV channels at home and abroad**.

Each episode offers **practical tools and troubleshooting advice**, interwoven with **case studies** that show how internationally known and award-winning programs were developed. **Interviews with top industry professionals**—producers, commissioners, and agents—reveal the lengths they've gone to in order to get their programs commissioned:

* John Smithson (Darlow Smithson) took **more than two years to obtain the rights** to a book called *Touching the Void*. It went on to be the most successful feature-length documentary in UK history.

* Thom Beers (Original Productions) **risked life and limb** in the worst storms in thirty years to film aboard an Alaskan crab fishing boat for a documentary special. He explains how he turned that footage into *The Deadliest Catch*.

* It took Alex Graham (Wall to Wall) **more than a decade to sell** a show on family history. *Who Do You Think You Are?* is now a BAFTA-nominated show that is seen around the world.

Experienced producers explain how they **generate ideas, write a compelling proposal, find talent, produce a pitch tape, and sell program ideas to**

domestic and international broadcasters. Viewers learn the importance of: having the right aptitude; understanding the TV landscape; multiplatform content; and alternative funding. And we expose the embarrassing mistakes that producers consistently make when pitching their shows.

This series is **a unique guide** for television producers, independent filmmakers and media students who want to get their ideas on TV; it provides **a master class** for the novice show creator, while more experienced producers can dip in and out for a refresher course.

Nicola Lees has developed hundreds of factual programs for network and cable channels in the UK and USA, including the BBC, Discovery Channel, Travel Channel, and TLC. She has written more than 300 factual television pro-gramme proposals, and has been directly involved in researching, writing, or pitching more than eighty commissioned programs, including RTS History Award winner *The Guinea Pig Club* and BAFTA-nominated *Earth: Power of the Planet*.

If I were pitching this book as a TV show, this is how the proposal might look. NB: as a program concept it needs some work.

Illustrations

Style Note

There are several terms used in the international television market that sometimes have similar meanings and sometimes mean something quite different. Throughout this book I use the term most pertinent to the territory to which it refers; I also provide alternative terms where appropriate so you won't get tripped up by an unfamiliar term in a meeting with a foreign buyer.

"Factual" refers to TV programs that are unscripted, also variously known as: documentary, alternative, reality, and even "unscripted drama."

I use "commissioner/commissioning executive/commissioning editor" to refer to UK TV channel executives in charge of buying new programs and "channel executive" to refer to US buyers (who are also known as development executives, a title that is also used in the industry for those people developing and pitching ideas, and therefore too confusing to use in the context of this book). "Buyer" is the term commonly used in the context of festivals and conferences, where it refers to channel executives/commissioners, distributors, and other funders. When talking generally I use "channel executive."

I use "development producer" as a catch-all for anyone originating, developing, and pitching program ideas; they could be researchers, assistant/associate producers, directors, or executive producers working in development or on a production.

For onscreen talent I use "host" when referring to American programs and "presenter" for UK programs and "talent" when talking generally.

Program details are given for first transmission: number of episodes x duration in minutes (e.g. 6x30') and channel. A full filmography with links to individual program websites (where available) can be found at http://www.tvmole.com/ 2010/01/greenlit-filmography/. Budgets are given in £(GBP) and $(USD) as appropriate.

Introduction

> *How do you develop ideas for television? It's bloody difficult.*
>
> —Ben Hall, Managing Director, Shine Network

The first idea that I pitched, a documentary called *The Guinea Pig Club*, was commissioned (verbally, at least) within a week of its conception. At the time I was a junior researcher working in my first development job at the BBC; little did I know that it would never be so quick and easy again. At best, fewer than one in one hundred unsolicited ideas are given a second look; one commissioner estimated that fewer than one proposal in a thousand gets commissioned. Of those ideas that do manage to catch a buyer's eye, most take months or years to get the final greenlight for production.

It turns out that I had, in my first ever pitch, stumbled upon some of the secret principles of successful development and pitching. I say secret, because since then, I've never heard anyone fully explain how the TV development and commissioning process works. In *Greenlit* I reveal those secrets. I want to share with you what I've learned over the past decade in the hope that you don't make the same mistakes that I did. This is the book I wish someone had given me when I first started out. It would have saved me a lot of confusion and frustration; it would certainly have helped me better understand the TV business.

Getting a factual TV idea commissioned is akin to getting all the planets aligned. If that makes you feel daunted, you're in good company. Until I started researching this book I imagined I was the only person who had struggled to understand the system. Why did the same producers seem to get all the commissions? Why did great ideas get turned down, when mediocre ones were commissioned? How do you get anyone to take notice of your idea if you're not "in the club"? What on earth is going through the commissioner's mind? Surprisingly, the experienced development producers that I interviewed also confessed to being baffled (and that was with a combined experience of nigh on thirty-five years); this book makes things clearer, whatever your level of experience.

Greenlit focuses purely on how to develop factual programming (also known as nonfiction, reality, or alternative programming in the USA). The range of factual programs on television is vast, encompassing subjects such as biography, wildlife, survival, health, business, lifestyle, food, exploration, anthropology, science, religion, and history. These subjects are presented in a variety of formats including: one-off documentary, docudrama, fly-on-the-wall, lightly constructed formats, heavily constructed formats, and competition reality shows, to name a few. (Game shows are a specialized genre and beyond the scope of this book.)

To find out exactly what it takes to get nonfiction TV programs commissioned, I interviewed more than fifty industry professionals from seven countries and four continents, including development producers, channel executives, and big-name international producers. They represent commercial and public service broadcasters, network and cable channels and span the world of factual TV production from competition reality programs to feature-length documentaries. Interviewees were selected because they are widely respected within the industry and have originated, developed, pitched, or commissioned award-winning and internationally successful programs. Interviewees were asked to speak candidly about their experiences, and they exceeded my expectations; some people, however, participated only on the understanding that they could remain anonymous (some feared for their job, others feared the wrath of their company's PR department). I respected their wishes: I preferred that people could speak honestly. I am grateful to everyone who generously gave their time to share their experiences.

To illustrate the various principles of development best practice, I've included detailed case studies of internationally recognized programs; some are included to show that, sometimes, you have to break the rules to get what you want. While talking to several people about the origins of a particular program idea, it became apparent that time and memory had clouded the exact recollection of events. As most of the examples in this book are programs that were originally developed and pitched a number of years ago it is fair to assume that other people involved in their development might remember different details; therefore, the accounts you read here are one version of events, intended to be illustrative rather than a forensic blow-by-blow account of the genesis of an idea.

It became apparent that TV channel executives are all looking for the same thing: a breakout hit show that will bring in good audience numbers and keep them in their job. They all share the same frustrations: a daily avalanche of inappropriate, ill-conceived ideas, rambling proposals, and unfocused pitches from unknown producers. Do they tell the hapless producers pitching these ill-formed ideas that they're way off mark? No. Why not? Because they're nice people and don't want to hurt a producer's feelings.

For the first time, you'll learn what channel executives *really* think about producers and their ideas, and get their advice on what to do—and not do—if you want to get *your* factual TV ideas commissioned. I'll give you all the tips, tricks, and insider knowledge you need to get ahead—whether you are trying to break into the domestic TV industry or are pitching ideas at an international level.

So, what do you need to get your great idea off the ground? You need passion, guts, determination, and a thick skin. And it helps if you don't mind rejection. Repeated rejection. But to have a chance of getting your factual idea commissioned, you also need an idea that:

is more than a subject area—it needs a story with engaging characters, obstacles to be overcome, transformations to be made, or unique insights to be revealed; **has universal appeal for a network**; or at least universal appeal within a niche channel; **is "big," "fresh," "noisy," and "exciting"** enough to appeal to channel executives, but not so big fresh, noisy, and exciting that it scares them away; **looks similar, but not too similar, to a recent runaway success; looks nothing like a show that recently failed to draw an audience; is presented in a proven format** that the audience wants to watch, week after week, season after season; **has an audience that the advertisers want to capture; has a killer title, and a one-page outline; has established and successful talent attached** to the idea; failing that, new onscreen talent that the channel can build future programs around; **has a pitch tape that looks like the finished show**, or showcases the wide-ranging talents of your inexperienced new host but costs nothing to make; **can be pitched in one line** in a corridor or conference bar; **looks glossy and expensive**, but can be made on a shoestring; **has someone to pitch it who knows how to tell a good story**, and knows when to shut up; **has an executive producer with an outstanding track record** of producing similar programs that attracted vast audiences, industry awards, and critical acclaim; and last but not least: **a commissioning executive who got out of the right side of the bed** that morning and still has money in their budget to spend.

Easy, right? No, of course not. But it will be easier once you've worked your way though this book and understand how the business works. It takes many years to build the experience and contacts that you need to be a major player in the industry, but if you start out with a clear vision of what you need to do, building your development skills as you go along, by the time you find yourself in a meeting with a commissioner you will present your ideas professionally and with confidence. If you already have plenty of production experience behind you and want to start pitching your own ideas, this book turbocharges your chances of success.

Each chapter explains a different step in the development and commissioning process:

* developing the right mindset;

* understanding the TV market;

* generating new ideas;

* finding the best story and program format;

* adding multiplatform content;

* writing a proposal;

* talent spotting;

* producing a pitch tape;

* pitching;

* alternative sources of funding; and

* getting the greenlight.

At the end of each chapter you'll find a list of tasks that will help you to jumpstart or fine-tune your skills and some useful resources* for you to explore. There are sample proposals, ballpark channel budgets, and a program budget outline in the Appendices. Although the development and commissioning process is laid out in a step-by-step fashion, development of an idea is not always linear. Read the book through once to get a good overview, and then dip in and out of various chapters as necessary for each new project.

Whatever your level of experience this book is for you if:

* **You are looking for your first job in television**—every employer will expect you to bring ideas to your interview.

* **You want to pitch ideas to an independent production company's development team**—find out how to present your idea so it gets noticed and you stay attached to it.

* **You are working in a development team for the first time and feel overwhelmed by the scale of the challenge**—you will be guided through the process of making your proposal bullet-proof.

* **You run a development team but you don't have time to train everyone from scratch**—give them a copy of this book and they'll start contributing immediately.

* **You are an executive producer pitching your ideas for the first time**—even experienced producers can find the pitching process brutal and soul-destroying. Learn what to expect and how to come out smiling.

* **You are the head of an independent production company looking to expand your business by selling your programs internationally or find co-production money for your shows**—find out how to make your programs appeal to foreign buyers and avoid being tripped up by cultural differences in the pitching process.

* **You run a digital agency and have been working with independent production companies on their multiplatform ideas**—you've got some TV

*Links to recommended resources can be found at www.tvmole.com/2009/12/greenlitbookresources.

ideas that you'd like to pitch. Find out how to make sure the TV channel executives take you seriously.

* **You are an independent filmmaker**—you might not aspire to get your ideas on TV but you will still need to raise the money to make your films. The principles for pitching (and sometimes the buyers) are the same.

Although development is a protracted and intensely frustrating process, it is also fun, intellectually stimulating, exhilarating, and, for the lucky few, extremely lucrative. It's a specialty within TV that draws a certain type of producer, one that thrives in a stressful, fast-paced, highly competitive environment. If you think that might be you, let's explore the world of development a little more, with an introduction to how development teams and channel commissioning teams are structured.

CASE STUDY
The Guinea Pig Club (1x60´ BBC4)

I was working as a researcher for the BBC's in-house Science Department development team and spent all of my time writing proposals for other people's ideas. It was not long after 9/11 and the start of the "war on terror" and I had been thinking about how war can drive medical innovation, such as the treatment of burns.

One day, when everyone else was out of the office, Emma Swain, the specialist factual commissioner, popped her head in the door to speak to my boss. I saw my chance and asked her if she'd be interested in a program about war and medicine. "No," she said, as she left the room. "That's too niche, I need something more specific."

That's a bit contradictory, I thought. But then I got it: she wanted to get at the wider issue through a more human story to which everyone could relate. That turned out to be some of the best advice I was ever given.

I started typing in some keywords to Amazon.co.uk and soon came across a book called *McIndoe's Army: The Story of the Guinea Pig Club and Its Indomitable Members*, by Edward Bishop. It told the story of a group of young WWII airmen who sustained horrifying facial burns after being shot down over the English Channel. They survived to become human guinea pigs for some of the world's first plastic surgery techniques. They had been treated at a small cottage hospital, in East Grinstead, Surrey, UK, so I called their press officer to see if I could find out more.

She told me that the Guinea Pigs, as they are still known, were holding an open day on the following Monday and she invited me down to meet them. The next day, I did some more Internet research and wrote a one-page draft proposal.

When I meet the Guinea Pigs, a few days later, they were charming and full of great anecdotes; I was convinced that their story would make a fantastic documentary. I looked around the small museum dedicated to the Guinea Pigs and got copies of photographs showing the Guinea Pigs before and after surgery.

Back in the office, I tweaked the proposal to include the stories I'd heard on my recce and added a photograph of the Guinea Pigs.

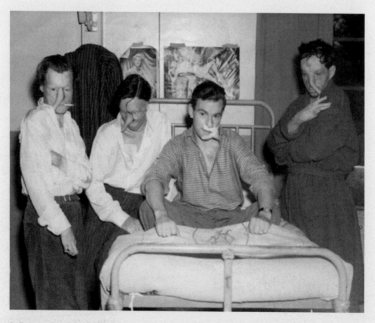

© Guinea Pig Club and Queen Victoria Hospital NHS Foundation Trust

A couple of days later we had a routine development meeting with our commissioner, Emma Swain. She still remembers the proposal: "It was very short, it was a quick read; had a good title that made me want to know more. I remember it had a good picture on it: a really arresting image—there was some extraordinary skin graft surgery in the image. I do remember that, and it's a long time ago!

"It was a well-written, clear story: this is what we're going to do, this is what the film is going to be like, and this is why it's important to make the film—because it *was* extraordinary, and it *was* a breakthrough.

"It was a mixture of powerful information and personal experience, and there were people who were going to tell you about it from their firsthand experience rather than just experts. It seemed to me to be a story that hadn't been told, or hadn't been told in that way before.

"It felt like a good subject for a film—it had all of the ingredients and it would make sixty minutes of strong television, not forty minutes."

Emma bought into the idea in that first pitch meeting, although I later wrote a longer proposal including reference to modern-day plastic surgery in order to secure the commission.

The Guinea Pig Club was shown on BBC4 (and later on BBC2), and TLC in the USA. It won the RTS History Award.

Development Master Class: Introduction

Key Principles

1. In the *Guinea Pig Club* case study, above, there are (at least) thirteen key principles of development that make success more likely. Can you spot them?[1]

2. I also made one potentially commission-killing mistake. What is it?[2]

Explore More

If you are interested in learning how other producers have successfully developed and pitched their ideas, read:

Peter Bazalgette: *Billion Dollar Game: How Three Men Risked It All and Changed Television*
The story of *Who Wants to Be a Millionaire, Big Brother,* and *Survivor* from the producer of *Ready Steady Cook* and *Changing Rooms.*

Bill Carter: *Desperate Networks*
An account of the LA TV industry over an eventful season in 2004–05, when hopeful producers were pitching programs such as *The Apprentice, American Idol,* and *Survivor*—and were all turned down.

Michael Essany: *Reality Check: The Business and Art of Producing Reality TV*
The former E! Channel talk show host describes how he launched his first show, aged thirteen, and explains how he turned his small fry cable access series into an internationally syndicated program.

---

1. **Principles of good development:** a blue-chip production team; regular contact with the commissioner; pitching ideas congruent with production team skills; responding positively to negative feedback; using a range of resources—internet, telephone and face-to-face interview—to find a unique story; securing the consent and trust of potential contributors; acting with a sense of urgency to catch one-off opportunities; writing a one-page proposal; using arresting images to illustrate the pitch; describing compelling characters; outlining the story arc; describing the approach—the different components of the film; demonstrating that there was enough rich content to fill the time.
2. **The mistake:** originally pitching a subject area instead of a program idea.

Iikka Vehkalahti and Don Edkins: *Steps by Steps*
A step-by-step account of how an international documentary project featuring thirty-eight films about HIV and AIDS in southern Africa was conceived, developed, and realized.

1 Welcome to Development Hell (A.K.A. What the Hell Is Development?)

Can't you just develop the ideas that will get commissioned?

—Executive Producer (Anon.)

A couple of years ago, I saw a video of a creative session held at a big UK broadcaster: the kind of session that reassures senior managers that their organization is on the creative cutting edge. The video showcased all the programs that creative facilitators had helped through the "development" process, but the clips were from programs already in production (some had been on air for years). Whatever the creative facilitators were doing it wasn't program development. For a moment I was baffled, and then I had a revelation: few people understand what program development is.

So what is it?

The development process starts when you have an idea and it stops when a TV channel has agreed the budget and editorial content and has given the project the greenlight to go into production. Before any program, let alone an international hit such as *Deadliest Catch*, *American Idol*, *Planet Earth*, or *Supernanny*, hits our television screens it has probably spent months, if not years, in development; being turned from a vague concept into a workable format. Before it reaches the pitch stage, an idea needs a clear narrative, suitable talent (a presenter or host) attached, access secured, a proposal written, and a pitch tape shot.

However, the development process doesn't always happen in that order: your starting point might be onscreen talent for whom you have to find a format; a blank page with a tight deadline; or sometimes even a commission. Often, you will make a taster tape, other times not; mostly you will pitch in a formal meeting, but you might find yourself pitching in a corridor; you need to write a proposal but it may never be read. And the program that ends up on screen will be different from the one you pitch, and may be unrecognizable from your original idea.

Everyone believes that to be successful in development you have to have good ideas, but the truth is that development is not just about coming up with good ideas. It's about market forces, audience trends, and channel executives' foibles. Development is about more than mere creativity. "It's about the timing, your relationships with the commissioners, it's about being one of the 'in' companies," says one development producer. "It's about getting past commissioners' PAs and being able to convince them to meet you. It's about being able to cater to what that channel wants, and it's not always about how good your idea is." Development is, in other words, all about the politics.

Independent production companies survive by selling ideas and TV broad-casters wouldn't exist without a ready supply of programs—so who are the people who are keeping the TV business alive?

Who's Who in Development?

Most independent TV production companies dedicate staff to the develop-ment of new program ideas (some TV channels also have an in-house development team); in a small company it might be one person, or in a larger company it's more likely to be a team of people. The team is lead by a head of development who reports to the company's creative director, managing director, or CEO (every company uses different titles). Working under the head of develop-ment is a team of producers, assistant/associate producers, and researchers. The team members might work individually (in their own specialisms, such as science or history) or together as a team. Team members regularly pitch their ideas to the head of development, who decides which ones should be developed further. The head of development then pitches those ideas to the head of the company, who decides which of those ideas should be pitched to the TV channels. In some companies the head of development conducts meetings with the channels, in other companies the managing director pitches the ideas. The executive or series producer penciled in to make the program may or may not be involved in the development and pitching process.

In a well-run team everything should run relatively smoothly with well-targeted ideas being developed, pitched, and commissioned on a regular basis but, inevitably, it's not that simple. Staff turnover in development can be high and the people charged with coming up with the next big idea are often the least knowledgeable about how the business works. "I just thought it would be that I would have a good idea and develop it a bit and then it would be commissioned," says one producer/director. "I really did think it would be as straightforward as that: I was very naïve!"

Development is a discipline that requires an in-depth knowledge of the industry. As most programs take many months to go from idea to commission, the people with the best chance of success are those who have strong, on-going relationships with the channel executives: their potential buyers. In other words, to be successful you need to be committed over the long term.

Development also requires a set of skills that are distinct from those of production. It can be hard for production people to get into the unique mindset needed for development—selling rather than making—and many find it immensely frustrating. One experienced producer/director who made technically difficult and emotionally demanding medical series said, "Development is the hardest job I've ever done," before fleeing back to the safety of production.

Filmmakers—understandably—want to make programs about issues they are passionate about, and channel executives want high audience figures in order to attract advertisers (read: funding). Unfortunately passion projects aren't always ratings winners, therefore, development producers have to balance pitching ideas they love with those they think will sell; alas, they will not always be the same thing.

Who's Who at the Channels?

Once an idea has attracted initial interest from a channel executive, the idea enters the channel's development process. Channels all have different development and commissioning structures. At some, particularly in the UK, network commissioners have their own budget and look after a specialty, for example, daytime or specialist factual (science, history, arts, religion, natural history) programs. They make a decision about whether your proposal fits their brief, and if so, work on it with you until they are happy to formally commission it (usually after they've obtained a confirmatory "twin tick" from their channel controller).

At other channels, particularly US cable channels, a team of channel executives (usually known as VPs/development), filter all the proposals that come into their office. The channel executives are the vital link between you and the people with the power and money to greenlight or reject your idea. They individually take pitches from producers and then pitch the ideas they like to the rest of their team on a weekly basis. As a team, they decide which ideas to pitch to the channel head and other senior decision-making executives, such as the scheduler and business affairs executive, at a regular commissioning or "greenlight" meeting. It's a competitive environment and an individual executive's reputation rests on pitching the most attention-grabbing idea, so they have to make sure that every idea is properly developed before they expose themselves to the gladiatorial arena of the channel pitch meeting. The senior executives are unlikely to have read your written proposal so your fortune rests on the shoulders of your channel development executive.

Cultivating a good relationship with a channel executive is the single most important thing you can do, and the more important they are in the channel hierarchy the better. "The truth of it is: once you've got a good idea, it's all about knowing the right people at the channel or you won't close the sale," says Ed Crick, Managing Director, Bullseye (and former director of development, TLC). But it can be hard to keep track of the channel executives, as commissioning can seem like one long round of musical chairs. "It pisses me off, how one minute you'll see [a commissioner] at a briefing and they're so committed to their channel," says a UK-based development producer, "and then two weeks later you see they've gone to a different channel, and you think hold on, where's your loyalty?"

As you'll find out, this tension between development producers and channel executives is never far from the surface. "TV is a funny industry in that no one is sure who has the higher status," observes filmmaker Adam Curtis. "The producers think they have more dignity than those who commission, but to be brutal, over the last ten years the commissioners have proved to be more creative than a lot of the producers."

The Commissioning Chain

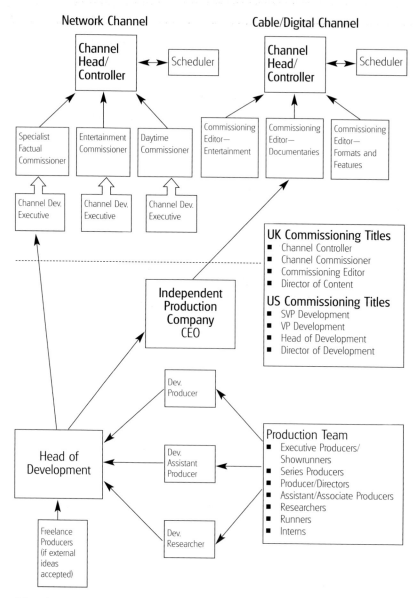

Follow the arrows to see the path that an idea might take through an independent production company development team and channel commissioning structure in order to reach the person who can ultimately give it the greenlight. NB: every channel is structured differently and has different titles for similar jobs.

Development Master Class 1

Know Who's Who

1. Google the names of the channel head/controller of your five favorite channels.

2. Go to the channel websites and find out who the commissioning/ development executives are in the genre of programming that most interests you.

3. Sign up for the weekly newsletter at www.tvmole.com to keep up to date with who is in and who is out in the world of development and commissioning.

4. Start a contacts book or online database. Become familiar with the names of people working in independent production company development teams or in the channel commissioning structure. Update your database every time they move jobs so you can keep track of who's who.

5. Join a professional association and start networking with senior people in the industry. For example, Women in Film and Television has more than 10,000 members in forty chapters around the world.

Explore More

Visit tvmole.com to see who currently works where in commissioning and development in the UK and USA:

* for heads of development at independent production companies: http://tiny.cc/headdev;

* for channel executives at channels in the UK and USA, visit: http://tiny.cc/channelcommissioners.

2 Do You Have What It Takes?

You're obviously suffering from delusions of adequacy!
—Alexis Carrington, *Dynasty*

When Mark Burnett was a British paratrooper fighting for his country in the Falklands War it would have seemed implausible that one day he would wind up working as a nanny in Beverley Hills and then selling $18 T-shirts on Venice Beach, LA. It would have seemed even more improbable that, fewer than twenty years later, he would have a reported net worth of around $300 million. How did he go from beach bum to multimillionaire? By selling TV programs.

Mark Burnett, award-winning US producer of *Survivor, The Apprentice*, and *Are You Smarter than a Fifth Grader?*, is one of the world's most successful TV producers, and has been named as one of *Time* magazine's "100 Most Influential People in the World Today." He's so prolific—having produced more than 1,100 hours of television, which air in more than seventy countries—that he is the first reality producer to receive a star on Hollywood's Walk of Fame. Tellingly, he's not just won TV industry awards, but also won *Brandweek*'s Marketer of the Year award.

In 1993, Burnett, thirty-three years old and fresh out of the army, satisfied his taste for adventure by participating with an American team in an extreme race called Raid Gauloises in Oman. The race involved traveling in teams of five over hundreds of miles by camel, horse, and on foot. This trip started a journey that led to Burnett being credited with creating one of the most watched television shows of all time, which regularly pulled in more than twenty million viewers.

At first glance, it seems that nothing in Burnett's background predicted his television success, but in fact everything he did foreshadowed it. When working in the army he learned to make decisions under pressure; while working as a nanny he was exposed to influential people and when selling his T-shirts he developed a talent for pitching for business. Burnett also found time to work in insurance and had a credit card marketing business, which taught him about demographics and consumer attitudes. He'd also raised sponsorship that helped turn his Raid Gauloises adventure into a series of extreme adventure competition television programs called *Eco-Challenge*.

Taken separately, this seems like a disparate set of skills, but together they prepared him to pitch an idea for a new television show to CBS.* Burnett suggested putting sixteen strangers on a desert island, dividing them into two tribes, and letting them compete for rewards such as fishing gear, blankets, or a spa treatment and immunity against being voted off the island. The last one remaining would win $1 million, and the show would be called *Survivor*.

Burnett won the pitch and much, much more. In addition to the estimated $10 million that he picked up for the first series in 2000, and the nearly $1 million per episode license fee he negotiated for the second series (it's now reached its twenty-first season), he has since won two Emmys, and his company has received fifty-five award nominations.

Anyone can have ideas, but not everyone has the skills, knowledge, and determination necessary to turn those ideas into commissions. You might think you are an "ideas person" but having an idea for a TV program is just the start of a long commercial process. To successfully generate and pitch ideas you need to be creative, have market knowledge and copywriting skills, be able to spot potential onscreen talent, build long-term relationships and—perhaps above all—be tenacious and unafraid of rejection.

Don't worry if you don't think you have a natural aptitude; in this chapter you'll learn how to strengthen your weak areas.

*British producer Charlie Parsons originally created *Survivor* and sold the US rights to Mark Burnett.

Qualities of a Successful Development Producer

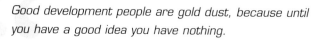

Good development people are gold dust, because until you have a good idea you have nothing.

—Keith Scholey, Big Cat Ltd.

Anyone can buy a cheap camera, edit footage, and upload their work online, but if you want to get paid for producing content treat development as a business. To succeed in a creative commercial environment you need most of, if not all, the following qualities and skills. Some are innate, some can be learned and others come through hard work and practice: life experience; production knowledge; social skills; team spirit; integrity; original thinking; journalistic instincts; story awareness; analysis, writing, and customer service skills; patience and resilience.

Life Experience

Some of the most interesting people working in television have also worked out in the "real world." They bring a sense of perspective and maturity to the job not often demonstrated by graduates fresh out of media school. If you've had a previous career, your experience gives you an advantage in TV development, as you have a unique take on the world.

Being an expert in your field is one way to get yourself noticed, but it's not enough on its own. "It's fun to have people who are phenomenal experts," says Tom Archer, Controller of Factual Production, BBC, "but they are much more of a luxury and you probably want to play them in at a particular moment," when a specialized program is in development. In order to keep yourself employed long term, be versatile enough to generate all kinds of ideas, not just those related to your niche. "Having a specialism is great but having a wide variety of experience gives you creative freedom," says one development producer. Take time to develop your expertise before meeting with TV executives and you will stand out from all the media wannabes.

CASE STUDY

Dr. Barry J. Gibb, Filmmaker

"I graduated in biochemistry in Dundee and was absolutely convinced I was going to be a scientist. I did eight years of post-doctoral research on neuroscience but I was always interested in more creative ways of portraying science.

"I decided to make documentaries, because there is no barrier to making a documentary, other than having a camera. Even if you can't edit you can always film stuff. And so that was when I realized documentary was my form and was what I wanted to do.

"It got a little more ambitious and a little more ambitious; all of this time I was practicing editing too. I approached the British Association for the Advancement of Science and I effectively begged them to let me make a film for them about stem cell research. That was my first foray into making something for an audience, although I only got a nominal fee.

"There wasn't a brief, and in those days my idea of a documentary was— I'm ashamed to admit it now—a series of talking heads. So I thought all I need to do is go out and film a lot of people talking about stem cell research. I funded myself to go to the Centre for Life in Newcastle and I interviewed this guy, who at the time was the biggest name in stem cell research. Instantly it felt like it had some weight to it, an anchor, rather than just a series of talking heads. So I put it together, and it went down really well.

"The British Council approached me because they'd seen *Stem Cells* and they wanted me to make something exactly like that but about climate change, so I did that to commission, and then I thought, 'I can actually make money!' Of course, if that happens in the first month of you going freelance you think, 'I'm going to be rolling in money'—the harsh reality is, it's not like that at all.

"I was making the most of 4docs,* which was brilliant, because there was no filter on it—apart from if what you sent them was so bad it was unscreenable—and you would get good feedback.

*An online channel that allowed anyone to upload their three-minute documentary films for criticism and review. The best were broadcast on Channel 4.

"I did something for the 4docs website, which was about photo-synthesis, called *Photo Synthesis*, which they liked. That was born of frustration: I had been told that botany was one of the most difficult things to teach in school because it's so boring. So I thought, I'm going to make an interesting film about plant life. And they liked it! All I know is that I wasn't trying to please anyone except myself.

"While all that was going on, I was having a bit of a crisis sitting in my bedroom, thinking, 'Am I going to sit here talking about being a filmmaker or am I going to become a filmmaker?' And it's powerful, this little transition: you realize the only way you are going to get people to know about you is to reach out.

"My films have now been shown on Channel 4's *3 Minute Wonder* and Current TV. You make your luck. You definitely make your luck."

Production Knowledge

Few people pursue a career in development without ever having worked in production, but it is not obligatory. "I can show you people who can absolutely deliver a show that is right for the slot, right for the budget and they can take it right the way through to the point at which it is commissionable, and there are other people who can execute that idea better than the first group of people," says Ben Hall, Managing Director, Shine Network. "It's perfectly legitimate to be one or the other. They are definitely different skills."

But the consensus is that it is important for development producers to have some production experience in order to understand what is and isn't possible within a certain timescale and budget. "You should be able to shoot, you should be able to cut, you should be able to spot talent," says Ed Crick. "If you are going to go into broad unscripted factual development—that's from specialist factual to talent-led to ob docs [observational documentaries] to factual entertainment formats—you need those skills. If you are going to be a games designer or a quiz show writer, that's different."

Undoubtedly, it is useful to be able to shoot and edit in order to produce pitch tapes, but there is usually somebody else on the team who has those skills. If you don't have much production experience, don't worry—you can partner with an established producer or production company.

Social Skills

Spend any time talking to anyone in television and they'll tell you that getting in on the business is as much about relationships as anything else. No matter what your other qualities are, if people don't want to work with you, you will get nowhere. "I think people who are very social and have a lot of chat in their life are great to have in development," says Tom Archer. "They're hearing all these different things and can bring that into their work; weird loners are not good."

You could be working with your development colleagues for much longer than you might on a production. "When I used to interview development people I used to think why do I want to spend the next year of my life talking about television with you? Because that's what we are going to do," says Ben Hall. "There are some people you don't want to be in a room with. You can't develop with people you don't want to be in a room with."

Having good relationships with potential buyers is an essential part of development too. "Really good developers have a lot of connections," says one NYC-based cable channel executive. "They know who to talk to about various things, and they're good relationship builders. They're the frontline for all of this, they'll do the dinners and the drinks and the schmoozing and all that stuff."

Team Spirit

Behind every hit TV program there is a team of people, although you wouldn't know it from the press. "You get quotes about 'the man behind the hit ...' But it rarely is one man, it's a whole group of people getting together brainstorming," says Nick Shearman, the BBC's former commissioning editor for in-house formats and features. "Part of that is brainstorming with the commissioning editor and being taken through a rigorous process. Commissioning is a team game and development is very much a part of that."

You might not be in a position to choose your teammates, but if you are it's wise to think about the mix. "In terms of the mix of people there's an alchemy, but you can't predict what ingredients you need to put in the test tube, or how many times to shake it. That makes it exciting and interesting," says Tom Archer. Ben Hall describes his ideal development team as having five different types of people: an originator, "who can actually have an idea, so when you are all sat there staring at the wall, someone who can go, 'How about ...?' There's an ideas nurturer, who can say, 'That's great,' but they probably can't come up with ideas.

Then you need someone who is a real ideas crystalizer so they can take an idea and write it up. Then there are the pitchers and the producers. And they are not all the same people."

The development team should also represent a cross-section of society. "Class and ethnicity are important, otherwise ideas tend to overwhelmingly mirror the same thing again and again," says Tom Archer. "Within the London factual production community, there was a period when there was a bunch of women who were all the same age, all had nannies looking after their kids and they probably all had 4x4s; their outlook was so narrow on a day-to-day basis that it was inevitable that their program ideas reflected that and therefore would not be that relevant to the wider audience."

CASE STUDY

Greenlit: *The Fast and the Gorgeous* (10x60' MTV India)

BBC Worldwide, Mumbai, India

"We developed a new format for MTV India, called *The Fast and the Gorgeous*," says Saul Nassé, General Manager and Creative Head, BBC Worldwide Productions, India. "They gave us a specific brief, which was: 'We want a show that is about finding four girls who are going to follow the Formula 1 team around the world.'

"Sonia Chowdhry, the creative head of the development team here in India, co-developed it with BBC Worldwide's central development team in London. That meant we got a mixture of local thinking about what type of content we could create, along with some international expertise on formats and how you can make games work and do eliminations. That collaboration was quite powerful and has worked well."

Integrity

"Being decent and treating people decently is important. Telly is one of those industries where people can be treated badly, and it also makes people behave badly, and that's a dangerous thing, particularly in development," warns a development producer. "You need people who you can trust, and you need people who aren't going to take all of the credit. Having a boss who unfairly credits the wrong person for an idea is the worst thing you can do to people in development." In development, reputation is everything, so guard yours fiercely.

Whether you specialize in high-end specialist factual programs or low-cost reality formats, believe that you are developing the best possible ideas, don't exploit anyone's naïveté or goodwill, and work for a company that makes programs you admire. Where you draw that line is a personal choice, but make sure you've thought it through, otherwise you will be miserable.

Original Thinking

A good development producer "exists in the ideas world," according to one US cable channel executive. "Producers and executive producers; those people are working out details like how do we execute this and what has to happen first … a development person says, 'What if we blew up the moon?'"

As well as having a well-developed imagination, you also need to be able to spot trends. "Television production is all about 'zeitgeist surfing,'" says Tom Gutteridge, founder of Mentorn and Standing Stone Productions. It's about "trying to anticipate public taste at least a year before anyone else (a bit like fashion or any design-based industry)," which means pitching ideas for which there is no precedent. But the most original ideas make channel executives nervous. "New ideas are usually unpopular ones," Peter Bazalgette, former Chief Creative Officer at Endemol, once said. In order to get an innovative idea commissioned there must be a series of risk-takers in the commissioning chain. From the person who originates the idea, through to the executive producer who agrees to champion the idea and the commissioning executive, they are all putting their reputation and job on the line by being part of a risky commission.

A good development producer will take risks, is not afraid of failure, and embraces rejection: the experienced development producer has at least nine rejections for every program commissioned. But the truth is: the better developed an idea, the less risky it will appear to the channel and the more chance you have of success.

Journalistic Instincts

Development requires you to get to grips with a wide range of subjects and to do so at speed. Key skills include, "turning ideas around quickly, knowing where to source your facts and stats to make your idea feel relevant and timely; also, having good relationships with journalists often helps as well," says one development producer.

Being friendly with journalists isn't enough; you have to think like one, too. "Everyone in TV reads the same newspapers and goes on the same websites and that's part of the reason that people come up with the same ideas all the time," says Nick Emmerson, President of Shed Media US. "There are two kinds of stories: those where you ring someone up and say that you're interested in their story, and they say: 'You and two dozen other people.' And there are those where no one's called them. It's like gold when they've never been contacted before—that's the Holy Grail."

Know your way around the Internet, but don't be afraid to be old-fashioned and pick up the phone and talk to people—it's often quicker and can turn up more interesting leads. You also need to know when you've found your story, ignoring the temptation to keep researching a subject until you know everything there is to know about it. "Bad development people get stuck into a lot of needless detail," observes Keith Scholey, Director of Wild Horizons Ltd. and Big Cat Ltd. and ex-controller of factual production at the BBC. "They hope that by burying themselves in detail that they are going to come up with some great television prospect; it's not going to happen."

Being obsessed with the details can be a sign of insecurity, or it can act as a cover for people who don't have their own ideas. "It's easy to hide at your computer and hone your document over and over, but some people can bang out ideas everyday," says Nick Emmerson. The detailed research can be left to the production researchers if an idea gets as far as being commissioned.

Knowing the Difference Between a Subject and a Story Idea

Program development is about finding stories in subjects. Every factual program needs a story that unfolds or tells the audience something they don't know—and that's as true of competition reality shows (who is going to waltz off with the prize?) as it is of serious documentaries (what effect is climate change having on polar bears?). "People constantly send in subjects instead of ideas," says Emma Swain, Head of Knowledge Commissioning, BBC. "They'll say, 'Henry VIII is interesting, there's an anniversary coming up, I think we should do a film about the life of Henry VIII'; it just looks like a Wikipedia description of it with a few experts thrown in and it looks quite dull. Often quite senior people say, 'Wouldn't it be nice to cover …?' No, not necessarily."

Whereas a subject area can generally be described in one word, a program idea has a story—beginning, middle, and an end. Something *happens.* And don't mistake an issue for a story. "Some people want to talk about the issue a lot and you have no idea about what that would be like as a documentary," says Claire Aguilar, Vice President of Programming, ITVS, USA. "Whenever you think you have come up with an idea, ask yourself, 'What actually happens? What would we *see?*'"

For example, here are some subject areas turned into program ideas.

Subject area: Fashion.
Program idea: We see what happens when a badly dressed woman is given a fashion makeover with the help of an unforgiving 360-degree mirror. What will she look like after her makeover? (*What Not to Wear*).

Subject area: Penguins.
Program idea: We follow a colony of Emperor penguins as they embark on an epic and dangerous journey across frozen wastelands in order to mate and bring up their chicks. Will they make it safely? (*March of the Penguins*).

Subject area: Parenting.
Program idea: A no-nonsense nanny goes into the homes of naughty children and teaches the parents how to use a "naughty step" to help deal with bad behavior. Will the children turn into angels? (*Supernanny*).

Subject area: WWII.
Program idea: Using new survivor testimony, interviews with SS members, archive footage, and drama reconstructions we discover how Auschwitz evolved from a prison holding Jewish political prisoners into a mechanized factory for mass murder. How could such a thing happen? (*Auschwitz*).

Subject area: Racial prejudice.
Program idea: Two families, one black, one white, trade races with the help of make-up, to experience life in each other's shoes. How will they fare? (*Black.White*).

Storytelling Skills: Myths and Fairy Tales

"The only rule in the world: Nothing beats a good story. Go to a commissioner with a good story and they will love you," says award-winning filmmaker Adam Curtis. Factual programs often borrow storytelling techniques from drama. It's useful to have a grasp of the common story themes as they can act as a shorthand description in a pitch. For example, before they know the specifics of the idea everyone understands what a David and Goliath story will entail. Other themes might be: man against nature; class war; love story; redemption; and battle of the sexes.

Programs such as *Survivor* and *The Apprentice* are heavily influenced by the work of mythology professor Joseph Campbell, who explored mythological, psychological, and religious archetypes in his books, *The Power of Myth* and *The Hero with a Thousand Faces*. Campbell was interested in the way hero stories reveal universal truths about an individual's role in society, self-discovery and the ability to overcome one's limitations.

There's no need to get hung up on storytelling theories. It is helpful though, when assessing your ideas, to ask yourself: what is the journey that my contributor, presenter, or viewer is about to go on, and what will they learn along the way? In other words, what's the story arc? If nothing changes from beginning to end, you don't have a story. You could still make a film, but it wouldn't be engaging or memorable.

You do, however, need to know the main storytelling techniques and conventions, such as "the hook," which engages the viewer so they start watching; the "cliff-hanger" that keeps them watching across ad breaks or episodes; and the "climax," which is the emotionally satisfying payoff.

Analysis—Not Paralysis

It's vital to accurately and quickly assess whether an idea is viable and work out who might want to buy it. "Very good development people know exactly who they are developing it for and exactly why they are generating an idea," says Keith Scholey. They are also "very good at saying, 'That is a non-idea' and not wasting their time." You might be spending a lot of time in the company of an idea, so you need to believe in it.

Writing Skills

In order to sell an idea three things are necessary: written, verbal, and visual presentations. A written proposal comes first. Some beginner developers (and some executive producers) feel that they have to tell the channel executive everything they know and produce a lengthy, detailed, and dense essay. This is a mistake. A program proposal is a sales pitch, not a university thesis, and needs to be short and to the point, no longer than one page. If a channel executive is interested they will invite you to a pitch meeting or ask you to send more details.

Channel executives are extremely busy people with a towering pile of proposals to read, and an overflowing inbox, so you need to make life as easy as possible for them. One commissioner received more than five thousand proposals when he started working at ITV and there was a rumor that one channel head multitasked to such an extent that she read her proposals on her exercise bike in front of the TV.

Writing succinct proposals is a skill that can be learned; it is necessary to be literate and able to write in different styles, self-edit and write quickly against tight deadlines.

Customer Service Skills: The Channel Executive Is (Almost) Always Right

To pitch an idea successfully, match your idea to a channel's needs. "You wouldn't ever pitch a social issues documentary to Discovery," says executive producer/writer/director Peter Rees. "Everyone has that passion project about their mother who died of cancer, or about going through the process of grieving after losing their daughter who died in childbirth, but Discovery's not interested."

Working in development teaches you "to consider the needs and the interests of who you are delivering your product to," says a UK producer/director. "It's horrible to talk about it like that, but it is a product, it's a commodity, you are a commodity and that's what makes it go round."

Development producer Dan Hall admits that it's easy to get carried away with your own ideas. "One of my problems is that I create an internal picture of what I want to see instead of what the channels want to see. I watched the wonderful *Mary Queen of Shops* and Mary had to say to this woman, 'You are a lovely woman and your shop is charming but you are selling clothes that you want to buy; and there's only one of you. That's why you are not making any money.' It makes sense."

Understand what the customer—in our case, a channel executive—wants and give it to them. That means listening to what they say; it's also about noting what's *not* said and questioning what is *really* meant. Opportunistic commissions can be won from noting casual asides made by channel executives during and after pitches. Pick up on one of these thoughts, turn it into a well-developed proposal and present the idea back to them and they will think you are wonderful; there's nothing easier than persuading a channel executive to commission their own ideas.

In one pitch, I showed tape of a potential new presenter to channel controller Janice Hadlow, and a group of BBC4 channel executives. It showed him standing in the middle of an empty, sterile room in the Royal Geographical Society, London, describing how it used to be full of dusty cabinets full of rolled-up old maps that numerous explorers, from David Livingstone to Roald Amundsen, had used to plan their historic expeditions around the world. When the tape stopped, the channel head remarked, quietly and to no one in particular, "I could sit and watch him walk round there all day." At the next meeting, we pitched an idea that involved the same presenter, Paul Rose, showing us around the most interesting museums in Britain, resulting in a commission for a six-part series called *Take One Museum*.

Good customer service also means getting to know executive producers and channel executives and working out how to manage your relationship to get the best out of them. Do they like to be hands-on right from the outset so they feel they have ownership, or do they work better when presented with an idea that they can critique and make suggestions for improvement? Working out their style will help you pitch them in the right way and save you a lot of wasted effort.

The trick is to give them what they want without compromising what you want to make. "The key way to pitch something is to go to them, work out what they want, offer it to them in the most imaginative way possible and then make it and let it evolve into something that has its own originality," advises Adam Curtis. "Then go back to them, and they won't mind even if it's a hundred miles away from what you pitched them."

Patience of a Saint

No matter how established you are, it might take years before a channel buys an idea: even Matt Damon took a decade to get his History Channel documentary *The People Speak* on TV. Your idea might not be salable in the current market for some reason; perhaps a similar program has been commissioned or it's an unfashionable format. But your idea could be perfect in eighteen months or two years. Keep key contributors and potential onscreen talent on your side, bide your time and be prepared to strike when an opportunity appears.

You'll also have to deal with people higher up the commissioning chain critiquing your ideas. "You have to rework things again and again and again, which is exhausting and demoralizing," says one producer/director. You also have to "try to interpret and understand exactly what that commissioner wants and incorporate it or completely rework your idea," in order to try to make it salable.

Resilience

> *A thick skin is a gift from God.*
> —Konrad Adenauer

Development is hard work and the pressure to come up with more and better ideas is relentless, as are the knock-backs and lack of recognition. "You think, I'll just get this one thing off and I'll go down in history," says one development producer. "No. You're nobody: you'll leave and they'll find someone else to come in and do it. They can easily find someone to come in to do your job. You have to love your job, you have to be doing it not because you are looking for credit or recognition, but because you enjoy it."

These are just some of the personal qualities and skills you need. So, if you're made of (nearly) the right stuff it's time to have some ideas, right? Wrong. Read on to learn to navigate your way around the current television landscape.

CASE STUDY

Greenlit: *Touching the Void* (106´ Theatrical)

Darlow Smithson

"Someone had told me, 'You must read this book [*Touching the Void*],' says John Smithson, Chief Creative Director, Darlow Smithson. "I did read it and thought it was brilliant, but I slightly forgot about it. And then Sue Summers, a journalist who was working with us, said, 'Have you read *Touching the Void*?' and I said, 'Yes, that's a good idea, let's try and chase it and find out what's what.'

"We found out that the book had been optioned by a number of film companies in the USA and Hollywood. Often good stories are taken off the market by film companies and optioned, and every year the option is renewed. Scripts had been written, but the project was stuck in development hell.

"Everything was in the book so we could only do the story with the co-operation of Joe Simpson, so we started negotiating with the publishers of the book to see if we could get the rights; it took well over two years to get the rights to the book. A long, long battle. But that was only the start of the story.

"What we then had to do, after we secured the rights to do a television docudrama, was to get it financed. We took it to the guy who then ran Channel 4 International, Paul Sowerbutts, who loved the story, so Channel4i helped us pay for the option fee. You pay an option fee and then you pay a much bigger price in the event you get the project into production.

"So then the challenge was to get Channel 4 interested. I managed to persuade two commissioning editors who worked in the same department, Sara Ramsden and Charles Furneaux, to believe in the project. The problem we then had was the feeling that mountain stories were not popular—when they had been done before they had not been a ratings success. So when they [Ramsden and Furneaux] took the project to the then director of programs at Channel 4 he was skeptical about its potential. But the commissioning editors were so passionate about it, that Tim Gardam, the director of television, was prepared to allow the project. He was worried about it working, but he was prepared to let it go into development. So we knew we had a UK broadcaster.

"We knew at that stage that we needed about £1 million to make it, and we probably had around half of that from Channel 4. There was an output deal that then existed between Channel 4 and PBS in America. PBS liked the story and came on board, so we got the same money from America as we did from Channel 4. So we had nearly £1 million, which was both a lot, and nothing like enough. Filming in the mountains is incredibly expensive. What to do?

"We'd been looking around for the right director: we needed someone who could handle the drama and be a brilliant storyteller and we needed someone with real star value and the idea came up to talk to Kevin Macdonald. Kevin had won the Oscar for *One Day in September*, and I thought that was a well-constructed film. Kevin hadn't done much with actors then, but I was impressed with his vision and we saw eye-to-eye on the story.

"*One Day in September* had got a theatrical release and we talked about doing *Touching the Void* as a theatrical release. I was pretty skeptical about theatrical documentaries; I thought it was a bit like vanity publishing. You could get your film seen more widely by doing it on television. But it seemed that it would up the ambition, so we started looking at theatrical.

"Paul Webster, then the head of Film Four, liked the story enormously, liked the hybrid approach we were going to do, mixing drama and documentary, liked the talent of Kevin Macdonald, and respected the track record of Darlow Smithson. Suddenly we were talking about it being a Film Four, Channel 4, PBS production and Film Four's involvement meant we could transfer it into a theatrical documentary. They came in for just under £500,000 so we now had £1.5 million but we felt we needed closer to £2 million as the costs go up dramatically when you are doing a theatrical— your shooting costs and your post-production costs all go up dramatically.

"So we were still short. The final piece of the jigsaw was to bring in the UK Film Council, who also came in for about a quarter of the budget. So we had about £1.8 million to make the film, but we'd only bought the rights to television so we had to go back again and do another rights negotiation that would allow us to make a feature film. It was an epic journey and it felt like we'd climbed quite a mountain before we'd started making it.

"It became the most successful theatrical documentary globally and I think ended up making $20 million or something and won sixteen awards or so, including the BAFTA for outstanding British film. People loved that film, people still talk about that film now."

Development Master Class 2

Develop Yourself

1. Make a list of your specialist skills and knowledge.

2. Talk to someone new at work this week. Find out what they're interested in and what they do outside of work.

3. Watch five factual programs: write down the subject and try to explain the story in one sentence.

4. Write a one-page outline of your favorite factual TV program (leaving out specific names and the title). Ask someone else to read your outline and guess which program it describes.

5. Give someone public credit for something they have helped you with. Get in the habit of doing this for every project you work on.

Explore More

Paul Arden: *It's Not How Good You Are, It's How Good You Want to Be*
With lots of pictures and big text (and easily read in the bathroom) this short book offers an injection of confidence if you ever doubt your creative ability.

Mark Burnett: *Jump In! Even If You Don't Know How to Swim*
Burnett explains why fear and procrastination are the biggest barriers to success, among stories of pitching and producing *Survivor*. Note that the first people he thanks in the Acknowledgments are the 1,500+ "show runners, producers, field producers, editors, assistant editors, loggers, casting associates, accountants, camera, sound, art department, unit, and challenge teams" on his successful shows.

3

Understanding the TV Landscape

> *Why isn't there anything good on television? In a word, economics.*
>
> —Kevin Allman

In 1982, the year Channel 4 was born, David Pritchard, a senior producer of BBC Plymouth's arts strand *RPM*, wandered into Floyd's Bistro in Bristol, UK. Over a boozy meal of clams and *steak frites*, David got to know the proprietor. Keith Floyd was a *bon viveur* with a cynical distrust of TV types; over a glass of wine or two he predicted, "Cooking will be the next rock and roll."

One day, a year later, David went to the Plymouth fish market and got chatting to a man who was filleting fish. "Look—all this gurnard, all this mullet, all this cuttlefish, all this squid—we don't eat any of that over here, it all goes to France and Spain," said the fishmonger. David's interest was piqued by the prospect of a program about the "travesty of all this fish being shipped off in big lorries," and remembered Keith Floyd, thinking he'd make the perfect presenter. He took Floyd down to the market to film a half-hour program.

David liked the program so much he commissioned himself to make another five programs, which became the popular *Floyd on Fish*. "It was," he says, with some understatement, "a lovely situation." He believes he would never have got that show commissioned if he'd had to pitch it to a commissioning editor. "If I'd had to convince somebody else, it would have been an uphill struggle, I tell you. I'd rather have pulled a steam engine along with a rope between my teeth than have to face anyone and say, 'Now, look, here is a flamboyant chap, he likes wine, he can cook and we'll cook fish aboard trawlers, straight from the net.' I can see the look on their faces right now." Indeed he reflects that, "It was a jolly good job that I could commission my own programs back then, because otherwise I probably wouldn't be making Rick Stein programs now."

Anyone working in TV today will tell you that it isn't what it used to be. According to the Research Centre, "Commissioning used to be about finding good ideas, spending money on them and seeing where they might work in the schedule: a bottom-up process ... Now, at all broadcasters, the process is much more top-down. The emphasis has shifted from a product-oriented to a market-oriented approach to programming, which requires a tighter focus on competitive scheduling." In other words, it's not about the ideas, it's about the audience figures.

Public Service vs. Advertising Revenues

So how did it come to this? According to Kevin Allman, former society editor of the *Los Angeles Herald-Examiner*, "The whole point of the television industry is commercials. Programs are merely the glue that stick product pitches together, and art is totally irrelevant to the process." In order to operate as viable businesses, commercial broadcasters on both sides of the Atlantic have to transmit shows that appeal to a demographic that is attractive to advertisers (usually young adults aged between eighteen and thirty-four or adults aged between twenty-five and fifty). A ratings success on an advertiser-funded commercial channel keeps both its advertisers and shareholders happy. A ratings failure means that advertising revenues, and profits, go down, resulting in less money for the channel to spend on new programming. Public service broadcasters such as the BBC aren't immune: they are competing for the same audience and must prove, via high viewing figures, that they are providing value for the public money that funds them.

Cable Explosion

With increased competition from hundreds of cable channels, it is increasingly difficult for channels to attract high audience numbers. Pre-Channel 4, there were just three TV channels in the UK. Today, that number has exploded, and the competition to get noticed is ferocious. From its heyday of twenty million viewers, BBC1 now attracts about five million to its primetime shows. Fifty years ago, a

US advertiser could expect 80 percent of American women to see an advert screened during a primetime TV show. Now advertisers have to run ads on a hundred channels to reach the same number of women. "We're competing in a market of six hundred channels so we need terrific stories and a unique something to be noticed," says Martin Morgan, Deputy Channels Director, BSkyB.

Channels are using different tactics in an attempt to attract the audience. Some go after "noise" or press coverage generated by outrageous titles, such as *Bridezillas* or *The Boy Whose Skin Fell Off*. "What channel controllers are interested in is having people talking about their channel," notes Adam Curtis.

Other channels try to implement a "fewer, bigger, better" strategy, which means that they spend their money on big blockbuster shows like *Britain's Got Talent* or *American Idol*. Cheap spin-off programming, like *Britain's Got More Talent* or *The Xtra Factor* (a spin-off of ITV1's *The X Factor*) on ITV2, give the channel more schedule-filling programming for their money. Which is great if you like reality programming; a disaster if you prefer highbrow documentaries.

Reality Hits

In 1992 MTV broadcast its first series of *The Real World*. Its creators, Jonathan Murray and the late Mary-Ellis Bunim, came from a background in news programming and soap opera respectively, and combined their skills to construct narratives from real-life situations. In the series, seven young people from different backgrounds moved into a house and had their lives documented over the course of several months. Over the years it has tackled difficult subjects, such as religion, AIDS, politics, and prejudice, turning it into a living "soap opera." It remains MTV's longest-running show, reaching its twenty-fourth season in 2010.

Unscripted television, such as *The Real World* or *Big Brother*, doesn't need writers, actors, or union labor. Network executives soon discovered that reality shows like these, without all the wrangling over artists' contracts, were not only cheaper but also faster to produce—and they attracted younger audiences in their millions. Channels began to order unscripted factual shows to fill their schedules. The second wave of reality TV came with *Survivor* in 2000, which sparked threatened walkouts by actors and writers, who claimed reality TV producers were formatting the show so heavily that it amounted to scripting. What started as a quick fix became fashionable, and then part of the television landscape: we now even have subgenres such as "celebreality" and "chefreality."

Reality television, the bastard child no one wanted, has grown into a noisy, unruly teenager that is keeping a lot of people in business.

According to Kevin Allman, the US networks "spend millions of dollars each year hiring people to produce not the best, but the most fiscally promising programming ideas possible. Sometimes an artistically successful show emerges, but that's just icing on the quarterly report. In the television industry, art is at best a by-product of the sales process." Julian Bellamy, Channel 4's head of programming, also recently observed that, "this is a culture that views factual programs simply as an economic rather than an editorial choice, a cheaper alternative to drama and comedy. This is a culture that, instead of looking out at the world and finding extraordinary ways of reflecting its themes, stories, and issues through television, too often fails to go beyond emulating what already works."

The explosion of cable channels provides great opportunities for the TV format producer, but three things conspire against innovative programming:

1. Cable channels (e.g. DIY Network and Good Food Channel) transmit programs that cater to small niche audiences who expect a certain type of program.

2. Channel executives are nervous about commissioning risky programs and so commission shows that are similar to their existing programs.

3. Independent producers play safe by pitching spin-offs or look-alike programs in order to win commissions.

The Cost of Creativity

But what's happened to the more edifying documentary? There are still channels where documentary makers can pitch their more traditional wares, but you have to look a little harder to find them.

Some channels, particularly the BBC and Channel 4, do broadcast one-off documentaries, but they prefer documentary series, for the same reasons that US cable channels want formats; a series of six, twelve, or twenty-six programs fills more of the schedule, and is cheaper and less labor-intensive than the same number of hours filled by one-off programs. Once you've fine-tuned an episodic (each episode consists of a self-contained narrative) format it can run and run, and can be repeated at random throughout the schedule to fill in gaps.

Channel 4 once worked out the relative costs of different kinds of programming:

* drama series such as *Queer as Folk* cost 18 pence per viewer;

* comedy series such as *Spaced* cost 10 pence;

* documentary series cost 5 pence;

* feature programs cost 3 pence;

* Graham Norton's chat show cost 2 pence;

* Factual entertainment programs cost 2 pence.*

While the world reveres the BBC for its smart, high-end (and expensive), factual programming such as *Planet Earth*, *Blue Planet*, and *Walking with Dinosaurs*, these programs are a luxury.

Shock Docs

In order to appeal to younger, more distracted audiences a new form of documentary programming has sprung up in the apparent no-man's land between serious documentary—informative, intelligent, and socially responsible—and more entertainment-driven programs. So in recent years, we've seen documentaries with shocking titles (much beloved of BBC3 or Channel 4), such as *Fuck Off I'm Fat* (BBC3) and *My Big Breasts and Me* (BBC3), and extreme, immersive observational documentary series, such as *Brits Behind Bars* (Bravo, UK) and *Deadliest Catch* (Discovery).

Now you know why broadcasters want certain types of programs and that some channels cater only to niche interests, you can decide where to position yourself in the market. It's up to you whether you want to join the reality bandwagon or stick to pitching more serious programs; but there's more money in the former than the latter (if you are lucky enough to have a format that goes on to sell around the world).

Whether you are working in a super-indie or as a one-man-band, if you have ideas to pitch, the principles are the same: know yourself, know the market and, most importantly, know your channel executive.

*These figures are out of date but give a good sense of relative costs of different types of programs.

Know Yourself: Science Geek or Entertainment Star?

In *Selling the Invisible*, Harry Beckwith describes how people often made unadventurous decisions, such as eating at McDonald's rather than a nicer-looking café in a strange town, because they were "not looking for the service they wanted but the one they feared the least ... People do not want to make the superior choice; they want to avoid making a bad choice." With McDonald's, you know what you're going to get. There's nothing unfamiliar or challenging about McDonald's; you go in, order, pay, eat, get out. There's no risk of unfamiliar food, an unexpectedly expensive bill, slow service.

Commissioning executives might eat at fancy restaurants at night, but at work they want McDonald's—they want to get the program they expect, at a good price, when they need it. To ensure they don't make a bad commissioning choice they buy it from a production company that has a proven track record in the kind of program they're pitching. If you specialize in highly constructed science documentaries, it's unlikely that a channel will believe that you can successfully execute a reality show, however good your idea. If they don't trust you, they won't buy from you. As one US channel executive explained, "If you are a small company you might surprise us by doing a great job on a docusoap but there are very few companies that can do big competition shows." If you are pitching "a big multimillion-dollar competition show—you need to have done that before, otherwise you'll drown."

Before you start developing and pitching ideas, consider which channels you understand and play to your strengths. For example, you might be their target demographic, or you might have specialist expertise or contacts that are relevant to the Military Channel or the Food Network.

In order to build trust, many successful producers become brands, specializing in a certain type of program. "My concept is simple," says *Deadliest Catch* producer Thom Beers. "High stakes, high rewards, in an exotic location. That's the Thom Beers Original Productions brand." Once you've built your reputation, things suddenly become a lot easier. "You scramble, scramble, scramble when you first start out, then you reach a certain point and the work begins to find you," says a US cable channel exec. "You don't have to look for the work, you can choose which of the work you want to do. Once you've proved you can produce a good-looking show, channels will seek you out to replicate that."

An executive at a different US cable channel agrees, "There's a lot of producers that we use because they're great executors but not necessarily great developers. We will bring them ideas that we have internally because we know they can execute them well, it's not like they bring us a ton of ideas." In other words, it's not about whom you know, but about who knows you.

Know Your Market: Niche Ideas vs. Broad Appeal

With so many channels it's hard to keep across them all: but if there's one thing you can do that will set you apart from the majority of your competitors it is to understand the difference between channels and know their programs.

Niche or BROADcast?

National networks such as ITV1, BBC in the UK and CBS, ABC, and NBC in the US, are aimed at a broad cross-section of viewers (hence *broad*casters) and have the money to commission expensive primetime shows such as *Strictly Come Dancing* or *American Idol* (but they spend less on programming for their daytime or early evening schedules). Cable, digital satellite channels tend to focus on a niche subject area, such as food or home improvements, or a specific segment of the population, such as women or young adults. Cable, digital, and satellite channels have much smaller budgets across all their schedules and usually commission only long-running formats, as economies of scale make them cheaper to produce per hour of scheduling time, therefore pitching an expensive show to a cable channel is a waste of time.

Make sure you are familiar with a channel before attempting to pitch to them. "My pet peeve is when people tell you the show is perfect for the channel and you get the tape and it's totally unlike anything else we've ever had," says one US cable channel executive. "How can you think that a show like that will sit next to x, y, and z, which are the cornerstones of our channel? It is totally dissimilar to everything else we have on the air—it skews to the wrong gender, it's thirty years younger or older than what we do, or we would never do this subject matter."

There's no excuse for this lack of market awareness, says Rudy Buttignol, President and CEO of British Columbia's Knowledge Network Corporation. "Going onto a broadcaster's website ... it can't tell you everything, but take the time and the courtesy to find out as much as you can, so when you meet a buyer you can actually dig in with more substantial questions than the most inane. 'So, what's your channel interested in?' That's a bad question."

Identifying Target Channels

If you have a good working relationship with a specific channel, it makes sense to generate program ideas to meet their brief. Alternatively, you can come up with an idea first and then look for a suitable channel to which to pitch it. If you don't yet know enough about your idea to know which channel it would suit, develop it a little more. At some point, your idea will reveal itself to be an adventure survival series aimed at men, or a "real crime" series that would appeal to women. As soon as you know the true nature of an idea, you can investigate which channels might be interested, based on their target market and current programming, and develop it further with them specifically in mind.

For example:

Blighty: One Nation Under One Channel.
Factual programming aimed at thirty- and forty-something British couples who want to engage with all things British.
Programs: *Made in Britain, My Brilliant Britain, Tales from the Palaces, The Real Little Britain.*

Spike TV: Get More Action.
US entertainment channel aimed at young men.
Programs: *Real Vice Cops Uncut, Pros vs. Joes, 1000 Ways to Die, Deadliest Warrior, Jesse James Is a Dead Man, Surviving Disaster.*

Virgin 1
Populist entertainment for adults with a British sense of mischief and humor.
Programs: *Sexcetera, Home Video Heroes, MacIntyre: World's Toughest Towns, Driving Me Mad.*

Discovery US: The World is Just ... Awesome!
US-based male-skewed, adventurous exploration of the world.
Programs: *Deadliest Catch, Dirty Jobs, Shark Week, The Detonators, Mythbusters, Verminators.*

Oxygen: Live Out Loud.
US entertainment reality shows for younger women.
Programs: *Janice Dickinson's Modeling Agency, Snapped, Bad Girls Club, Addicted to Beauty, Dance Your Ass Off.*

Living
British female-skewed, aimed at under-forty-five-year-olds.
Programs: *Most Haunted, Four Weddings, Jade, Top Model.*

A&E: Real Life. Drama.
US channel with big characters and extreme situations.
Programs: *Dog the Bounty Hunter, Intervention, Obsessed, Tattoo Highway.*

truTV: Not reality. Actuality.
Behind-the-scenes, real-life US stories and true crime.
Programs: *Forensic Files, Inside American Jail, Disorder in the Court, Operation Repo.*

Be especially careful if you are pitching your ideas internationally as seemingly similar UK and US channels can be very different. Lucy Pilkington, who commissioned for Bravo in the UK, expressed mystification at being pitched sewing shows, but a quick look at the US Bravo channel reveals why there may have been a mix-up:

Bravo (UK)
Male-skewing programs aimed at sixteen- to forty-four-year-olds that entertain, amuse, and shock.
Programs: *Danny Dyer's Deadliest Men, Armed and Dangerous, Brits Behind Bars, Sin Cities.*

Bravo (USA): Watch What Happens.
Reality programming for eighteen- to fifty-four-year-olds with a strong metro-politan and gay following.
Programs: *Project Runway, Top Chef, The Real Housewives of . . . , Launch My Line, America's Next Top Model, Tim Gunn's Guide to Style, The Fashion Project.*

Sometimes an idea is right for a channel in terms of its narrative and tone, but the channel executives turn out to have an aversion to a whole subject area. Chuck Braverman of Braverman Productions pitched a show to Discovery about smoke jumpers and people who put out fires. He was told, "Fire doesn't work on Discovery" ("That was ten years ago: things change," he says, wryly). David Broome, executive producer of *The Biggest Loser*, recalled that channel execs had repeatedly said that weight loss would never work in primetime. It's now in its ninth season on NBC and is seen in nearly a dozen countries around the world.

CASE STUDY

Pass: *Mountains and Fire*

Braverman Productions Inc.

"I had a great show for Discovery," says Chuck Braverman of Braverman Productions. "I wanted to do a show about a ski mountain resort—they were doing a series called *On the Inside* and I thought this would be perfect—on the inside of a ski resort.

"We would go to Aspen or somewhere in the later summertime when they were preparing and hiring new staff for the winter, and it would be like the opening of a big Broadway play when the first big snow came down.

"So I went to the executive of Discovery and they said, 'Mountains don't work.' I almost fell off my chair. 'Mountains don't work.' He said that to me!

"He said they'd done a number of shows about skiing but their audience (at the time—about ten years ago) was a bit more blue-collar and therefore they would have a hard time relating to skiing. According to him the people who were watching Discovery weren't into skiing. It made sense."

While you should know the differences between different channels and their audiences, don't be in thrall to them, or you risk producing derivative and predictable program ideas. In *Art & Fear*, David Bayles and Ted Orland note that, "In the simplest yet most deadly scenario, ideas are diluted to what you imagine your audience can imagine, leading to work that is condescending, arrogant, or both. Worse yet, you discard your own highest vision in the process." I rarely find it useful to think about a destination channel before I start generating ideas, as I find that's too constraining. I prefer to collect ideas and, before I put in any real development effort, do a quick feasibility check to see if it feels right for any of the channels with which I have a relationship. If an idea doesn't fit it's not worth pursuing. I record it in my database for possible future use and move on to something else.

Once you've got an overview of a channel's character, dig a little deeper into their schedule to understand what they're about.

Scheduling Real Estate

There are two main parts of the TV schedule, daytime and primetime, usually overseen by different channel executives. Channels also sometimes refer to early evening or "shoulder peak," which roughly equates with 5PM–7PM.

Channels often schedule different types of programs on different nights: Saturday night is the traditional night for big entertainment shows, for example. TLC, a channel that focuses on a mainly female audience, currently dedicates Thursday nights to programming that appeals to men, such as *American Chopper.*

"There's an incredibly useful exercise that Richard Dale, director of Dangerous Films, got us to do," says Dan Hall, "which was to go through the schedules and mark all the different factual programs—blue was documentaries, green was specialist factual—so you can see what the slots are. What's frightening is that you can see how few factual slots there are. There's no point developing, say, a 3x60' pre-watershed program, if there are no one-hour pre-watershed slots. If you think they will change the schedules to fit your idea, they won't." (Pre-watershed programs are suitable for children and are transmitted before 9PM. Post-watershed there is a gradual relaxation on the amount of swearing, violence, and nudity that is considered acceptable.)

CASE STUDY

The Speaker (8x60′ BBC2)

BBC Entertainment Manchester

"*The Speaker* was a public speaking competition for teenagers," says Mirella Breda, Executive Editor, Entertainment Commissioning, BBC. "In principle, it was a good idea; there was a good premise at the beginning of it. Public speaking is one of the greatest fears in adult life, so the idea that you could take the YouTube generation of monosyllabic bedroom dwellers and turn them into enigmatic, charismatic public speakers was quite an interesting and exciting journey I thought we could go on.

"Actually, the premise of watching a TV show about something we all dread and we all fear, isn't the most exciting or appealing option at eight o'clock at night and I think that's the problem we had. People didn't want to come to a program about a subject that they themselves feared; it's something we choose to avoid rather than aspire to.

"*The Speaker* had a core audience of one million people, which for us is a bad result, but it was constant and it actually had some of the highest A.I.s of any factual entertainment show this year, so the people who watched it loved it, it just didn't attract enough people. I see it as an honorable failure."

What's on TV Now ... and Next?

It's important to know the schedules of your target channels, and the types of programs they currently transmit, but it's also necessary to look out for new upcoming programs across all channels. Channel executives are attuned to rival shows that get critical acclaim or become surprise breakout hits as they'll want to emulate or capitalize on their success: you'll know when a show becomes a hit as the program gets coverage in newspapers, contributors appear on radio or breakfast TV, and people are talking about it at the bus stop (or around the proverbial water cooler) or on Facebook and Twitter (the digital water cooler).

Look out for highly hyped programs that don't seem to take off as expected and try to work out what went wrong. "None of us can watch TV all the time," says Emma Swain, "but when something's been a success or when something hasn't performed, or when something has been marketed a lot: those are the things you absolutely do have to watch." Channel executives expect you to know the hits and howlers as well as they do and get irritated if they have to explain the latest hot format to you in a pitch meeting.

Don't do what some (surprisingly senior) people do and rely only on reading what the TV critics say before forming your opinion about a show. That's no better than using *Cliff Notes* to pass your English literature exam. Analyze why a program does or doesn't work and be able to defend it. Is it an exciting new approach to a subject? An innovative use of emerging technology? Or, conversely, is the talent wrong? The format contrived? Does the story lack drama or intrigue? Visit fan forums such as digitalspy.co.uk (or explore the Most Commented link on tvmole.com) and find out what the viewers think too.

It pays to be informed about recently commissioned programs that haven't yet hit the screen (there can be a time lag of a few days to several years between the announcement of the commission in the trade press and transmission). Knowing that a channel has recently greenlit a program about a high-end spa will prevent you wasting time pitching them a similar idea. Read the trade magazines and websites listed in the resources at the end of this chapter to keep up to date.

Who's Watching What? Measuring Eyeballs and Bums on Seats

It's best not to have an opinion about a show until you see how big the ratings are.

—Mike Darnell, Head of Alternative Series, Fox

Track which programs are doing well and which are sliding out of favor by keeping abreast of the viewing figures in the trade press. Channel executives are hooked on their audience viewing figures and wait anxiously for the daily audience viewing figures to be published (don't attempt to have a meeting when the figures are due or you will have to endure them glancing distractedly at their PDA every couple of minutes). Their mood—and receptivity to your ideas—often depends on the strength of last night's audience ratings. "The only feedback you get is 'Are you delivering in terms of ratings and reputation?' That's the only thing you stand or fall by—it doesn't matter how you deliver," one UK channel executive told the Research Centre.

In the UK, the figures are measured by BARB (Broadcasters' Audience Research Board) and are reported in millions of viewers. They record the viewing habits of 11,500 viewers in 5,100 homes via set-top monitors. A popular unscripted show, such as *Strictly Come Dancing* on BBC1, attracts around 9 million viewers, but 3–5 million is more usual.

Share

"Share" is the percentage of the viewing audience who are watching that program rather than any of the other programs on TV at that time. For example, in the case of the final episode of *Britain's Got Talent* 2009 on ITV1, a 72 percent share means that, of all the people who were watching TV at that time, 72 percent of them are watching *Britain's Got Talent*. Digital channels (on both sides of the Atlantic) have an audience in thousands or low millions, and their share is calculated against other cable channels as well as against all the available channels.

In the US, audience figures are measured by Nielsen's "People Meters" (a box attached to the TV in sample homes allows individual family members to record exactly what they are watching via a remote control). The figures are a little more complicated to understand but essentially also represent audience in millions and share. ABC's *Dancing with the Stars* (the US version of *Strictly*) gets an average of 20 million viewers and a 20 percent share.

Reach

You may also come across "reach," which describes how broad the audience is demographically: whether it is reaching young people and older people, the wealthy and the not so well off. Due to its public service remit, reach is of particular importance to the BBC.

Appreciation Index

The Appreciation Index (A.I.) is used in the UK to measure how much people enjoyed a program and is expressed as a number between one and one hundred. A score of eighty-five is excellent, below sixty is considered a poor result. If a program attracts only a small audience but they mightily enjoyed what they saw, then it is deemed to have at least had some public service value and therefore the low viewing figures can be defended. As a rule of thumb, serious factual programs tend to get lower viewing figures but high A.I. rating, while factual entertainment formats get a lower A.I. and higher viewing figures. Either way, it is a trade-off.

Audiences respond to different types of programs at different times of day. In the early evening, they're getting in from work, dealing with homework and putting the kids to bed and getting their dinner, so programs between 7PM and 8PM tend to be structured so that you can dip in and out of them (and the reason why you get so many recaps and "coming up ..." segments in early-evening programs).

By 8PM and 9PM people are settling down with a cup of tea or glass of wine and are in the mood to sit back and be engaged and entertained. If the channel commissions something that doesn't match the mood of the audience it will drive them away and the next morning the ratings will stink.

Channel Briefs: Gazing at Crystal Balls

A channel usually publishes its program wishlist on its website, via a newsletter, or at special briefings sessions hosted a few times a year by the channel. "At Current we regularly send out an updated briefing document with details of what you are looking for. Make sure that you have read that," says Emily Renshaw-Smith, Director of Content, Current TV,* "because not doing that gives a bad first impression."

But briefs can be unreliable as they go out of date fast. "[Channels] don't update their websites enough, so they'll have the same brief up there for ages and you know that's not what they're looking for," says one development producer. "Only a few companies will be privy to the most recent information and that's annoying; I hate that."

What's more, channel executives don't know what they want until they see it, and so offer vague briefs. "We got a commissioning brief in today: it was absolutely pointless," says another development producer. "They said they wanted new talent. Fancy that! Actually what they want is famous people to do something they've not done before. They're not looking for new talent at all. They want someone who is new to their channel but already established on another channel; few will consider a complete unknown."

*Emily Renshaw-Smith has since left Current TV to join Rare Day as Head of Development and Production.

And producers are often too literal in their interpretation of a brief. "The danger with saying I'm interested in a territory," says Nick Shearman, "is that people will give you back something that is exactly what you've just said. So if you are listening to someone saying 'I'm interested in wine,' try to give them something different from the other one hundred people in the room. The goal is to come up with something different." Martin Morgan agrees: "The more prescriptive you are, the more all the proposals look the same. If we are looking for programs around bravery and secrets you can't say much more than that."

The trick is to take a subject area and inject it with the DNA of the channel. Tom Gutteridge, creator of *Robot Wars*, told Beth Ridley at the University of York's student newspaper that you should look between the lines for opportunities. "You talk to the commissioners and find out what they think they need," he said, "and then surprise them with something they haven't thought of."

Know Your Channel Executive

Channel executives are usually responsible for commissioning specific types of programs: daytime, current affairs, documentaries, features, and formats or specialist factual (art, history, natural history, religion), so you need to work out which executive at a specific channel is likely to be most interested in your idea (this information can usually be found on their commissioning website or via your agent in the US). As well as knowing *whom* to pitch to at each channel, it also helps to know what they are like as individuals, as their personality will influence their commissioning style and decision-making.

Stop Press: Channel Executives Are People Too

If great ideas are the currency of program development, personal relationships are gold. It's an open secret that producers who have an existing relationship with a channel executive will sell more shows. According to the Research Centre, "Programs tend to be commissioned on the basis of conversations, over time, between commissioner and indie, rather than the unsolicited proposals which have been the mainstay of some indies' practices."

It helps to have regular contact with the people you are pitching to. Over the course of many conversations you get a good sense of their personal likes and dislikes, and this intelligence is invaluable. "You learn as a journalist to go and sit with a person and very quickly find out who they are and what's at the back of their mind," says Adam Curtis. "You need to do the same with commissioners."

As you build your relationship with a channel executive it becomes easier to guess what kind of ideas will interest them. "You find out how they look at the world," says Adam, "and then you fit what you want to do with their view of the world."

Sometimes, however, it can be impossible to build bridges with certain channel executives, and the reasons might be unfathomable. "The commissioning editors I find it hardest to forge a relationship with are short, straight men," said one senior male production executive. "With every other commissioning editor, I can form a good relationship with them; but not short, straight men. Weird, huh?"

If you don't yet have relationships with the relevant channel executives, do as much as you can to gather information on them. Read the industry press. Find out who works where, what they've commissioned, what's worked for them and what hasn't. Read personal interviews and gather any information that will help you understand their viewpoint and offer them something that will resonate.

Any gossip you can glean is also useful. One channel suddenly started commissioning relationship shows soon after the channel controller got divorced. Is your channel executive married with a family? Parenting might work. An extreme sports enthusiast? Get celebrities to jump out of planes. The art of pitching program ideas is like buying the perfect birthday gift. Don't be the unthinking husband that buys his wife a food mixer. Present her with a diamond.

Horses for Courses

Not all channel executives can make the imaginative leap required to turn a well-described concept into a TV program. "As a generalization, most commissioning execs come from a production background," says Chuck Braverman but, "occasionally you run into people who don't understand filmmaking."

When you are dealing with channel executives who don't have a program-making background, you might discover they talk a completely different language—that of the marketer or scheduler—and that's how they assess ideas, not in terms of editorial content. They are imagining where an idea will fit in the schedule, or what it might look like on a billboard. Mark Burnett capitalized on this by mocking up the front covers of *Time* and *Newsweek* with headlines that declared *Survivor* to be a national phenomenon. (*Survivor* appeared on both the cover of *Time* and *Newsweek* within three months of the show's debut.) If you want to get them excited you have to present your idea to them in terms they understand.

Other channel executives respond to having their egos stroked. "Some commissioning editors love to be made a fuss of," says Ed Crick. "Some people want a performance, to be indulged, and made a fuss of. And sometimes that's fine because they are decent people and just flamboyant characters and sometimes it's a pain because they are megalomaniac psychopaths!"

CASE STUDY

Greenlit: *Sole Survivors: Yellowstone Bison* (1x60´ Animal Planet)
Braverman Productions Inc.

"I think I have good instincts about what would make a good television show and what people want to watch," says Chuck Braverman of Braverman Productions, "but I might be pitching a good idea at the wrong time to the right network.

"I pitched a show to Animal Planet with some talent attached and was flat out rejected. A year later, I was at Silverdocs conference and heard an Animal Planet executive saying that they were looking for new series with exciting new talent.

"Of course all the executives had changed at the channel, so I made an appointment and went in with the exact same show and the exact same talent, and sold the show and made a pilot. Same idea, different people."

The Fear Factor

Those channel executives who come from business and marketing backgrounds are likely to be more ratings-driven, than ex-program-makers who want to have some editorial input and a row of shiny awards on their desk. Whatever drives them—eyeballs or ego—"All commissioners are fearful," says Keith Scholey, "they are scared of losing their reputation and their jobs." This fear can manifest itself in conservative commissioning choices. "Commissioners sit there and say they want 'original and edgy,'" says Adam Curtis, "when what they mean is: 'we want pretty much the same stuff but full of new content, and every now and again we want something a bit different.'" Peter Rees agrees: "I think the networks' declining ratings are a result of them not being that interested in new material or taking risks with new producers and new formats."

What channel executives are looking for, especially at the more formatted, entertainment end of the factual spectrum, is a safe bet, something that's already worked. What they *really* want is for that safe idea to become a breakout hit when it airs. They want a win-win situation: the rewards without the risk. To be successful, it seems that you have to know what works, and why it works, and then give them more of the same.

One way that producers are assuaging this fear (and making money), is by selling a proven hit format to foreign channels. "There's never been such a desire to buy formats internationally; broadcasters all want to buy a hit, because a hit is reassurance," says Ben Hall. "At the same time, no one wants to buy a new show; everybody wants to buy a show that has been proven somewhere else. But a hit has to be a new show at some point, so we are all looking at how we help broadcasters take the risk of commissioning a new show."

When developing new shows producers trying to reduce the risk of rejection can go into survival mode, and play it too safe. "The lack of ambition astonishes me," says Adam Curtis. "People say, 'The commissioners will only allow the same stuff through,' but what [producers] come up with is the most clichéd stuff that we've heard a million times … I think to be fair to commissioners they are waiting for people to come up with good stuff."

Julian Bellamy, head of programming Channel 4, told delegates at the Televisual Intelligent Factual festival that, "getting people to think differently about ideas is more challenging than it's ever been. It takes real nerve to jump into the dark not knowing how a risky idea will turn out, or how viewers will react to seeing something completely new and different. But it's vital factual television does this."

CASE STUDY

Taking Risks

Simon Dickson, deputy head Channel 4 Documentaries and Documentary Series

"It is relatively straightforward to commission lots of 'programming' but commissioning good telly takes nerve, and luck. Crucially, you've got to surround yourself with the best, most talented people to have a chance of achieving something great.

"I'm not one of those people that can do this job in my sleep. In order to progress, I keep setting myself a higher and higher challenge. For example, *The Boy Whose Skin Fell Off* proved I could commission a program that would pull in an audience and win lots of awards; but it was only a single documentary. So, how could I do that for a series?

"*Meet the Natives* came along and it achieved similar sort of recognition and was quite innovative, so how do I supersize that? How do I do a bigger series? Can I play with the form of television and try to change the landscape a bit?

"*The Family* was originally my idea, but it was made by a brilliant production company, Firefly. That series was nine hours of television and it got big ratings and a BAFTA nomination. So what else can we do as a multi-camera observational documentary? How about observing life in a maternity hospital? We're currently filming with 50 cameras in a maternity hospital for a month.

"So I'm trying to be recognized as somebody who is a good guy to bring ideas to, who has the confidence to do things on a big scale and is available to help the production company to execute those ideas.

"I definitely get a high from it. When I know I've got a great idea in front of me, and I believe in it, it's quite exciting. The biggest high for me is when I see a program in the cutting room and I know that it's good. I'm an audience member at that point. If I like it, then I know there will be other people out there who do as well.

"I guess in a cruder way, I'm also excited when things I've commissioned get recognized through industry awards and that's always important. The

> ideal thing is to achieve both audience ratings and industry recognition.
>
> "My biggest fear is that my stuff doesn't make an impact; that you put stuff out on television and people merely say, 'That was quite good.'"

So, you have your team, and know the market inside out. It's time to come up with some ideas, preferably programs that, contrary to Kevin Allman's cynical observation, become the glue that stick the ads together.

Let's have some new clichés.

—Sam Goldwyn, attributed, possibly apocryphal

Development Master Class 3

Map and Navigate the Landscape

1. If you've not already done so, sign up to the weekly newsletter at www.tvmole.com to have factual TV industry news delivered to your inbox every Monday.

2. Alternatively, set up an RSS feed from each of the magazines listed below (look for the small orange, square button with a radio signal symbol on their homepages). Scroll through it daily to catch up on the latest industry news.

3. Look at the schedules of a couple of different channels (either online or in the TV listings magazines) and mark all the factual programs. Identify whether the channel schedules blocks of similar programs on certain nights.

4. Make a point of reading commissioner/channel executive interviews in the industry press to find out a little about their programming likes and dislikes.

5. Visit some channel commissioning websites to get their latest briefs (where available). Try Googling [channel name] + "producers" or [channel name] + "commissioning" to find the right page.

6. If you can't find the latest briefs, call the channel commissioning team (usually listed on the channel website under "Commissioning") and ask if they can send you the latest brief and put you on their distribution list. In the UK PACT also has information for its members on upcoming producer briefing sessions to be held at the channels.

Explore More

Broadcast: weekly magazine and subscription website devoted to the UK TV industry, including commissions, premières, and interviews with top industry players http://www.broadcastnow.co.uk.

BARB (Broadcasters' Audience Research Board): provides daily audience viewing figures (overnights) for UK TV programs http://www.barb.co.uk/.

CableU: part of a development/distribution/representation company, CableU is a subscription-based website that analyzes US network performance, covers commissions and cancellations, and offers detailed network profiles, including current briefs and pitching tips. Full access is currently $850 per annum but you can sign up to the CableU blog for free, which has industry insights and interviews with producers and channel executives http://www.cableu.tv/cuconfidential/.

C21: news and features about the TV industry. Various free newsletters can be delivered to your inbox; some articles can be read online, for other others you need a paid subscription http://www.c21media.net.

Cynopsis.com: daily email newsletter with new commissions, programs in development, hirings and firings across the US TV industry. There is a separate newsletter for digital news http://www.cynopsis.com.

The Hollywood Reporter: daily and weekly entertainment industry magazine with a TV section, and a number of daily email newsletters http://www.hollywoodreporter.com.

Nielsen: provides audience viewing figures for US TV shows http://en-us.nielsen.com/rankings/insights/rankings/television.

PACT: UK trade association for TV, film, and digital media companies https://www.pact.co.uk.

Realscreen: international magazine devoted to nonfiction programming. Sign up for the free email newsletter which is delivered Monday, Wednesday, and Friday each week htttp://www.realscreen.com.

TV Mole: website aimed at factual TV producers, which logs new commissions in the UK, US, and beyond. A weekly newsletter delivers all the latest information to your inbox once a week http://www.tvmole.com.

Variety: weekly magazine focusing on the US entertainment business but with an international readership. There is a free daily email newsletter with all the headlines, but you must subscribe to get full access to online content. Currently, non-subscribers can access five pages on online content per month http://www.variety.com/.

The Wit: another subscription-only site that gives you access to factual and format programming, commissioning, and development news from around the world. You can also follow them on Facebook http://www.thewit.com.

4 Generating Ideas

You can't wait for inspiration. You have to go after it with a club.

—Jack London (1876–1916)

In 2000, ex-advertising executive and internet consultant Elise Doganieri asked her partner, TV producer Bertram van Munster, what was new in the world of TV. "Same old, same old," he said. "You guys need to come up with some better shows, then," replied Elise. So Bertram challenged her to come up with a great idea, and gave her five minutes. "By the third minute, she'd come up with the basic concept of *Race Around the World*: teams of two racing around the world, the first one that gets back to the United States of America wins the proverbial $1 million."

The Amazing Race, as it became known, debuted in 2001 on CBS in the US. It has since won seven primetime Emmys, including six for "outstanding reality-competition program," has been transmitted around the world, from Brazil to Israel, Finland, and Vietnam, and aired its sixteenth season in early 2010. Not bad for a show thought up in three minutes.

Stephen Lambert's wife, Jenny, had the idea for the award-winning format *Faking It* as they lay in bed one night. She asked, "Why not do *Pygmalion* for real?" He told her to go back to sleep, but called Channel 4 the next day. It ran for nine series and sold around the world.

If only it were always that easy! More often than not, shows are created only after many conversations, and many months of hard work. There are, of course, some people who like to perpetuate the myth that the best ideas spring fully formed from the brains of geniuses (read: executive producers), but that's not true: after all, Elise Doganieri wasn't (yet) a TV producer. But she had an insight into human behavior from a European backpacking trip she went on with her best friend after college; part way through the trip they fell out so badly that they ended up taking off in different directions. The stress of traveling is relatable, and *The Amazing Race* capitalizes on that universal experience, while testing the contestants' relationships to their limit.

You have to get your ideas from somewhere. Stephen King once said if you are an "ideas person," ideas are all around you. "Good story ideas seem to come quite literally from nowhere, sailing at you right out of the empty sky; two previously unrelated ideas come together and make something new under the sun. Your job isn't to find these ideas but to recognize them when they show up." But not everyone has ideas sailing out of the sky at them. "Most people don't have a lot of ideas. My experience is that a lot of people don't have one good idea," says Peter Rees, so you have to be a little more proactive.

If you are high up in the TV production food chain, your main source of inspiration might come from your conversations with channel executives. "Ideas quite often get talked into existence through conversations between commissioners and television production companies," says Simon Dickson, deputy head of Channel 4 Documentaries. That "tends to be the way that something gets born." Indeed, one producer said, in a survey compiled by the Research Centre, that "Around 80 percent of his company's commissions were due in part from commissioners' ideas or desires, and that his division does not send in ideas that are unsolicited." If you are in the privileged position of having regular meetings with a commissioning executive, you should find it nigh on impossible *not* to get a commission.

If you are not fortunate enough to have a channel executive feeding you ideas, you must come up with some of your own. If you are working in development it is expected that you will come up with ideas, and lots of them. "Development producers have to be like those tennis ball machines that just fire them out and don't care if they come back; they have to be smart ideas machines," says Lucy Pilkington. You can find inspiration in two ways: expose yourself to various stimuli and hope that inspiration strikes, or you can attempt to engineer an idea by using various "creative techniques."

Ten Ways to Prime Your Mind for Ongoing Inspiration

Nothing can be created out of nothing.

—Lucretius (d. 55 BC)

Here are ten things you can do that will provide you with a range of raw materials from which you can draw inspiration. Try them out and mix and match to suit your needs and interests. Be on the lookout for other sources and add them to your arsenal.

1) Get out more: turn off the TV and go and do something more interesting instead

You should make a point of trying every experience once, excepting incest and folk dancing.

—Sir Arnold Bax, composer

Peter Bazalgette, then head of independent production company Bazalgette (so the often-told story goes) paid a visit to his local garden center one day and noticed that people weren't buying seeds; they were walking out with their arms laden with fully grown plants. At the time, gardening shows in the UK were sedate affairs that appealed to the more mature viewer, featuring genteel presenters patiently sowing, pricking, weeding, and fertilizing their seedlings into mature plants.

Bazalgette had a flash of insight: the people at the garden center checkout didn't want to wait around waiting for labor-intensive young plants to grow, they wanted a garden makeover and they wanted it now. And so *Ground Force*, one of BBC1's most successful and long-running formats, was born. At its peak (helped, no doubt, by the braless charms of Charlie Dimmock), it was the third most watched program in the UK.

Don't confine idea generation to office hours. "Once you've started, you've never finished in development: you are always thinking about how you could use this talent or what you could do with this idea, and maybe that's not a bad thing. But sitting at a desk all day *is* a bad thing," says Dan Hall.

Sign up to museum, gallery, and cinema mailing lists and make a point of going to different events at least once a month. A change of scene does wonders for creativity—be adventurous in your choices, even if you specialize in a certain genre or subject area. For example, if you are a history development producer in London, over the course of a couple of months one summer, you could have seen a child's-eye view of World War Two at the Imperial War Museum; heard Joe Kerr, author of *Autopia: Cars and Culture*, talk about the history of Detroit, from "Motor to Motown," at the Victoria & Albert Museum; and dressed up for a 1950s tea dance at Bethnal Green Working Men's Club, in London's East End.

If you develop science programs in NYC, you could have met Richard Ellis, author of *Tuna: A Love Story*, at the American Museum of Natural History; sat in a bar in Brooklyn to listen to Dr. Leslie Vosshall, head of the Laboratory of Neurogenetics and Behavior at Rockefeller University, talk about the science of smell; and taken a stomach-churning Taxidermy Tour of Chinatown with artist Nate Hill, who salvages animal carcasses from trash cans and sews them together to create fantastical new creatures.

Any of these nights out could have inspired new ideas. The taxidermy tour might suggest a documentary presented by Damien Hirst, a fly-on-the-wall series set in a Chinatown restaurant, or a series that follows a taxidermist who specializes in stuffing the dead pets of celebrities. It's good to have random nights out with your development team or friends, so you can refer back to the event months later when a related idea emerges. Having fun with your team is a great way to bond and get on the same wavelength.

Try it: get your team or friends together over a beer and give them each a piece of paper with one of those talks and events written at the top. Give them ten minutes to come up with three program ideas each, then swap and repeat with another event. The trick is not to be too prescriptive, encourage them to think laterally. After a couple of rounds compare notes to see what you've all come up with. Try the same exercise with the current issue of *Time Out* or other listings magazine.

CASE STUDY

Greenlit: *Meet the Natives* (3x50´ Channel 4)

KEO Films

"I was cycling to work one day and I was going along at speed, hunched over my bicycle, in my yellow fluorescent jacket, my silly helmet and ridiculous-looking raingear," says Simon Dickson, deputy head Channel 4 Documentaries and Documentary Series. "There's a building with a mirrored front around the corner from the Channel 4 office and I caught a glimpse of my reflection in the glass, and I remember thinking how stupid I looked.

"I'd been watching *Tribe* the day before, where Bruce Parry goes to places like the Amazon and hangs out with tribes. All the tribespeople look strange and exotic to him, and he reflects on how peculiar their ways of life are.

"As I cycled past this building, I thought, 'It's all very well for a white, middle-class, well-educated, ex-Army man to go over and think the natives look a bit strange; but they would think that our world is pretty weird too, if they were to experience it.' I got to the next set of traffic lights and realized that I'd just had an idea.

"I got to the office and realized that if I didn't act on it quickly, I would forget about it or I would stop believing in it, so the next thing to do was to decide whom to call about it.

"I knew instinctively that I should call a company called Keo Films, who make incredibly good anthropology films. I knew that they would do the development properly, and I knew that they would tell me honestly whether it could be done. Some companies are better at some things than others, and part of my job is knowing whom to call about certain types of projects.

"I called them and said, 'I've got an idea I'd like to talk to you about. I'm not going to tell you about it over the phone, because I want to see the look on your face.' They came in a couple of days later, and I described it to them and they laughed and said, 'You can't do that; it's going to be awful, there's no way you can do this.' But by the end of the meeting, they said, 'We'll have a look at it for you, but we're not promising anything.'

"I thought, 'Great: if they do some work, fall in love with it, and conclude it can be done, then they are the right people to do it and I should commission them.' Other companies would have come in and said, 'That's a great idea, let's do it,' but they would be the wrong companies.

"I gave them a few grand [development money] and they came back a few weeks later and said, 'It's not going to be easy, but we think we might be able to do it, and we have a group of people we could do it with.'

"They told me about this tribe that I'd never heard of in the South Pacific, in a place called Vanuatu, who believe that Prince Philip is a living reincarnation of their island god and they've always wanted to meet him.

"Keo went out and met the tribe and came back with a tape of them all saying how they'd like to come to Britain, so I thought, 'Let's do it.' Originally, we were going to do a different tribe each week, but it's a lot of work for not much return, and in the end, it was nicer to stick with the one tribe.

"It was a great series, it was made with complete sincerity and it won a load of awards. We are now doing a follow-up with some Amish teenagers."

Meet the Natives won, among others, the RTS Documentary Series Award, and the Televisual Awards Best Documentary Series and Broadcast Award for Best Series, as well as receiving nominations from BAFTA and the Grierson Awards.

2) Stay in and watch TV

It's important to know what's currently transmitting, so you can pick up new trends, get inspiration for a new approach that you can apply to your subject area, and have a point of reference for discussing ideas with channel executives. "I think TV is largely an evolution," says Ben Hall. "Sometimes there's something big that moves the goalposts but by and large it's evolutionary, so knowledge counts for a lot."

For example, there have been a number of fly-on-the-wall documentaries chronicling the lives of ordinary families. *An American Family* followed the Loud family in Santa Barbara, California (1973); *The Family* profiled the Wilkins family in Reading, England (1978); and *Sylvania Waters* followed an Australian family (1992). All these series were popular with audience and critics, but how could this well-established "real-life soap" approach be updated? Enter *The Osbournes*, which followed aging rocker Ozzie Osbourne and his unconventional family. It premièred on MTV in 2002, and won the channel its highest audience ratings and a Primetime Emmy Award for Outstanding Reality Program.

Watch every new program in your specialist genre. So, if your company specializes in science documentaries, watch all the science documentaries on TV. Time-shift recording and viewing technologies such as Sky+, Channel 4's 4oD, the BBC's iPlayer in the UK, or TiVo in the US, make this easier than ever, as you can plan your viewing, or catch up with programs you've missed. At the very least you should look at the TV listings at the beginning of each week, and know what's on, noting any new programs.

Be aware of channels that have annual seasons of programming for which you could pitch content, for example, *Shark Week* on Discovery Channel, or *Expedition Week* on National Geographic Channel (US).

Watch as many new formats as you can. A format is a program that has the same recognizable elements repeated in every program, with only the characters changing week to week. In *Wife Swap*, the families are different in each program, but every episode has the same structure: two women from contrasting backgrounds leave home and move in with each other's family. They observe their host family's rules before trying to improve things by imposing some of their own. At the end of the program, the couples, reunited with their partners, meet to discuss their experiences, resulting in a confrontation and/or tears. In a competition format, such as *Survivor*, or *Strictly Come Dancing*, each episode presents its participants with a series of challenges that must be completed or overcome. At the end of each episode, someone is ejected from the series. In either case, a formatted program is essentially the same week to week, so there's no need to watch a whole series (unless you become a fan).

Some producers only admit to watching award-winning or critically acclaimed programs. You should make a point of watching terrible programs too, as honing your critical skills will help you critique your own ideas.

CASE STUDY

Greenlit: *Miracle of the Hudson Plane Crash* (1x60´ Channel 4)

Darlow Smithson Productions

"I decided I wanted to look at the Hudson story, when I saw the news bulletin," says Simon Dickson, deputy head Channel 4 Documentaries and Documentary Series. "I was at home when it came on the news. I was struck by the image of an airplane in the middle of the Hudson River. I didn't think about it, it was an instantaneous feeling that we should do a film, because what would it feel like being on an airplane thinking that you were going to die, then minutes later, after the most extraordinary crash landing in aviation history, realize that you are alive?

"Before the news item finished, I went into my hallway, picked up the phone and rang John Smithson. I knew I needed somebody of that caliber to be looking at the story. I left one message for him, and one for another well-known production company, and resolved that whoever called me back first, I would ask them to look at it; John was the first to call me back.

"He was in America at the Sundance Documentary Festival, so that was helpful, because he was in the right time zone. I realized that he could potentially bump into people at Sundance who might want to put money into the film. He started talking to broadcasters in America within minutes of me ringing. I said that I would pay for them to spend the weekend in New York; there wasn't any risk involved in funding Darlow Smithson for a couple of days.

"I spent the weekend doing normal weekend stuff, but I knew that by Monday, Darlow Smithson would have spent a couple of days in New York doing a little bit of filming, making some contacts with the coastguard and the emergency services and the airline, and so forth. They'd also done a film for me in the past about the construction of the Airbus, the big airliner, so I knew they had some contacts with Airbus, who were the company that made the airplane, so Darlow Smithson were the right fit for that idea.

"There are a number of companies in Britain who have a reputation for doing fast turnaround documentaries. The characteristics that companies who do those sorts of programs need include: a stable company that is well respected internationally, because these fast turnaround films typically need co-production money from different international broadcasters and you may find that your story requires you have access to journalists in different countries; and you've got to move quickly, quite often on a global scale.

"By Monday, they'd done good development on it: they had a list of things the film would include, and a list of things they'd like the film to include, but they couldn't guarantee.

"More than one commissioner at Channel 4 had a call from more than one company saying, 'Do you want us to pursue the plane crash?' So when Julian Bellamy said, 'We're getting a lot of pitches in on the Hudson thing, what do you guys think?' I was able to say, 'I've had John working on it since Friday,' and described to him the kind of film I thought we would get. What marked this commission out was that John and I didn't wait for anyone's permission. I didn't wait for anyone to come and ask me if Channel 4 wanted the film—I knew that we did.

"When you see something like that, you do spring out of your seat and you call an indie, because you are ambitious to be the person to bring that film to the audience. You want to be associated with it.

"*Miracle of the Hudson* was my idea but I'd say that it got commissioned because I reacted to an event. It's not the same as me conceiving of something; that's a different ballgame."

3) Go to work

If you are working on a production, there could be ideas for new programs right under your nose. Is there an interesting character in the background of the story who deserves a program of their own? Or an interviewee with an unusual area of expertise who could host a whole series? Does a contact reveal an interesting story lead during a coffee break that's worth following up?

CASE STUDY
Greenlit: *Deadliest Catch* (8x60´ Discovery)
Original Productions

"I had just left Paramount, I had no job, I had no idea what I was going to do next," says Thom Beers of Original Productions. "I'd moved to Los Angeles after eleven years at Turner broadcasting; I had a reputation as an executive but not a strong reputation as a producer.

"Steve Burns, who was running the Discovery Channel, called me. He'd lost a producer who'd decided he couldn't do a show called *Extreme Alaska*. He said, 'Thom, I know who you are, and I'd like you to do this.' So I was commissioned by the Discovery Channel to make a two-hour special.

"I researched everything I could about what was extreme in Alaska; Burns had sent me a whole package of what the producer had done for research, and there was a news story in there about the deadliest job in the world, and it was crab fishing.

"So I went up to Dutch Harbor in the Aleutian chain, and walked the dock in search of boats. This was late 1998, and the King Crab season was over (the Opilio Crab season is in January/February). The only way you meet captains in Dutch Harbor is in the Elbow Room bar, where I found a guy called Rick Mezich who was the skipper and owner of the *Fierce Allegiance*. Over a couple of shots of Jack Daniel's and a couple of pints, I talked my way on to his boat.

"He said we could join the January Opilio season. My plan was to go out for four or five days and cut a twelve-minute segment for *Extreme Alaska*. When I joined the boat with a cameraman and a sound engineer, we did not anticipate running into the worst storm in thirty years. Within twenty-four hours we were two hundred miles out at sea with the winds whipping seventy miles per hour and the waves cresting at forty feet. It was a brutal season: that year, three boats sank, seven men drowned and they never found the bodies. I thought we were all going to die, but I thought, 'Let's keep rolling.'

"These guys were fishing twenty-four hours a day, there was no 'Let's shoot for eight hours and have a lovely meal and enjoy a movie.' These guys worked night and day and slept two or three hours. We thought, 'Wow, this is an amazing pace,' so we had to get into that pace. We were shooting night and day.

"I had a camera in an underwater mount that I put on a mast pointing down because I knew the action was in a 20x20ft area. I had a Hi8 camera, which had a slow record mechanism, which was great because it meant we only had to go up the frigging mast in a massive storm six times a day to change the tapes! It was brutal.

"You don't just walk on to a crab boat and say, 'OK, I'm the auteur director ...' To be a successful producer you have to ingratiate yourself with the crew. We got up earlier than anyone else and cooked breakfast. We washed the dishes, I washed clothes, I made sure the skipper had plenty of hot coffee. I'd be filming with one hand and sorting crab with the other as the boat's bouncing all over the place.

"So I'm rolling, and the storm's getting worse and worse and there are white snakes on the water, these white tubes of water. They say when the birds sit down things are bad—I looked out and there's all these birds hunkering down; then the storm got real bad ...

"I was convinced the boat was going to sink. I had a Pelican™ case and every night I put the tapes and the script notes into the case; I was convinced that when the boat sank, the Pelican™ case would be carried by currents due south one thousand three hundred miles and be washed up on Malibu Beach to be found by an editor's son who would take it home and his dad would think, 'Hey there's a brilliant TV show in here!' You go a bit crazy out there.

"We came out of the storm and went back to shore. It changed me: it was cathartic. That's what you are looking for as a producer; to me it's about the adventure, the journey.

"I came back and I started looking at the footage, and I thought 'Whoa! This isn't just twelve minutes, this is extraordinary—no one's ever seen this: men being knocked over by a storm.'

"I went to Discovery and said, 'Look, I've got the most incredible show here.' He said, 'What do you need?' 'I need $125K and I will finish the show. I will put twelve minutes in the *Extreme Alaska* show but I will also make you an hour that will live on long past your and my time at Discovery.'

They believed me so they gave me the money. I made a sweet deal where I hung on to the international rights for ten years, which was an impossible thing to do, but I said, 'Look, I'm not going out there again risking my life just to get $4,000.'

"I went back to Seattle and did all the transitions and inserts and did some reconstructions of guys going overboard—I basically fleshed out the story that I had.

"The show went on the air in late 1999 and it blasted; the numbers were outrageous. I wanted to go out and do this thing again but it took me three years to persuade them and they would only give me three hours. I went back out again, and it was amazing; a guy went overboard and they saved his life.

"But the scheduler—the bane of every producer's life—never had any faith in these shows, so they put the three hours on a Sunday night at 8PM with no promotion. Normally Discovery was getting a 0.8–1.0 rating at that time. It started at 8PM with 0.8; at the end of three hours, it went to a 3.5. Five million people tuned in without a single loss per quarter-hour. The build was a perfect set of stairs.

"That's when Billy Campbell, president of Discovery, said, 'Oh my god! When can we get more? I want more in three months.' I said, 'Dude, the season doesn't start for seven months. There's no way in hell.' He said, 'What are you talking about—let's get out there and catch some crab.'

"Jane Root arrived as GM at Discovery as they commissioned a series, and she wanted to turn it into a competition where whoever won the most crabs in a season won $250,000; it was so wrong. And then they wanted to put Mike Rowe out there as a live host on the boats, 'in the moment.' I'm like, 'What are you doing? I've got this great show and all of a sudden you're trying to make it into *Survivor* meets *Dirty Jobs*.' It went in a very bad direction.

"Fortunately, the press and the sea captains and coastguards said, 'Look, people are risking their lives already; we don't need people to do it for money,' so I got to make the show I wanted to make."

Deadliest Catch has won an Emmy for Outstanding Cinematography (and been nominated for several more) and is shown in 150 countries.

4) Network

Networking is second nature to some people, others (especially Brits) would rather poke their own eyes out. But networking is an essential skill. It's not about desperately handing out your business cards; it's having the ability to talk to strangers; to engage new acquaintances in meaningful conversation and find something interesting out about them.

For example, talking to BBC presenter Paul Rose is always fascinating. He's an ex-British Antarctic Survey base commander, and has had such extraordinary life experiences and is so interested in, and curious about, the world, that ideas fly out of his mouth like butterflies ready to be caught in a virtual butterfly net. Program-makers talk to extraordinary people on a daily basis (often without realizing it) in order to produce their programs. And once you master this skill you will not only always have your next job lined up, but you will never again endure a dull party. If you find yourself stuck with a bore, you are asking the wrong questions. And it's amazing what people will tell you if you ask—exploit that!

Make sure you broaden your networking circle outside of your television contacts. If you're nervous there are many ways to make it easier. Increasingly, the internet is providing ways to meet people in person and, unsurprisingly, marketing and advertising people have capitalized on it far better than most TV folk.

For example, Likemind.us holds monthly breakfasts in more than fifty cities around the world. There is no agenda other than getting an interesting mix of creative people together, and as an extra incentive there is often free coffee. I have met, among others, the head of a Madison Avenue ad agency, a producer from current.tv, a trend spotter, a climate change scientist, several multiplatform content producers, a hypnotist, a photographer, and a journalist who specialized in writing about plastic surgery. It makes for a stimulating and inspiring couple of hours. Try it, or something similar; you have nothing to lose except an hour or two before work. If there isn't one where you live, apply to be a host via the www.likemind.us website, and set up your own.

Remember, everyone is feeling as anxious and self-conscious as you, so smile, say hello and ask them how they heard about the event. If they don't respond enthusiastically, move on to find someone friendlier. Once you've found someone you like and have a connection with, get the goodwill ball rolling by offering some tidbit of information or introduce them to someone who might be able to help them in some way, so they will be comfortable helping you out in future. If it's not something you're used to doing, you'll get an enormous buzz from having taken the initiative. Cultivate these contacts, as you'll never know when they might come in handy.

At conferences, book readings, or press receptions, make it your goal to talk to at least one stranger. You'll hear of other interesting events, or experts that you would never find by doing research at your desk.

Take time to make contact with PR people, curators, agents, and publishers and get on their mailing lists. Take the friendly ones out to lunch occasionally so you're top of their list when there's something interesting on their radar.

5) Look into the past

Look at the programs in your company's back catalog. Is there anything in the archives that could be revitalized with a modern twist, or a format that fell out of favor a few years ago, but could be perfect right now?

Dancing with the Stars is currently one of the most popular programs in the world, and transmitted in thirty-eight countries. It is a modern twist on an old British format, *Come Dancing*, which aired on the BBC from 1949 to 1998. The original series was a genteel ballroom dancing competition that appealed to a diminishing, aging audience.

In 2004, the BBC launched *Strictly Come Dancing* in the UK, a much glitzier version that cleverly retained its appeal to traditional *Come Dancing* viewers, but also attracted younger viewers by pairing professional dancers with untrained celebrities. With a nod to *Strictly Ballroom*, Baz Luhrmann's cult ballroom dancing movie familiar to younger audiences, it made formal dancing sexy and aspirational. By introducing reality sensibilities, a dusty old format was reborn, and then reproduced internationally as *Dancing with the Stars*, a global, award-winning success that has spawned several spin-offs, a live tour, and a video game.

Likewise, *Britain's Missing Top Model*, in which eight disabled women competed for the chance to appear in *Marie Claire*, was a twist on *Britain's* (and *America's*) *Next Top Model*.

6) Peer into the future

TV channel executives like a "hook" or a "peg" for a program idea; in other words they want a reason why they should commission this particular idea right now. A useful way of finding a peg is to research upcoming anniversaries. For example:

* 2014 is the seventieth anniversary of D-Day;

* 2015 is the eight hundredth anniversary of the signing of Magna Carta;

* 2018 is the fiftieth anniversary of the assassination of Martin Luther King, Jr.

Focus on anniversaries that are at least eighteen months away so you have time to pitch the idea and produce the program or series before the actual date of the anniversary. "Producers try to pitch us anniversary programs ten days before the anniversary," says Martin Morgan, but "we are planning our schedules, especially for big anniversary events, two or three years in advance."

CASE STUDY

Greenlit: *Falklands: The Islanders' War* (2x60')

Point of View Production Company Ltd.

"I've always had an interest in history," says Mike Ford of Point of View Production Company, "and I was looking for ideas for the History Channel. It suddenly occurred to me that the twenty-fifth anniversary of the Falklands conflict was coming up. As a young news cameraman back in 1982 I had covered all the naval ships and Royal Marines leaving Plymouth and then coming back at the end of the war.

"So I said to myself, 'How do we make something different about the Falklands that hasn't been done before?' I knew the military side had been well covered, as had the political side with Maggie Thatcher, so it would have to be another angle.

"I tapped into my computer 'Falkland Islands conflict islanders' because I believe that the strongest stories are about real people and sometimes ordinary people get caught up in extraordinary things. Within seconds this book title came up: *Falkland Islanders at War* by Graham Bound. I contacted the publisher, who put me in touch with Graham. As it turned out, he'd written the book for the twentieth anniversary and had tried to get interest from broadcasters then, without success. So when we came along he was eager to help. A working relationship was born and Graham, a native Falkland Islander, was able to open doors for me on the islands, which can be quite a guarded and insular community.

"I wanted to make a short pilot and luckily there were a few Falkland Islanders now living in the UK. For instance, there was a veterinarian who had acted as an intelligence gatherer using his camera; he also used the pliers he used as his animal castrating scissors to cut communication wires. The tragedy was that three Falkland Islanders were killed by friendly fire, and one of those was the vet's wife. So that was obviously a powerful story. I then made a pilot, which was about five to seven minutes long. Having interviewed six or seven islanders, I made a seven-minute pilot and took it to the History Channel in the UK. They loved it immediately because it was a fresh angle."

Martin Morgan, deputy channels director at BSkyB, was the commissioner. "For the twenty-fifth anniversary of the Falklands War we had twenty or thirty proposals about the war, and they all had soldiers yomping about, as you might expect, but one stood out. It told the story from the perspective of the Falkland Islanders and the resistance movement that had sprung up. After twenty-five years the story hadn't ever been told.

"Most of those other producers had come at it thinking that it was an easy thing to make: lots of interviews, lots of archive, you can get to the Falkland Islands relatively easily, but they hadn't asked themselves: what's the new angle?"

Falklands: The Islanders' War won the Broadcasting Press Guild "Best Multichannel Programme 2007" Award.

7) Read everything on the newsstand

Commuting time, airport delays, lunch, breakfast in bed are all opportunities to read something. Don't read with the sole intention of finding stories, as it makes it a joyless task; just stay alert for interesting subjects, contributors, or potential presenters.

Wife Swap was originally inspired by a *Daily Mail* article that contrasted the spending habits of different occupations, such as nurses and lawyers. The original pitch focused on swapping people from different financial backgrounds, but it evolved prior to filming to include people with different value systems from all sorts of social backgrounds.

"I think it's important for producers to put in the research to find good stories," says Peter Rees. "There are new stories out there and there are certainly new ways of telling old stories. I'm not a believer in the industry adage that there are no new stories; if you agree with that, then you shouldn't be in the business."

"The thing to do is read LexisNexis a lot and read newspapers and things will occur to you," says Adam Curtis. LexisNexis is a comprehensive database of public records, including criminal and marriage and divorce records, newspaper articles going back to 1986 and public records, available via (expensive) subscription, which your company might give you access to. If not, there is a free version at lexisnexis.com/news, which has the front-page stories from newspapers such as the *Boston Globe*, *South China Morning Post*, *USA Today*, and the *LA Times*. There are also transcripts from news bulletins from ABC, NBC, CBS, and Fox News.

This kind of research led to a commission for Adam Curtis. "I discovered that Sigmund Freud had invented public relations in the 1920s and I thought that was a good story. I went to Jane Root at BBC2 and said, 'I want to do a story about the Freud dynasty and public relations and its history.' She said fine, so I made a series called *Century of the Self*."

Don't make the mistake of reading only newspapers that agree with your political/intellectual leanings; your audience is diverse and, whether you agree with their politics or not, know what concerns them. Being forced to think about subjects in a different way than you would normally is a great way to stimulate ideas. "Your imagination may be creaky or timid or dwarfed or frozen at the joints," said Walt Disney, but even "the *Reader's Digest* can serve as a gymnasium for its training."

If you work within a specialist factual genre, read the relevant magazines, such as *Wired*, *Popular Science*, *New Scientist*, *History Magazine*, or their online equivalents.

CASE STUDY

Greenlit: *Supernanny* (11x60´ Channel 4)

Ricochet

"As an executive producer, you often fall into development between other projects," says Nick Emmerson, President, Shed Media USA, "and it was one of those moments at Ricochet when Ed Levan, Nick Powell, and I were knocking around ideas together.

"This was in 2004, in the summer, and there weren't any big news stories, just lots of PR-led stories. We noticed there were lots of self-help and parenting books being promoted, and we realized parenting, as a theme, wasn't covered on primetime TV at all. What's a bold and noisy way of tackling a dry subject? We could get a nanny in.

"When we had the basic format, we went to see Danny Cohen at Channel 4. The format was: plea for help; Supernanny goes in and observes and then does an intervention; she leaves for a few days, and we keep filming; she looks at the footage and then we do an update.

"Danny was very, very collaborative and he was helpful in honing things, and working out the techniques and middle of the show. He commissioned it early in the process and said, 'Let's go find the nanny.' We actually had an airdate before we found the nanny."

Jo Frost also stars in the UK and US version of *Supernanny* (ABC), and the format has been sold to fifty territories. Romania, Israel, Poland, Brazil, Germany, and China have their own local *Supernanny*. The series received nominations for the People's Choice Award and an International Emmy Award.

---

8) Surf with intent

Find some good blogs and keep checking back to see what they're writing about. If you don't know where to start, explore Technorati.com, which tracks more than 112 million blogs in real time, and monitors what people are posting about, with thousands of updates every hour. According to Technorati, there are more than 175,000 new blogs every day, and 1.6 million new posts per day, so you should find something of interest. Posts are organized into categories such as Entertainment, Politics, Lifestyle, and Business, making it easier to find blogs on a certain subject.

Set up an RSS (Really Simple Syndication) feed from your favorite blogs and updated content will be automatically collated on a single page for you. To read your aggregated content you first need to download a Feed Reader such as Google Reader, Bloglines, or Pageflakes. You can subscribe to a blog's RSS feed by clicking on the small square orange button on the site you want to monitor.

Surfing blogs can be addictive, so ration yourself; the aim is to prime your mind, not procrastinate.

9) Subscribe to other creative industries' online newsletters

Marketing and advertising people are constantly scouring the planet for new trends and insights. The advantage of dipping into their world is that you'll get a sense of the zeitgeist much faster than if you waited until it is featured in a Sunday supplement where everyone else in TV will read it too. Trendwatching.com, coolhunting.com, and springwise.com (which specializes in new business ideas) are good places to start.

Keep a separate, personal, email address for all your email newsletters so your subscriptions don't clog up your normal inbox and you don't have to unsubscribe and resubscribe every time you move to a different job. An email account with a search facility such as Gmail makes it easy to search for articles with keywords weeks or months after receiving the original email.

10) Talk to your colleagues, family, and friends

Too often development teams are isolated from their production colleagues, but it's hard to come up with ideas on your own. Mark Burnett was talking to his team when they realized they all had trouble helping their ten-year-old children to do their homework, and that conversation sparked the development of *Are You Smarter than a Fifth Grader?* (known as *Are You Smarter than a 10 Year Old?* in the UK). It's essential to kick ideas around with other people. "The thing about development," says Ben Hall, is working out "how do you have the conversation you haven't had yet?"

Some managers attempt to rectify a lack of interaction by introducing weekly "clippings sessions" where everyone has to bring a newspaper or magazine cutting from the past week to share with everyone else. While these sessions can be a useful tool for training junior staff to recognize which articles can be spun into program ideas, the forced creativity of these sessions can be stifling and counterproductive for the more experienced development producer. They force a person to spend their weekends actively looking for ideas, which not only ruins their weekend, but produces forced ideas from the same sources that every other TV producer is reading, which is not conducive to original thought. Good developers are always on the lookout for a good story, and it's not something they switch on and off to suit some kind of creative schedule. Instead, this kind of discussion about what's on the news and in the newspapers should be happening organically on a daily basis.

In a well-run team, a discussion about last night's television and this morning's papers happens naturally as people arrive, log into their computers and get their first cup of coffee. Your team should feel able to stop work and chat without fear of being censured for not "working."

Keep interesting clippings on a pin board where everyone can add their articles or comment. Don't keep your clippings in a file because that's where they'll tend to stay, unseen and uninspiring. Let your clippings wall grow organically, and periodically cull out-of-date or irrelevant cuttings.

Crushing Creativity

There are a number of things that can conspire against the creation of original ideas, including having people in charge of "creativity" who are narrow in their thinking.

The Bad Boss

No matter how creative or motivated individual members of the development team are, they will quickly become demoralized if they are working under someone who is rigid, autocratic, fearful of failure, or pursuing their own agenda. Unfortunately all of these scenarios are common. "Your job," says Adam Curtis, "is to play games to get around them. It's a good discipline because it forces you to be creative."

Executive producers can get fixated on pitching only ideas that they are interested in, even if the market isn't buying programs in that subject area or format. This results in execs killing ideas that don't fit their own agenda, even when those ideas might be exactly what the channel wants.

Ideas can also be crushed if the boss is prescriptive, with aspirations for a show like a current hit. "We had the *Walking with Dinosaurs* brand hanging over us like the sword of Damocles," says one producer/director, "but if you are constantly banging people over the head with the example of something, they get hung up on that and stop thinking laterally and creatively, so they don't come up with the goods. It's the equivalent of writer's block. I think there's too much impatience from senior people in development; they are under pressure to deliver, of course they are, but their anxieties are manifested in unfortunate ways. Some people respond well to pressure and can come up with a good idea, but you can crush really good ideas early on with impatience."

In *Art & Fear*, David Bayles and Ted Orland tell the tale of two groups of students in a pottery class:

The ceramics teacher announced on opening day that he was dividing the class into two groups. All those on the left side of the studio, he said, would be graded solely on the quantity of work they produced, all those on the right solely on its quality.

His procedure was simple: on the final day of class he would bring in his bathroom scales and weigh the work of the "quantity" group: fifty pounds of pots rated an "A," forty pounds a "B," and so on. Those being graded on "quality," however, needed to produce only one pot—albeit a perfect one—to get an "A."

Well, came grading time and a curious fact emerged: the works of highest quality were all produced by the group being graded for quantity. It seems that while the "quantity" group was busily churning out piles of work and learning from their mistakes the "quality" group had sat theorizing about perfection, and in the end had little more to show for their efforts than grandiose theories and a pile of dead clay.

In order to find the best idea, generate lots of ideas and don't worry about quality in the first instance. You'll undoubtedly generate some ideas that aren't worth pursuing, but that's OK. In fact you wouldn't be doing your job properly if that weren't the case. "Failure is inevitable," says Ed Crick, "and you might as well make your mistakes quickly and then you can make your successes quicker as well." As those potters did.

All creative endeavors require the creation of drafts that are reworked or discarded until the final, best piece emerges. "The first third of ideas are obvious; the second third are more interesting; the final third show flair, insight, curiosity, even complexity, as later thinking builds on earlier thinking," says Emmy-winning choreographer Twyla Tharp. There's no point wasting time on ideas that are weak, derivative, expensive, or uncastable, but until you have had a lot of ideas it's hard to spot the outstanding ones. If you have only one idea you naturally think it's the best; because it *is* the best in your sample size of one. Put it up against another ten or twenty ideas, though, and its relative strength soon becomes apparent.

Executive and senior producers must be open to talking about all ideas, even if they don't immediately see their appeal. "There's nothing worse than having someone shrug their shoulders at an idea," says one development producer, "it kills an idea flat." After a verbal kick around an idea might turn into something amazing, or it could turn out to be a dud. Either way, you have a result and you can move on.

There's another type of producer who is stuck in the past, and wants to keep rehashing a program that was a huge hit ten years ago because they want to replicate their earlier success. Every idea they come up with is a version of an old-fashioned show. If the market has moved on, they are wasting time and energy that could be used to generate fresher ideas. "Fear breeds rigidity in executive producers," says Adam Curtis. "Fear communicates itself down to assistant producers and everyone becomes rigid. But everyone has to feel that they can try new things." The key is not to spend time on the weak ideas. "The interesting thing about a good idea," says Keith Scholey, "is that the best ones are always the ones that seem obvious. You know you've got one because it's so obvious that you are terrified that someone else is going to think of the same thing."

When senior producers listen to younger producers it can give them the edge, particularly when pitching to the smaller channels, notes Lucy Pilkington, senior commissioning editor at Virgin Media Television. "A big bugbear is producers not understanding the difference between being able to make a show for BBC2 and being able to make a show for us," she says. "If anything we get that from more established producers, because they've made their money doing things for Channel 4, or for the BBC, so they do things in their particular way, whereas the younger producers, they tend to watch us, they are much more light on their feet about knowing what the new trends are."

Cranking Up Creativity

"If you can make it fun, people enjoy what they're doing and it frees up their creative processes," says one development producer. "If it's all very serious they are scared of being laughed at and humiliated and you don't want people to feel like that." John Hesling, SVP programming, BBC Worldwide, America, agrees: "We used to come up with lots of one-liners, silly stuff, which is an important part of the development process. If you stop people coming up with absurd things then they're never going to come up with anything."

It's also important that senior members of the team communicate everything to their team. "I think development teams who don't have senior producers or executive producers or their creative heads with them, talking to them many times every day, that undermines their effectiveness, to be sure," says Tom Archer. "It's easy for people in the higher echelons in television to not pass on all the pieces of information that they accrue in a working day—little bits of gossip, little bits of intelligence. You don't know what crucial thing you have in your brain that's going to spark off something in the development team. So I think that contact is important—there's no point in doing that sort of thing by paper or even a phone call—it's talking with many people in the room, interacting. As a creative head I always put myself in an adjoining room to development and always spent any spare time I had sitting there eavesdropping, intervening, asking, that kind of stuff, generally being a semi-detached part of the team."

How to Generate New Ideas Quickly

You should, by now, be seeing new ideas wherever you go, but let's assume you suddenly need to come up with some completely new ideas. How do you generate ideas from scratch? "You come up with ideas through reading, consuming influence or you come up with ideas through a spark of genius, but usually you come up with ideas through a creative collaboration," says Ed Crick, "but it's useful to have a framework for that, which might be a particular development technique or a focused channel or slot need, or it could be particular resources like a piece of talent."

Here are five suggestions:

1) **Create your own brief**—It is difficult to generate ideas while looking at a blank page, where anything is possible, so set yourself some parameters: having boundaries and limitations forces you to think more creatively. "I personally feel, if you are stuck you need to start with a brief, even if it's a made-up one, because it at least gives you something to talk about," says Ben Hall. "You can at least talk about what is already there. Take talent shows: is there a market? What's out there? Is there room for another dancing show? If you think there is, how do you make it different?"

2) **Spend the day out of the office with your team**—Base yourselves in a bookstore café for the day and see what interesting biographies or popular science books you can find. Or visit a museum together. Just being out of the office can stimulate new conversations.

3) **Free associate**—Go and sit somewhere quiet with a notepad and write down anything that comes to mind. Free associate around different subject areas. "Sometimes I will write down lists of things I'm interested in," says Barry Gibb, filmmaker and science multimedia editor at the Wellcome Trust. By writing down words around cybernetics and machines he came up with an idea for a film about cyborgs, which he successfully pitched to Emily Renshaw-Smith at Current TV.

4) **Look at past, current and upcoming movies**—Is there a factual take on the subject? For example, *Batman* might have led you to develop *Who Wants to Be a Superhero?* (Sci Fi Channel). *Oz and James's Big Wine Adventure* "was vaguely based on *Sideways*," says Nick Shearman, "and I often think that movies are a good basis for good format ideas." Likewise, *Rock School* was influenced by Jack Black's *School of Rock*.

5) **Expand a brand**—Look at the programs your production company currently has on the air—are they likely to return, and if so, can you spin off new shows from them? "You don't need that many good ideas," says Keith Scholey, "because once you have a good idea a whole financial chain springs out from that," for example, "*1900 House* became a brand with *1940s House*, *Frontier House*, and so on," says Alex Graham, CEO of Wall to Wall.

In reality, the proactive development producer has little need to actively generate new ideas because they have more ideas on their slate than they can realistically develop into commissionable proposals. So where do all these ideas come from?

Apart from the ideas generated from all the sources listed above, the development team are, at any one time, also working on ideas brought to them by executive producers and on ideas generated during meetings with channel executives. According to research done by the Research Centre, many commissioners "said that they thought up program ideas themselves, seeing it as a very important aspect of their role. When asked about the approximate percentage of commissions that had such input, many put it between 20 and 50 percent of their commissions."

Organization

Prioritizing Ideas: All Ideas Are Not Equal

Generally, channel executive-generated ideas take priority. If a channel executive has already invested emotionally and intellectually in an idea you have a much better chance of getting it greenlit.

The fast turnaround documentary, such as *Miracle of the Hudson Plane Crash*, is the flashing-blue-light-emergency version of an idea. "If it's a breaking current affairs or entertainment story you have to act fast and you need to get it to a commissioner on the day the story breaks," says one development producer. "If they are interested they will call you back, and it might be commissioned by the next morning—it does happen."

Ideas from executive producers are next on the priority list, especially if they have a good track record of salable ideas (you'll soon get to know who they are) and the channel trusts them to deliver. Some executive producers will develop and pitch their own ideas, others need a lot of help to research, write, and prepare their pitch.

Next in the pecking order is you, the development producer. In order to successfully work up your own ideas it's vital to leave your ego outside the door, otherwise you can spend an inordinate amount of time developing an idea in which only you are interested. The ability to objectively assess your own ideas requires discipline and ruthlessness. To succeed, concentrate on the ideas that best fit a channel brief and kill any idea that doesn't.

Then there are the ideas that come in from the wider production community. Usually, these need the most work, and as they are most likely to be presented as a subject area rather than a program idea, they get pushed to the bottom of the priority pile. The lesson here, if you are a producer trying to get Development to listen to your ideas, is to make it easy for the people acting as gatekeepers. You don't need to give them a full proposal; a couple of paragraphs that make the idea easy to visualize and give an indication of which channel might be interested will take your idea to the top of the list, especially if you are lucky enough to tap into a current channel need (we look at how to protect your ideas from unscrupulous operators in the next chapter).

Time Management: The Art of Juggling ...

Keep calm and carry on.
—Ministry of Information, 1939

Good time management is vital if you are to successfully generate and pitch ideas on an on-going basis. If you regularly meet with a channel executive, work backward from the meeting date and mark in your diary the deadlines for practicing your pitch, writing your proposal, developing your ideas, generating new ideas. Then work forward, adhering to the amount of time available for each activity. This will prevent you lapsing into firefighting mode. "You can't come up with an idea if someone is banging on your door saying we need it at six o'clock tonight. It's very difficult," warns Keith Scholey. If you are working on something that isn't ready by the deadline, be honest with yourself, and pull it from the pitch until it is ready.

However, a controlled sense of urgency can be a great antidote for procrastination and a good tool for scaring you into actively developing your ideas and writing your proposal. If you don't have a looming deadline, a self-imposed deadline can break your deadlock. "Development is difficult," says Keith Scholey. "New ideas are few and they are very hard, so people get stuck in all sorts of escape mechanisms of how to get away from difficulty, and I think the people who struggle try to lose themselves in other activities."

Don't let the creative process become more important than the idea; by the time you've "processed" your idea, your competitors have made off with the business. You need be fast on your feet to compete. For this reason, don't schedule in formal "creative sessions": they often take weeks to organize and just waste time. If someone has a creative problem, they should be able to turn to anyone in the team and brainstorm it there and then, or over a coffee. If it's done spontaneously, other people can chip in then or later if a thought occurs to them. Keep it organic and creative and trust your team to call a brainstorm if they need one. Don't put boundaries round creativity.

If you are lucky enough to have a team, allocate their work wisely, playing to their strengths. Some people are great at ideas generation but hopeless at writing, some great at pitching, others are good all-rounders. It helps if ideas are developed by people who are passionate about them, so make sure that the most appropriate person is working on an idea.

Manage your team's workload. Keep them busy, don't allow them to get bored or they will lose momentum. I use a series of notes stuck to the wall, each with a title of a program. On a daily basis, after triaging the slate in light of recent meetings or channel executive feedback, I rearrange the titles into deadline order, with the most pressing priorities at the top. Each team member selects a title to work on from those with the closest deadline and works on it until it is developed and a proposal written. They pass the proposal to me for feedback and select the next project from the priority list. I've found that this system builds healthy competition among the team, which keeps the momentum up, and they self-select the ideas they're most passionate about, which increases quality and productivity.

If a team is well trained, know their deadlines, are given the tools with which they need to work, for example easy access to lightweight cameras and editing software, and they are kept fully informed of all the commissioning gossip, they will be able to make the best use of their time. Good development teams are "incredibly focused and targeted and they know exactly what they are doing every day," says Ben Hall. "They don't waste any time, and if they don't have anything to do they go home. They don't stay really late." However, I know from experience (from both a team and manager's perspective) that if you trust your team and don't try to schedule their creativity, they will be engaged and enthused enough to still be there at midnight if they're editing a promo tape that they're excited about.

Sometimes, in an all-hands-on-deck situation, you might need to pull in production staff to help you write proposals. Having a clear proposal template and definitive house-style makes it easier for them to produce what you need and a breeze for you to edit.

Ensure that you also have house rules for recording research—make use of footnotes or some other agreed system so that if anyone "gets run over by a bus" or more likely, goes off to work on a production, anyone else can pick up from where they left off. Likewise for conversations with contributors, talent, and agents: nothing is more annoying for them than having to repeat conversations with new people every time they're in contact with you.

Get a well-respected executive producer on side with your idea as soon as possible, as they will add weight to your pitch. The earlier they're included in the process the more enthusiastically they will champion your idea, and they may well relieve you of some of the workload as they get emotionally and intellectually drawn in by the idea.

Keeping Track of Ideas ... and Not Dropping Any Balls

The key to sustained and successful development of television ideas is good organization, which boils down to good record keeping and good housekeeping. Some people carry a notebook at all times; others find it easier to keep a stash of postcards in their pocket. You could use blank business cards. Choreographer Twyla Tharp collects all the thoughts, articles, and artifacts that influence her choreography in a box, which she excavates like an archeologist when she needs inspiration.

Keep a database of all your ideas. "I have an ideas master list that I keep with me wherever I go on a Word.doc, which I back up regularly," says one develop-ment producer. "Every week I start a new paragraph and all of the ideas that I have had or have sent to anyone, I add to the list. Keeping a list helps with ownership too."

Keep separate sheets for ideas in active development, those that have promise but aren't a priority and those that have been rejected. Be meticulous in your record keeping and you will never embarrass yourself by offering the same idea to the same person twice, or be unable to recall whether you've already pitched an idea.

"If I'm out of work, I don't do much with my ideas, they tend to sit in a notebook or on my laptop," says one development producer, "and then when I go to work for a company I can go back into my stockpile and see if there's anything that would work for that company." Having a good back catalog means you never start from scratch, and it works as a safety net: having it gives you the confidence of knowing that you can come up with ideas.

If people are pitching ideas to you, record the title, date of origination, a one-sentence description (no point going into too much detail as it will be constantly evolving), who had the idea originally (important for giving credit and feedback), whom you've pitched it to, and what stage it's at. "All those ideas need to be written down and put in a file and revisited every three months," says John Hesling, "because whether it's reading the paper or looking at song titles or whatever, ideas don't come from nowhere, they need to be sprung from somewhere."

It's a good strategy to build a relatively broad portfolio, as you would when investing in the stock market: invest the bulk of your development effort in safe stock, such as ideas in which a channel executive has expressed interest, and much smaller amount of effort into wild-card ideas. Challenge yourself to develop and pitch riskier, and more ambitious ideas, because if you rely too much on one type of show, for example property flipping shows, and there's a market downturn, or property shows fall from favor, you're suddenly left high and dry. If you have a more diverse development portfolio, chances are you've been steadily gaining a reputation for another type of program, and therefore able to ride the market and dodge bankruptcy.

It is important to keep your active ideas database free from clutter. This involves triaging and killing ideas that you no longer have any passion for, and expending effort only on the ideas with the most promise. Doing this at the earliest stage of development will save you a lot of wasted time later on. The triage process should be repeated at least monthly on all ideas in development so you keep ideas moving toward commission, or remove them from your slate. In the earliest stages of the process, when you are yet to fully develop an idea, it's hard to imagine its potential, but you must train yourself to be objective and ruthless. Get someone else to do it for you if you are emotionally involved in your idea. First, ask yourself whether your idea is suited to television or whether it might be best left as a scientific paper, academic book, photography exhibition, or museum exhibit. For a television program to work, you need a strong intellectual and/or emotional journey, or a question that can be answered *and* a visual way of presenting the narrative.

Your Active list should be fairly short and manageable. No idea should be on there unless there is something happening to it—a proposal being written, talent being found, a pitch tape being shot, or a channel executive meeting sought.

When an idea has been rejected move it to the Archive sheet for future reference. Sometimes these ideas can come back to life if there's a change of channel head. Conversely, it's a useful reference for new staff to know what's already been pitched and failed.

A talent database is vital too, with photographs, website addresses, contact details, previous television experience, personal interests, and a record of correspondence. Keep it up to date and it will be invaluable, when you find an idea that would be perfect for that cake decorator you discovered eighteen months ago.

To check if your records are adequate, ask yourself a question: if you were run over by a bus tomorrow, would someone be able to take over seamlessly using only the information in your records? If yes, congratulate yourself, and keep your fingers crossed they will never need to. If the answer is no, sort it out.

To find out if your fledgling idea has potential and should be put through to the next stage ask yourself a series of questions:

1. Does the idea feel original and exciting? Perhaps a bit "dangerous"?

2. Is it topical?

3. Is it similar in content, tone, or format to a successful program but with its own unique twist?

4. Is it a good match for a particular channel's brief?

5. Is it more than a subject area?

6. Is there a narrative, with a strong character, goals, obstacles, a climax?

7. Does it tap into a universal theme? For example:
    a. Man against nature—*Touching the Void, Man vs. Wild*
    b. David vs. Goliath—*Gladiators*
    c. Redemption—*I'm a Celebrity Get Me Out of Here!, The Dog Whisperer*
    d. Battle of the Sexes—*Wife Swap, Beauty and the Geek, The Bachelor*
    e. Triumph over adversity—*Deadliest Catch*
    f. Good vs. Evil—*Dog the Bounty Hunter*

8. Will viewers want to watch? Will it satisfy them intellectually and/or emotionally?

If you can't answer yes to at least four of these questions, stop and kill the idea. If it ticks most of the boxes, your idea lives to fight another day. It now needs to be developed further, but how do you do that?

Development Master Class 4

Generate Ideas

1. Sign up to get free newsletters from coolhunting.com and trendwatching.com or a couple of other newsletters relevant to your areas of interest.

2. Read a different newspaper every day of the week and at least one new magazine every week.

3. Compare three different formats. Write down their format points—the things that are the same from week to week that drive the narrative. Could you swap the formats about and create a new kind of show?

4. Visit a museum or gallery you've never been to, or attend a book reading.

5. Sign up to a couple of museum newsletters, one in your country and one somewhere else in the world.

6. Commit to going to one networking event every three months and meticulously record the details of anyone you find interesting; LinkedIn.com provides a constantly updated database of people's current job and contact details, which prevents you having outdated contacts in your address book.

7. Think back through all the productions you've worked on and list any interesting people you met or subjects that could be expanded into a new series.

8. Research anniversaries coming up in the next five years: keep a list of interesting dates for future reference. Wikipedia has a database of anniversaries: http://en.wikipedia.org/wiki/List_of_historical_anniversaries.

9. If you work at an independent production company with a back catalog, riffle through to see if there's anything that can be revived or reworked.

10. Start a spreadsheet and log all the ideas you've been gathering. Have one sheet for ideas in active development and an archive sheet. If you pitch an idea and it is rejected, move it from the Active page to the Archive page. Return to the archives periodically to see if there are any ideas worth dusting off and giving another whirl.

Explore More

Likemind: monthly breakfast meeting for creative people, usually held on the third Friday of every month in approximately fifty locations around the world http://likemind.us.

Meetup: another international networking organization that is based on special interests. There are groups in more than 11,000 cities around the world who are interested in everything from personal growth to procrastination and postpartum issues http://www.meetup.com.

BUBL: extensive archive of internet resources on all academic subjects run by Strathclyde University, Glasgow http://bubl.ac.uk/index.html.

Lexis Nexis: subscription news service with more than 4,000 sources. You can get free access to selected front-page news stories, US military press releases, news program transcripts, missing person information, among other things http://www.lexisnexis.com/news/.

TV Mole: news stories, trends, exhibitions, and new books are uploaded five times a week and categorized into art; books; business; documentary; history; lifestyle; multiplatform; natural history; reality; religion; science; technology innovations; videos. Click on the category list on the right side of the page to go to a specific category where you'll find dozens of short articles that will start sparking ideas http://www.tvmole.com.

Paul Arden: *Whatever You Think, Think the Opposite*
Very quick and easy read: ideal for shaking you out of a creative funk.

Mihaly Csikszentmihalyi: *Creativity: Flow and the Psychology of Discovery and Invention*
Drawing on more than one hundred interviews with creative people this book muses on the nature of the creative process. Good for procrastination if you are feeling "stuck."

Twyla Tharp: *The Creative Habit: Learn It and Use It for Life*
An inspiring book by an acclaimed choreographer who explains her creative process and how to make creativity part of your daily life.

Roger von Oech: *A Whack on the Side of the Head: How You Can Be More Creative*
Not aimed specifically at TV but it acts as a primer to get you in the creative mood.

5

Developing an Idea

*Many of life's failures are men who did not realize how
close they were to success when they gave up.*

—Thomas Edison

On a drizzly Thursday in September 1997, three men were confined to an office
in north Holland. It was late at night, or possibly early the next morning; none of
them can quite remember. But what happened next changed television forever.
Patrick Scholtze and brothers Paul and Bart Römer were kicking around ideas in
a lackluster meeting with their boss, John de Mol.

Paul Römer had read about, and was intrigued by, a webstite called
"JenniCam." About eighteen months previously, a nineteen-year-old American
college student, Jennifer Ringley, had set up a webcam in her college dorm room
and broadcast her life to the world via images that refreshed every three minutes.
JenniCam recorded everything from mundane everyday routines to more racy
activities such as an impromptu striptease and sex with her new boyfriend
(which created a stir when it turned out that he was also someone else's
boyfriend).

The team also talked about the increasing use of CCTV cameras in everyday
life and mused about sabbaticals, but they weren't getting anywhere with
generating program ideas; they were all talked out and ready to go home.

As they were getting ready to leave Bart Römer mentioned an American
experiment called Biosphere II, in which seven people lived together for a period
of two years in a totally enclosed and atmospherically controlled series of
greenhouse-like structures in Arizona. Suddenly the various conversations came

together to spark a bigger idea: what would happen if they locked up a group of people in a house and filmed them? John de Mol's imagination ignited.

De Mol suggested that they put people together in a confined space, film them 24/7 and made them do monthly challenges to earn the right to telephone their loved ones. Scholtze and the Römer brothers sat down, knowing it was going to be a long night. By the time they eventually left that office, Project X had been born.

Peter Bazalgette describes how Project X developed (and ultimately led him to be named as one of ten "Worst Britons" by the *Daily Mail*) in his book *Billion Dollar Game*. Over the next week, the team kept adding details: six people would live together in a luxury house for a year, at the end of which they could win a million guilders, but throughout the year they would be subjected to endurance tests designed to make them want to leave the house.

Paul Römer was put in charge of *The Golden Cage* (as the top-secret Project X became known to insiders). Römer started working on the logistics: he consulted psychiatrists from the University of Amsterdam, and technical experts at Sony. He put some colleagues in a room together and noted that it took less than an hour for them to get on each other's nerves. He invited six strangers to spend a few hours in a bare TV studio and filmed them as a voice-of-God broadcast instructions to them, making them angry and emotional. He worked out the program would need a budget of £11.5 million, which was 50 percent of some of the Dutch broadcasters' programming budgets. Römer was beginning to think it was impossible.

Other Endemol executives began to hear about the idea, and they weren't thrilled—one even thought it could bring Endemol down—but John de Mol was determined to press ahead with it.

Römer scaled down the ambition of the house, turning it into a cabin, and introduced a housemate eviction vote, so they could guarantee there would be only one winner of the million guilders. De Mol decided that the housemates would vote for two people and the audience would vote for which of them would actually be evicted. De Mol pitched the idea to RTL4 and SBS in the Netherlands, but both turned it down.

De Mol told Römer to make a taster tape, which was set to Carl Orff's dramatic oratorio *Carmina Burana*. Over archive footage of a NASA rocket launch, a portentous voiceover described the format: a group of strangers stranded together in a remote building for one year, completely cut off from the outside world. Intercut with the archive was an interview with a German professor theorizing about the dire psychological impact of such an experiment, where the volunteers are "totally isolated. Constantly observed ... Wherever they are, whatever they do, whatever they go throug ... every breath will be recorded and broadcast." The tape then cut to an interview with Jennifer Ringley and footage of the six people shot by Römer in the TV studio voting out a bewildered-looking man. Over CCTV footage the narrator warned that, "'Big Brother is watching you' is never truer than in *The Golden Cage*."

Around this time, the Dutch producers asked Peter Bazalgette if he could sell the show in the UK for them. His faxed response was: "The rats-in-a-cage-who'll-do-anything-for-money is something that I doubt we could sell onto terrestrial television."

De Mol's ambition was to have the winner leave the house on New Year's Eve 1999, and this self-imposed deadline was fast approaching with no buyer in sight. He reduced the duration of the filming to one hundred days, dropped the prize money to two hundred thousand guilders, and renamed it *Big Brother*. He pitched it to Pro Sieben, a German TV channel, which said no after two of the execs thought that the treatment of the housemates had Nazi undertones.

De Mol was running out of options and time, so he changed tack. He offered to sweeten the deal by sharing the financial risk with the broadcaster; of course he would also expect to share in any advertising revenue profits too, which was hitherto unheard-of. Unico Glorie, at Holland Media Group, which oversaw the younger-skewing channel Veronica, took the bait (and almost lost his job when his boss found out).

When *Big Brother* premièred on Veronica to a barrage of press outrage, it drew a 33 percent share of the audience, a huge improvement on the channel's normal 8 percent share. RTL in Germany and Telecinco in Spain quickly bought the rights to the format. Peter Bazalgette photocopied a full-page article in *The Times* about a romance between two of the Dutch *Big Brother* housemates, and faxed it to Sky One, ITV, Five, and Channel 4. Liz Murdoch at Sky didn't respond and David Liddiment at ITV turned it down. Alan Yentob at the BBC was interested, but Bazalgette thought the corporation's committees would put it through a creative "hot wash" and ruin it. Five couldn't make the budget, so Channel 4 bought the show. Bazalgette and Channel 4 tweaked the format, introducing weekly evictions, and the show subsequently sold around the world and was seen in nearly seventy countries.

Bazalgette later put *Big Brother*'s success down to it being the right time for it: the internet and mobile phones meant that the audience could consume the content and interact with it in a way they couldn't have a few years previously. He told *MoneyWeek* magazine that it was a convergence of different technologies like "Elvis and the electric guitar."

But actually there were a few things at work: a big audacious idea, a producer who championed it relentlessly, a channel executive who was willing to risk his job for it, an imaginative and daring commercial deal. It was these factors, together with the technological breakthroughs, that eventually led to *Big Brother*'s eventual runaway success. And, of course, there was the lengthy development process that took the idea from an impossibly expensive collection of random elements and turned it into a distinctive format that was commercially viable. "A great idea is a fine thing but if you can't back it up with how you are going to turn it into a television program it's not a pitch," notes Emily Renshaw-Smith.

Developing a new idea requires a series of structured decisions that ensure development effort is focused on creating a marketable and sellable proposition. Every creative decision you make has an impact on your idea's budget, production values (e.g. glossy and beautifully shot or shot with hand-held cameras), shape, and ambition, which in turn influence the number of channels to which you can pitch and its international market appeal. Therefore, "you need a sense of where you are headed," says Ben Hall. "Is it half an hour or an hour? Is it a primetime entertainment show that will take you into Europe?"

When you start developing your idea, invest some serious thinking time. This is the hardest but most important part of the process. It's not as concrete as writing your idea down, nor as exciting as pitching it, but the thinking you do now affects everything that comes later. Skip this part and cracks will suddenly appear in your idea, usually at the pitch meeting, and you will spend an uncomfortable thirty minutes doing a good impression of the Little Dutch Boy as you attempt to plug the holes while all hope of a commission leaks away.

Keep a couple of key things in mind as you develop your idea: your production experience and target market. Those important way-markers will stop you driving your idea down a dead end.

Growing Your Idea

If you are a documentarian, you first need to find a focused narrative—driven by characters and/or chronology (perhaps through history or corresponding to physical journey)—which necessitates research around your chosen subject. You might start by reading news and magazine archives, doing an Amazon book search or calling some academics. Follow interesting leads, and stay open to new possibilities as you sniff out interesting characters, details, and unexpected consequences: the best story might not be the one you'd initially imagined.

CASE STUDY

Capturing the Friedmans (107´ Theatrical)

Director: Andrew Jerecki

When Andrew Jerecki decided to make *Just a Clown*, a documentary about clowns in New York City, he interviewed high-class children's entertainer David Friedman, who works under the name Silly Billy. Jerecki wanted to explore who these adults were who liked to hang out at children's birthday parties; he thought it was a little weird, so he expected to find something interesting, but he wasn't sure exactly what. "In a documentary you are not the boss of the story, the story is the boss of you," says Jerecki, "it's important to just listen to the material."

After a couple of months' filming Friedman hinted at a family secret. Jerecki did some research and discovered Friedman's father, Arnold, and younger brother, Jesse, had been convicted of paedophilia in the late 1980s.

Arnold Friedman had taught his three young sons how to make short films using a Super 8 camera, and they'd always recorded family events such as birthdays and religious holidays. Continuing that tradition, David Friedman filmed the events around the arrests, and had also recorded a video diary; it turned out that David had twenty-five hours of archive footage that he was willing to share with Jerecki.

Suddenly, Jerecki was no longer making a documentary film about children's clowns, but a quite different archive-based film documenting the destruction of a family.

When developing a new factual entertainment format, the trick is to take a familiar subject and give it an unexpected treatment:

* When business met *Big Brother* we got *The Apprentice*.

* When business met *Idol*, we got *Dragons' Den*.

* When cooking met stadium sports we got *Iron Chef*.

* When WWII met reality TV, we got *Bad Lads' Army*.

Alternatively, at the entertainment end of the spectrum your aim is to find an idea that makes you think, "You can't do that!" as it is more likely to be original and exciting:

* You can't lock up ten strangers for ten weeks with no contact with the outside world—*Big Brother* (Channel 4).

* You can't send celebrities to live in the jungle and make them eat live insects and fish eyes—*I'm a Celebrity Get Me Out of Here* (ITV1).

* You can't show an animal being slaughtered and then watch people eat it.—*Kill It Cook It Eat It* (BBC3).

* You can't put amateur singers in a primetime slot—*American Idol* (Fox).

This is a strategy that Fox's president of alternative entertainment, Mike Darnell, subscribes to. "I like to twist things. I like to get a reaction out of people. I like the audience to go: 'What? What are they doing?' But in a way that shocks you, but generally doesn't turn your stomach."

In *Desperate Networks*, Bill Carter describes some of Darnell's more ambitious ideas. "Some of his ideas were too much even for Fox. For one proposed show, Mike wanted to sink a ship at sea live—it proved too costly. For another, he tried to get a stuntman to actually parachute from the stratosphere in something he was titling 'Space Jump.' Some Fox lawyers balked because it seemed there was a really good chance of killing the guy. Most infamously, Darnell came up with an idea to crash a 727 (Mike originally wanted a 747) jetliner into a mountain or in a desert (after the pilot had bailed out, of course). Darnell planned to fit the plane with numerous cameras that would capture the disaster in all its destructive glory." Although he didn't get to crash his airplane, in November 2009, *Broadcast* announced that Dragonfly had been commissioned by Channel 4, National Geographic, and Pro Sieben to film two pilots crash a 300-seat passenger plane after baling out over a desert.

Prêt-à-Porter Formats—Format Shapes to Suit Your Idea

There many ways of classifying types of factual TV programs, and the language used is often confusing, especially across international boundaries. Even within the same country, different people understand the same word to mean different things, depending on their production background (and level of pretentiousness). Let's cut through the jargon to look at the different ways that stories might be constructed, starting at the classic documentary end of the format spectrum and working toward entertainment (these classifications, based on my own analysis, aren't definitive, so you might want to add to them). In each subgenre there are a couple of examples to show how flexible these categories are.

Documentary

1) Classic Documentary—tends to be a one-off film that objectively explores or teaches us about a subject. However, in any documentary format the filmmaker "constructs the truth," to a greater or lesser extent, as they select and juxtapose material. "There is no such thing as reality. Reality is just the stories we tell each other," says Adam Curtis. "It doesn't mean you're being dishonest, it's just how you put the fragments together." (Note that Curtis uses "reality" in this context to mean "truth" rather than a genre of programming.)

A voiceover artist drives the narrative, in between interviews with academics or eyewitnesses who support or illuminate the main narrative. Archive footage or rostrum shots of contemporary newspapers, photographs, or letters provide the physical proof of the veracity of the story. Beautifully framed shots of landscapes or architectural details fill any visual gaps. This kind of documentary is intended to inform and educate the audience, and usually attract an older, male viewer. It is most often seen in science or history programming, for example:

* *Blue Planet* (BBC1/Discovery);

* *When We Left Earth: The NASA Missions* (Discovery);

* *NY77: The Coolest Year in Hell* (VH1);

* *Auschwitz: The Nazis and the Final Solution* (BBC2/PBS).

A variation is the talent-led documentary, in which an expert leads us through a subject, synthesizing and simplifying the subject so it's easy to understand. The presenter might interview experts, asking the questions the audience might ask. The defining feature is that the story can also be told without the presenter; in international versions the original presenter is often edited out and replaced with a voiceover. This talent-led approach is often used in documentary series. Examples include:

* *Earth: Power of the Planet* (BBC1/National Geographic);

* *The Human Body* (BBC2/Discovery);

* *Andrew Marr's History of Modern Britain* (BBC2).

2) Documentary Strands—it is hard to find a channel that will commission single documentaries; there is, however, a workaround in the shape of "strands." A strand is a series of single, but similarly themed documentaries, made by different producers and strung together to make a series. For example:

* *Horizon* (BBC2)—science;

* *Dispatches* (Channel 4)—current affairs;

* *Wonderland* (BBC2)—quirky human stories;

* *POV* (PBS)—independent "documentaries with a point of view";

* *Passionate Eye* (CBC, Canada)—provocative and award-winning documentaries from around the world.

3) Docudrama—a factually accurate story of a person or a period in history (or occasionally, the future), that uses documentary techniques such as voiceover, expert interviews, and contemporary documents, interspersed with dramatic scenes featuring actors.

Docudrama is a loose term with many variations and is used interchangeably with drama documentary, but for our purposes docudrama is more focused on the accurate telling of the facts than the entertainment values of the drama. The term "dramatic/drama reconstruction" indicates scenes featuring (usually non-speaking) actors who re-enact events. Drama reconstruction has fallen out of favor after channel executives tired of seeing badly acted historical scenes performed by actors in ill-fitting wigs (a.k.a. "men in tights"). Examples of successful docudramas include theatrical releases:

* *Touching the Void;*

* *Man on Wire.*

CASE STUDY

Greenlit: *Touching the Void* **(106´ Theatrical)**

Darlow Smithson

John Smithson faced the problem of telling a retrospective story in *Touching the Void*: "To tell the story, the two key protagonists Joe and Simon were obviously still alive, but there was no archive footage, there were just a few black-and-white stills. So how do you capture the drama? How do you visualize what they were talking about?

"It was a film about the universal themes of life and death, and what to do when you are in this appalling predicament, which is what happened when Joe dropped into the crevasse. It happened to be about mountain-eers, but it wasn't about mountaineering—it was about friendship, it was about the will to survive. So using dramatic re-enactment, and intercutting it with real-life testimony, became the obvious way of telling the story."

Touching the Void became the UK's most successful documentary feature film and won a BAFTA as well as multiple other awards and nominations.

---

4) *Drama Documentary*—a fully dramatized telling of a factual story. It became fashionable for documentary producers to produce dramatized documentaries, made on a much smaller budget than a comparable narrative drama budget. However, this approach sometimes led to criticism for low production values and poor storytelling. In this approach, although the narrative is based on facts there may be some dramatic license taken in order to make the narrative satisfying, which can be problematic when viewers are left unsure whether they are watching a factual story or a drama. Documentary fans find a lack of concrete facts deeply unsatisfying to watch, and drama lovers can feel bogged down in all the factual exposition. Examples in the genre include:

* *Supervolcano* (BBC1/Discovery);

* *Walking with Dinosaurs* (BBC1/Discovery), which replaced actors with computer-generated dinosaurs.

5) *Point of View Documentary*—this subjective approach is authored by the filmmaker or protagonist, and is strongly skewed toward a certain viewpoint. The argument can be made in voiceover and illustrated with archive film, as in *The Power of Nightmares* (BBC2), or it can be a personal take on a subject, such as in *The Boy Whose Skin Fell Off* (Channel 4), in which Jonny Kennedy narrates the story of his own death. The POV documentary is also a common vehicle for filmmakers with a campaigning agenda, such as:

* Jamie Oliver in *Jamie's School Dinners* (Channel 4);

* Morgan Spurlock in *Supersize Me* (Theatrical);

* Michael Moore in *Bowling for Columbine* (Theatrical).

6) *Immersive Documentary*—in the immersive documentary, the protagonist goes on a physical journey to investigate or discover something about the world. This subgenre includes travelogues. The host/presenter isn't an expert in the subject they're investigating, and therefore approaches it from an "everyman" perspective (and they usually *are* men). They don't tell us about their subject, they actually live it. Examples include:

* *30 Days* (FX/More 4);

* *Dirty Jobs* (Discovery);

* *Ross Kemp on Gangs* (Sky One);

* *Tribe/Going Tribal* (BBC2/Discovery).

7) Observational Documentary—also known as docusoap or fly-on-the-wall (especially in the UK), vérité or reality (especially in the US). This kind of documentary gives us unique access into the day-to-day lives of organizations or individuals. A narrator might set the scene, or the subjects themselves explain what's happening. Observational documentaries follow the same characters from week to week and are likely to return for more than one series. Each episode tends to have a self-contained story that is resolved by the end of the show. Careful casting ensures the characters are compelling enough to sustain a whole series. Examples include:

* *Ace of Cakes* (Food Network);

* *Dog the Bounty Hunter* (A&E);

* *American Chopper* (TLC);

* *The Family* (Channel 4).

In a variation on this theme, the environment becomes the main character and plays the role of antagonist, against which an ensemble cast must endure and survive:

* *Deadliest Catch* (Discovery);

* *Trauma: Life in the ER* (TLC);

* *Airport* (BBC2);

* *Ice Road Truckers* (History).

Although events unfold naturally, a story producer works with the editor to pull out specific story threads and weave them into a narrative with a beginning, middle, and end for each episode. For example, if we are following the story of a delayed flight, we would meet a number of affected passengers at the start of the program, see them becoming increasingly frustrated over the course of the program as they try to get information from the airline or organize alternative transport, and at the end of the show, discover whether they made it to the wedding on time or decided to cancel their vacation.

Formats

A 'formatted' program is one in which the narrative arc is the same each week; only the contributors change. "A format is a blueprint for a show," says Ben Hall. "If you can describe last week's show without having seen it, it is a format." Ex-BBC commercial affairs executive Matt Ogden adds that, "If you can't write a [format] bible and take photos, it's not a format."

The format narrative is driven by a number of "format points" that happen at the same time and in the same way in each episode. Successful formats are particularly sought-after as once the format is worked out, it is relatively cheap and easy to make week after week, as the production team doesn't have to find and create a completely new story for every episode.

For example, in the UK version of *The Apprentice* (format points in bold):

A **group of contestants** with **business backgrounds** live together in a **communal luxury penthouse**. A **telephone call summons** the contestants to the **board-room**. There they meet **Sir Alan Sugar and his two assistants** and are split into **two teams**. Sir Alan gives the two teams a **business-related challenge**, which they must complete against a **deadline**. The teams each select a **project manager** for the task. The cameras, and **one of Sir Alan's helpers** follow each of the teams as they **attempt the task**. After the challenge is completed (**two-thirds of the way** into the program) the two teams are summoned to Sir Alan's **boardroom**, where it is revealed **which team was the more successful**. The winning team is **given a reward and retires** from the boardroom. The losing team face Sir Alan in a **showdown** to determine which of the team will be fired. The **project manager is asked to select up to three team members** they believe to be most responsible for the team's failure. The **rest of the team is dismissed** and the remaining members face a **confrontation** in which they must fight for their reputation and their right to stay on the program. **Sir Alan fires at least one** of them with the words *"You're fired!"* The fired contestant leaves the boardroom and gives their **response to the verdict** in the back of a taxi as they are driven away in disgrace. The surviving contestants **return to the house** to join the others. The format is repeated each week until only the finalists remain and **one is hired**.

This format is based on the original US version of *The Apprentice*, which is set in NYC and presided over by Donald Trump. There are also Danish, Croatian, German, and Australian versions of the format.

1) Factual Entertainment—these are lighter factual subjects, such as fashion, property, or food, usually hosted and with the emphasis on entertainment. Every episode is a self-contained narrative, which makes it easy for the channel to repeat single episodes whenever they have a hole in the schedule, without having to commit to repeating the whole series. Within Factual Entertainment, there are a number of subgenres:

a) Talent-Led/Observational—a lightly formatted approach where a host with expert knowledge observes contributors effecting an authentic change in their lives—they would still make those changes if television cameras were not present. The host might offer advice but doesn't impose her (it is most often a woman) will on the contributors. Examples include:

* *Property Ladder* (Channel 4);
* *Location, Location, Location* (Channel 4);
* *Grand Designs* (Channel 4).

b) Talent-Led/Interventionist—a more heavily formatted approach, in which the onscreen talent forcibly effects a change in an unsuspecting or reluctant contributor's life. There are specific plot points that the audience recognizes from week to week; formats can become so familiar that some viewers tune in for the introduction of the problem and then watch something else, returning only for the dénouement. Examples include:

* *Supernanny* (Channel 4, ABC);
* *How Clean Is Your House?* (Channel 4/BBC America);

* *10 Years Younger* (Channel 4/TLC);
* *How to Look Good Naked* (Channel 4/Lifetime);
* *What Not to Wear* (BBC1/TLC);
* *Ramsey's Kitchen Nightmares* (Channel 4/Fox).

In a variation of this approach Intervention (A&E) tackles serious subjects such as drug addiction and compulsive behaviors but the expert doesn't intervene until toward the end of the program and we never see the transformation.

c) *Fish-out-of-Water*—ordinary people are taken out of their normal environment and introduced to people who don't share their beliefs, values, or opinions, in an effort to change their worldview, as in:

* *Wife Swap* (Channel 4/ABC);
* *Faking It* (Channel 4/TLC);
* *30 Days* (A&E).

d) *Magazine Format*—a classic studio-based format where one, two, or a team of presenters link between several different items in one show. The items might be studio-based—involving a guest or experiment, perhaps—and/or pre-recorded clips.

2) *Reality*—a much-derided term, but a type of format that is extremely popular with the younger audiences much sought after by advertisers. In the US the term reality is applied to a broad range of factual formats, ranging from observational documentaries to competition shows, but for our purposes, it refers to a group of people, carefully cast for greatest diversity and conflict, who are put together in a situation constructed entirely for television. The participants are usually placed under an extreme amount of emotional pressure. Seeing how people deal with aggression, rejection, confrontation, and disappointment is not only emotionally involving, but allows viewers to witness highly charged situations play out and then discuss the subsequent consequences with their friends or online.

There is often a clear format and a competition element, in which people are voted out of the environment by the group or the audience. The prize might be money, or a job contract. These shows have a serialized format, that is, each episode is designed to be watched in the order the producers intended. It is expected that viewers will be drawn in during the first episode and then return each week to see what happens until the final show's climax, therefore the show demands greater commitment from the audience. Reality programs include:

* *Beauty and the Geek* (The CW/E4);

* *Joe Millionaire* (Fox/Channel 4);

* *Big Brother* (Channel 4/CBS);

* *Survivor* (CBS/ITV);

* *I'm a Celebrity Get Me Out of Here* (ITV/ABC);

* *Hell's Kitchen* (ITV/Fox).

Reality programming traditionally attracts a young female audience, but savvy producers managed to draw in reality-scorning men with business-focused reality formats, such as *The Apprentice* (NBC/BBC1), and history-reality formats such as *Bad Lads' Army* (ITV) and *Frontier House* (PBS).

In nearly all cases, the environment to which the participants are subjected becomes an integral part of the show, usually acting as antagonist—a creepy-crawly-ridden jungle, an all-seeing house, a 1950s army boot camp. Sometimes it seems to be on the side of the participants—a millionaire's mansion, a gorgeous London landscape, an idyllic wilderness—but this often turns out to be a cruel illusion.

Entertainment

Entertainment shows are formatted studio-based competition shows with high production values and broad appeal. These shows play on the networks in primetime, sometimes with several episodes per week. Each episode has a contained narrative, perhaps focused on auditions in a particular city, but each episode is a building block of the bigger series' narrative arc, which is designed to build to an exciting series climax. These shows draw the most viewers and are highly sought after; they are, however, expensive to make and the risk to the channel is high. One successful show tends to spawn several look-alikes, each one feeling like a watered-down version of the original.

Hit entertainment shows include:

* *Strictly Come Dancing/Dancing with the Stars* (BBC1/ABC);

* *Pop Idol/American Idol* (ITV/Fox);

* *America/Britain's Got Talent* (NBC/ITV);

* *American Gladiators/Gladiators* (NBC/Sky One);

* *Iron Chef* (Food Network/Channel 4).

It is highly likely that your program format will slot into one of these genres. "What I find amusing is that people think it's possible to create an entirely new genre or show. It doesn't work like that. I think that's a waste of time and effort and hot air, predominantly from a proud and post-rationalizing producer or by channel heads defining their latest needs," says Ed Crick. "Things move in cycles: Lifestyle programming was huge and has now gone down, game shows were huge and have gone down and come back. Factual Entertainment was seemingly a novel genre, but the shows that built the genre already existed; they just needed affordable technology to become achievable in volume."

Tipping the Scales in Your Favor

If you are still undecided about the best approach, it might help to start by choosing your ideal genre based on the channel or audience you want to attract. All programs sit somewhere along the following continuum:

Classic documentary ◄——— Fact Ent ———► Entertainment

1. One-off ◄————————————————► Serialized formats

2. Male-skewing ◄————————————————► Female-skewing

3. Older audiences ◄————————————————► Younger audiences

4. Cable channels ◄————————————————► Networks

5. Niche audience ◄————————————————► Broad appeal

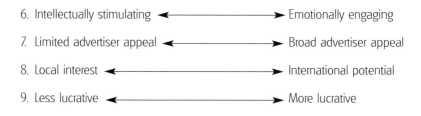

6. Intellectually stimulating ◄————————► Emotionally engaging

7. Limited advertiser appeal ◄————————► Broad advertiser appeal

8. Local interest ◄————————► International potential

9. Less lucrative ◄————————► More lucrative

Now you have a broad overview of established genres, it's time to add some detail to your idea.

Developing the Detail: What's the Approach?

Imagine you have an idea about zoos with the working title *Behind Bars*. It features an animal behavior expert called Abel Handler, and is aimed at the (fictional) Zoo Channel. What is the best way to tell the story?

Behind Bars could be told as a classic one-off documentary, exploring animal welfare and psychology, via interviews with a variety of experts. We could find out how zoo design affects animals' behavior and discover how zoos of the future might reduce the negative effects of a caged environment.

Or, it could be reworked as a point-of-view/campaigning documentary if Abel Handler is an eminent animal psychologist, who is on a mission to improve living conditions in zoos. He could spend several months in one zoo, attempting to change the oppressive management culture and empowering the keepers. Or it could be an undercover exposé of the world's worst zoos alongside a campaign to raise awareness of animal rights.

Alternatively, in a more factual entertainment approach, Abel could be the go-to expert that keepers call in to troubleshoot specific problems with their charges. Each week, Abel receives an SOS from a zoo. He spends three days working with the keepers to get to know the animals, before giving his diagnosis of the problem. He spends the next week teaching the keepers new handling techniques that will improve their relationship with their animals. Meanwhile, a specialized team makes over the enclosure to make it more animal-friendly. Finally, Abel steps back to watch as the keepers and their animals adjust to their new routine and environment. Has he succeeded in improving their lot?

Or, using a reality angle, Abel Handler takes a group of delinquent youths and puts them through a zoo boot camp where they are taught responsibility, teamwork, and initiative. We discover how the youngsters' challenging backgrounds affect their ambition and self-esteem, and watch as they slowly make a connection with the animals. For those who make the most progress and show the most commitment, there is the offer of a junior keeper job. Those that fail to muck in and muck out are escorted from the zoo grounds, free to resume their old lives. The final sequence reveals what has happened to the young people since the program was filmed.

Each of these approaches has potential, but which one you decide to pursue depends on your main area of expertise and for which channels it would be a good fit. For example, a series on zoos seems perfect for the Zoo Channel, but if their programs focus exclusively on animals they are unlikely to consider a series that concentrates on the problems of disadvantaged youths, so you would need to take a more animal-centered approach, or pitch to a different channel.

Mixing It Up: Simple Creative Techniques (You Can Use on Your Commute)

Play around with your idea before deciding on the ideal approach. In his book *Applied Imagination*, Alex Osborn outlined a checklist of techniques that you can use to develop your idea and make it different to anything else:

1. *Substitute*—use a different approach, host, era, or unusual location. When Adam Curtis was editing *Pandora's Box*, a film about how science had been used for political purposes over the last century, he realized it was boring, and decided to adopt a new tone. "I got desperate so I started to play around with it and made jokes; in parts it was silly and in other parts it was serious. By doing this I developed a style," he says.

2. *Combine*—bring together two different experts, or apply a new format to an old subject, or use a narrative device usually reserved for dramas. "The big next thing to come along will be a hybrid," says Adam Curtis. "Take something that's moribund and put it together with something else that's moribund."

3. *Adapt*—do you have a current or old series format that you could modernize or use to spin off a new show in your subject area?

4. *Magnify or minimize*—use more or fewer people, have a longer timescale or a severely restricted filming period, tell a bigger story or make it personal.

5. *Put it to other uses*—think about extra content that could be uploaded on the Internet to complement your program—contributors' diaries, outtakes, behind-the-scenes or "making-of" footage.

6. *Eliminate*—get rid of anything you don't need. The strongest ideas are often the simplest.

7. *Reverse or rearrange*—tell the story in a different order, or reverse convention. In most makeover shows, the intervention comes at the start of the show. In *Intervention* (A&E), the hit comes at the end. Adam Curtis is the master of turning subjects on their head: "I'd noticed that programs had become rigidly segmented, there were science programs and documentaries and what was called current affairs or news," he says. "Science programs had been completely captured by the scientists' view of the world. Documentaries were obsessed with this idea of 'the real' and were incredibly boring. And Current Affairs was captured with the idea that power was to do with politicians. I started to notice that you could pull them apart and put them together again."

To these classic techniques you can also add:

8. *Take a different vantage point*—are you looking at your subject or telling your story in the same way as everyone else? "If you want to be noticed, you've got to pull back like a helicopter and look at the thing you are making a program about and see it in other terms," says Adam Curtis. Take the example of 9/11. A number of documentaries have been made, all of them with a different viewpoint:

   ❋ *102 Minutes that Changed America*—a documentary told in real time through the home video footage of people witnessing the attack from the street or their apartment;

   ❋ *The Falling Man*—inspired by a photograph of a man falling from one of the towers;

❋ *9/11: Telephone Calls from the Twin Towers*—based on the voice recordings of people calling their loved ones from the twin towers;

❋ *Inside 9/11*—a two-part documentary covering the lead-up, the day, and the aftermath, using archive footage, witness and expert testimony;

❋ *Fahrenheit 9/11*—Michael Moore's critique of Bush in the aftermath of the attacks.

CASE STUDY

Greenlit: *The War Room* (96´)

Directors: Chris Hegedus, D. A. Pennebaker

Producer: R. J. Cutler

"When I pitched *The War Room* to George Stephanopoulos it was a movie about Bill Clinton and [George] said no to me so many times," says R. J. Cutler, president and founder of Actual Reality Pictures. "He was so regretful that he had to say no that eventually I thought, 'Why shouldn't it be a project about him?'

"I asked about making a film about him and he was open to the idea of me doing that as opposed to me doing a film about Bill Clinton."

The War Room was nominated for an Academy Award and won two awards from the National Board of Review.

---

9. *Make use of new technologies*—smaller, lightweight cameras, new graphics software, or emerging platforms can make possible what was impossible only a few years ago. For example, innovative computer-generated graphics bring new commissioning opportunities, which companies such as Pioneer Productions have capitalized on with science documentaries such as *Naked Science* (Nat Geo) and *Animals in the Womb* (Channel 4, Nat Geo), as have Dangerous Films with *Human Body: Pushing the Limits* (Discovery) and the BBC with *Fight for Life* (BBC1/Discovery).

New filming technology also makes some ideas idea viable for the first time, which is what happened for Thom Beers and *Ax Men*, a series that follows the dangerous work of loggers. "Filming timber on hundreds of square acres at a time on a tight budget I had to be able to have enough small cheap cameras so I could have three cameramen to cover it. I was thinking about that show for a while but I was waiting for the technology to catch up and be cost-effective." *102 Minutes That Changed America* and *Tsunami: Caught on Camera* both used amateur footage that was only available due to the ubiquity of cheap video and mobile phone cameras.

Necessity also forces invention. During filming of *Spy in the Den*, British wildlife filmmaker John Downer wanted to film lions without disturbing them, so he disguised a remote-controlled camera to look like a rock (which became known as "bouldercam"); he also disguised cameras as elephant dung to film wild elephants for *Spy in the Herd* (BBC/Discovery USA).

As digital special effects (SFX) get cheaper and a new generation of excellent graphic designers emerges from the gaming industry, producers can be tempted to use SFX to jazz up their programs. But just as an unconvincing dramatic reconstruction weakens a program, so do poorly executed effects. Your audience has grown up with Hollywood special effects, and you risk disappointing them if yours look a little homemade.

Mike Davis, of Lion TV, told *Broadcast* that he believes fantastic ideas should drive the development of new visual effects rather than producers succumbing to the temptation of using computer-generated images just because they're available. Are you in danger of your program being style over substance or does it add something new to a strong narrative? Do the effects add something new to your proposal or are they a distraction? Is there a better way to tell the story, through personal testimony, eyewitness accounts, or animated photographs?

10. *Lucky Dip Formatting Grid*—use the grid on page 111 to help you develop your approach. Work across from left to right and choose one element from each column. Alternatively, put each of these format elements on separate cards and choose them at random to see what you come up with. Or choose one component of your program idea, such as Setting and or POV, and swap the various options in that column into your idea to see if you can improve it.

Lucky Dip Formatting Grid

Select one element from each column, reading left to right

Genre	Characters	Point of View	Approach	Narrative Guide	Setting	Audience Motivation	Time Frame
Classic doc	One contributor	Objective	Fly-on-the-wall	Presenter-led	Studio	Educational	One hour
Point-of-view documentary	Many contributors	Expert view	Archive footage	Out of vision narrator	Work place	Guilty pleasure	One day
Expert intervention	Presenter/host + one contributor	Extraordinary person's view	Photographic archive	Filmmaker asking questions off camera	Behind the scenes	Practical tips	One week
Immersive	Presenter/host + many contributors	Judging	Closed-circuit television	Filmmaker in vision	Indoors	Aspiration	One weekend
Competition	Several presenter/hosts + one contributor	Polemical	Animation	Interviewed experts	Outside	Intellectual journey	A fortnight
Magazine format	Several presenters/hosts + many contributors	Investigative	Hidden camera	Contributor interviews	Private space e.g. private home	Emotional journey	A month
Observational	Invited audience	Celebrity viewpoint	Audience-generated footage	Video diaries	Constructed space e.g. Big Brother house	Revelation	Three months
Docudrama	Teams	Campaigning	Audience voting	Archive sound	Changing scenery	Fantasy	Six months
Reality	Animals	Satirical	Computer-generated images (CGI)	Music	Confined space	Humor	Ticking clock countdown

Developing the Detail: What's the Story?

All good stories have a beginning, middle, and end. A classic drama narrative usually involves: a set-up; a protagonist; an inciting incident that turns the protagonist's world upside down; the protagonist embarking on a journey full of obstacles; an antagonist. Resolution comes after a climactic confrontation between the protagonist and the antagonist.

What does this mean for the factual development producer? While you don't need to get bogged down in story theory (there are lots of excellent books if you are interested), it is useful to understand the principles. An simple short cut is to follow Robert Thirkell's lead: the producer of *Troubleshooter, Blood on the Carpet* and *Jamie's School Dinners* always looks for a fairy-tale narrative or Hollywood movie in his programs.

You can borrow story elements from any classic story, however unlikely it might seem. One Christmas, when I was working up a number of proposals for a big pitch meeting in January, I had almost everything prepared by the time I left the office for the holidays. Just one proposal was still outstanding: the commissioner had expressed a desire for a big landmark series on geology. I found myself alone at my desk on New Year's Day struggling to come up with a coherent narrative. I had found lots of interesting geographical landscapes and scientific projects to film, but I couldn't work out how to make them all hang together. Defeated, I headed home, where I noticed my old school Bible. In desperation, I opened the book at Genesis, and lo and behold, there was my narrative: "In the beginning God created the heavens and the earth … and God said, 'Let there be light'; and there was light … And God said let there be a firmament in the midst of the waters …" and so on. It's not a classic science text, granted, but it helped me order my proposal into a coherent narrative, starting at the beginning with the Big Bang and continuing via the formation of the planets and the oceans and mountains, etc. through to the present day. It was enough to secure secondary development money for a series producer to spend some time working it up and *Earth: Power of the Planet* was eventually commissioned by BBC2.

Finding the Story in Your Idea

1) *What is this story about?* Where is it set? What question needs to be answered? "Sometimes the story can be obvious and in the front but the real

story is some other subtext," says Chuck Braverman. "We did a film called *Abused* on spec, which we ended up selling to A&E. On the surface it's about: 'Did she murder this guy?' She did. But the real story is: 'Why did she shoot him and should she have gone to prison for nineteen years?' And when you know the real story you realize she should have been given a medal ..."

2) *Who is this story about?* Why should we care about them? What background information do we need?

3) *What happens to kick-start the narrative?* A question? An injustice? An intervention?

4) *What do your characters want or need?* Information? Transformation? Revenge? Redemption?

5) *What's standing in their way?* What emotional or physical obstacles must your characters overcome?

6) *How do the characters overcome the obstacles?* What reversals of fortune do they endure, what emotional highs and lows?

7) *What's the climax?* This could be a physical or emotional confrontation. If you are developing for a commercial channel, construct your narrative around the ad breaks, with something new happening in each segment, and cliff-hangers and reveals on either side of the breaks to keep the audience in their seats and their fingers off the remote control buttons.

8) *What's the payoff?* What does the audience get out of it? Revelation? A feeling of superiority? A happy ending? *Schadenfreude?*

What's the Shape? Cutting Your Story Cloth

When you start developing a series its shape will probably change as the elements change, but there are a few things to bear in mind, which might influence how the show develops. You have two decisions to make here: length of program and number of episodes.

Schedulers are generally looking for either 30´ episodes or 60´ episodes. If you are pitching to a commercial broadcaster that transmits commercials, a 30´

episode translates to roughly 22´ and 60´ needs approximately 42´ of program footage. In a half-hour episode, factor in two ad breaks (three program segments) and five ad breaks (six program segments) into an hour-long show (but check the requirements of specific channels).

If you are developing for a channel that doesn't carry commercials, you need to fill the full thirty and sixty minutes, which is a lot more material, so make sure you have enough to fill the time. Many documentary subjects make a great 40´ program but struggle to sustain over a full hour, which is a problem when there are no 40´ scheduling slots. In this instance you must decide whether you would be better pitching a 30´ show or find extra material to make an hour compelling.

Channels are rarely keen to schedule one-offs. It makes it difficult to sell advertising, and they are expensive to produce in comparison with a series of programs. If you have an idea for a one-off program and don't want it to die, your best bet is to spin it into a three-part series by adding two similar, related stories.

For example, Simon Winchcombe, an assistant producer at the BBC, had an idea about a historic scientific expedition to South America that was full of conflict and drama. It would have made a great single documentary but it was too niche a subject to sustain a series. I'd also had another idea, from Paul Rose, about a scientific expedition to map India, also full of drama. One idea on its own was not enough, but two similar ideas began to look like the basis for a series. After more research and a number of discussions with BBC4, *Voyages of Discovery*, a five-part series about pioneering scientific expeditions, was commissioned with Paul Rose presenting.

Channels much prefer to commission longer runs of programming, as they tend to be cheaper and they can sell blocks of advertising. Again, the exact length of series depends on the channel. In general, the UK broadcasters will usually commission runs of 6x60´ or 12x30´. In the US, it's more likely to be 13x60´, or sometimes 45x30´, but every channel is different. Daytime series have more episodes than primetime.

Don't overstretch your idea. "Thinking big doesn't mean taking what would be quite a nice one-off and writing 26x60´ on the front of it," said Richard Melman, speaking at the Intelligent Factual Festival. "I'm still slightly astonished, after all the years I've been doing it, where people come and sit in my office and say, 'Thirteen hours on the reformation of the Church of England.' And you think, I'm not going to watch Program Two, why should I expect the audience to? So it has to, if you are thinking big, you've got to say this has got to be the 'I must watch this tonight,' or at least set my Sky+ [TiVo] for it. It's got to have that impact, not just do lots of them."

As with everything on your proposal, your episode numbers are just an indication of intent and ambition, so can be changed after discussion with the channel. However, do make sure that if you are pitching a series of thirteen episodes, each one featuring a different family with sixteen children, that you can deliver what you are promising: in this instance you'd be advised to reduce the episodes or rethink your approach before you pitch.

If a channel likes your idea, the scheduler will immediately start imagining where it might play and the channel will tell you what length of series they'd like. So, you might pitch a series of six programs and the channel asks for twelve, or vice versa, but that's a discussion for later.

Structuring a Series

A series narrative runs from episode one through to its resolution in episode six, which is common in reality series. This structure makes scheduling repeats difficult, so some channels prefer episodic narratives, that is, stories that are self-contained within an episode, which are more common in factual entertainment shows. An episodic narrative allows the channel to repeat the programs at random wherever they have slots in the schedule, which makes a series more appealing logistically.

Whatever the overall structure, also think about how the story will work within each episode. "I always get people to write episode breakdowns, every single stage," says John Hesling. "You need to see how the acts will break down, and break down a whole episode, and then how the series will break down."

One final thing to consider is where you envisage your program playing in the schedule. If you are pitching to the UK, channels cannot broadcast programs with adult content (nudity, swearing, violence, sex, or references to drugs) before 9PM in the evening. It is wise to flag up any such content early in your development discussions with the channel, as that will affect their scheduling decisions. It may be that they have a need for post-watershed programming, in which case this would be an advantage; conversely, their post-watershed slots might be full and so you might need to tone down the content in order to secure a commission for an earlier slot.

The US broadcast networks operate a "safe harbor" for "indecent" programs after 10PM. Premium (paid-for) cable channels, such as HBO, have more leeway with the content they show, and their audiences are often motivated to subscribe safe in the knowledge that they will get more adult-themed programming.

Reality Check: Step into Your Channel Executive's Shoes

By now, you should know what your program looks like: its subject, genre, story, and structure. Before you commit your idea to paper, walk round your idea and kick its tires. Put on a channel executive's hat, stand back, and look at your idea objectively.

* *Can it be pitched in a sentence?* If not, you need to do some more thinking to refine it further. "Poor developers often overcomplicate the idea. The basic rule is: if you can't sell an idea in two lines, it's probably not an idea," says Keith Scholey.

* *Can the program be made in the necessary time frame?* If you are pitching an idea in June intended for Discovery's *Shark Week* in July, you have no chance of doing the deal, crewing up, filming, and editing before the transmission deadline.

* *Can it be cast?* If your proposal is about the lives of five tall women, you can be confident you could cast the show. If the proposal promises five women who are eight feet tall, be sure you have already located them and have tape to prove it.

* *Do you have exclusive access?* If you are proposing an access documentary, have you secured the co-operation of the people concerned? Or are you just floating the idea so you could pursue access if there is interest? Be careful when pitching something that relies on access: I once pitched a one-line idea about a hospital ship to a commissioner to gauge her interest. She was non-committal, but she called me at 9AM the following day to say that a slot had opened up in the schedule and the idea, *African ER*, had been commissioned by BBC3 for transmission in three months' time. I had to make some frantic

phone calls to the ship's PR people to persuade them to let us film with them. We managed to pull it off, but it would have been easier for the production team if a relationship had been nurtured over a longer period.

＊ *Is there an authentic narrative?* Different channels are more or less tolerant about the level of narrative construction. Some like a structured format, where the show is essentially the same each week, such as *What Not to Wear* and *Dragons' Den*, others prefer the format to provide an inciting incident of some sort and then for the narrative to unfold naturally depending on the characters of the people taking part, such as *Kitchen Nightmares* or *30 Days*.

＊ *Who is the onscreen talent?* If you plan to employ onscreen talent, who might it be? Again channels have their own ideas about this, so it's safest to suggest names of people who have the right tone and approach, rather than risk alienating them by insisting on someone of your choice (who, unbeknownst to you, has recently fallen out of favor). If the whole show is built around an unknown host, a pitch tape is vital. More about onscreen talent in Chapter Eight and pitch tapes in Chapter Nine.

＊ *What's the budget?* While you don't need a detailed budget at this stage, you do need a broad awareness of what your program is likely to cost. There is no point pitching a million-dollar show to a channel that has a budget of $100,000 per show. If your program ambition and channel budget don't match, rework your idea so that it can be made more cost-effectively, or consider pitching to other channels with larger budgets.

See the Appendix for a guide to channel budgets and a basic budget template.

Ways to decrease your budget include reducing the period of filming, self-shooting on DV cameras, moving from a television studio to an alternative setting, filming domestically rather than abroad, having a C-list rather than an A-list host etc. Talk to experienced producers and your production manager for advice—they have clever ways of eking out the budget.

Primetime entertainment format *Total Wipeout* is filmed on a specially built set in Argentina, which is used by twenty international producers who fly in their production teams and contestants to make their own local versions. Filming back to back on the location makes the most of the set and allows broadcasters to benefit from a spectacular set at reasonable cost. "*Who Wants* to Be a Millionaire was a brilliant example," says Ben Hall, "because you could make the prize fund work, and it was quite flexible because you could run it every day, you run it from week to week, you can run it in primetime, you can do specials, you can do celebrity specials, couple specials, you can flex it every which way."

If you are developing a show that has a cash prize, and you want to sell your format abroad, make sure the cash amount can be scaled up and down without compromising the integrity of the game, as not all channels have the same budget to spend.

If you are proposing a music documentary, be sure that you can clear the music and that it will be within your budget limits. The same applies to film archive: might the cost of licencing the footage be prohibitive? Take expert advice if you are unsure.

✳ *Does it fit the channel brief?* If you had a target channel in mind when you started developing your idea, you might find that you have moved away from the channel brief. Either tweak it back to fit, or if your new idea is stronger, consider a new target channel.

Keep a keen eye on this, especially if you are working up an idea that a channel has already expressed some interest in. I've pitched an idea that a channel liked, and then lost the business because the final proposal looked nothing like the original pitch—we'd developed ourselves out of a commission.

✳ *Does it have substance?* Is there something more to your idea than clever graphics or a glamorous setting? Is there a question answered? Or a journey? A previously unknown story revealed? Human drama and conflict? A resolution? *Walking with Dinosaurs* (BBC1/Discovery) successfully took paleontology, a traditional "talking head" subject, and gave it a natural history program treatment with the aid of spectacular computer-generated graphics, which allowed viewers to see dinosaurs moving through the landscape.

✳ *Is it revealing something new?* A number of subjects that have perennial appeal for television audiences—Ancient Egypt, WWII, Romans, Victorians, dinosaurs, volcanoes—have all been tackled many times. The trick is not necessarily to come up with a new subject, but to reveal something new about an old subject. Can an old mystery be solved by new forensic technology? Have you found an engaging academic with a controversial take on a subject? Or a never-before-seen viewpoint—WWII from a child's perspective, perhaps?

* *Is it timely and relevant?* Why should the channel show this program now? Is it a fashionable subject or approach? Is there a forthcoming anniversary to celebrate? Is there new knowledge about a familiar subject? Is it a historical subject that sheds light on the zeitgeist?

* *Does it avoid cliché?* Is there something different or surprising about your subject matter, your host or your approach to storytelling? Does it feel fresh and new? Have you created a new hybrid format?

* *Can it be visualized from a paper proposal or do you need a pitch tape?* If you are pitching an idea centered on new talent, or a character-based observational documentary series, the performance of your onscreen talent will make or break your series, so you must present a pitch tape to prove they can carry the show. If you are pitching a classic documentary approach, a tape is not always necessary or desirable.

* *Is there scope for multiplatform content?* There is an increasing drive toward having program-related content on the Internet. Some channel executives expect to discuss multiplatform content alongside the television pitch; others will start to consider it only once the television proposition has been commissioned.

Once you've thoroughly interrogated your idea with your channel executive's hat on, and you've made any necessary adjustments, you have a strong program idea for which you can write a solid proposal.

But there are a couple more things to do before you move on to the next stage: making sure you haven't infringed someone else's intellectual property, and protecting your idea from being stolen.

Avoiding Lawsuits

If you are creating a new TV series, you will inevitably refer to other programs as you develop yours. It's perfectly legitimate to be inspired by another series. "The shows that punch through are nearly always derivations of something else—done better or done differently, and with great timing, for sure—but definitely done before at some level," says Ed Crick. If you do take another show as your starting point, you must modify yours to make it substantially different. "There is a very fine line between mere inspiration and unlawful copying and a copycat must proceed with caution to avoid crossing this line," says Christoph Fey, attorney with the media law firm, Unverzagt von Have, Berlin. "Caution may demand one or the other minor change. However, the overall impact of all these little changes might very well weaken the show and thus result in a poor imitation, which is doomed to failure. More often than not, knockoffs simply do not perform as well as the fine-tuned original."

It's important to be aware of the boundaries, when using other programs or formats as inspiration. "In principle, one is free to take mere ideas, themes, facts, and methods of creation, such as style and technique, as these items are not considered copyrightable and, therefore, belong to the public domain," says Fey. "Ideas are as free as the air. It is not the idea behind a format that is protected—only the original expression of the idea is entitled to copyright protection ... the greater the originality, the thicker is the protection." In other words, it's the way in which you put the various elements together that matters, just as it is "'the original combination of words or notes that leads to a protectable book or song' ... ideas themselves cannot be protected, a compilation of ideas can," explains Fey.

"Unless you are deliberately trying to create a next-of-kin program, then absolutely you need to examine the format to make sure that yours is distinctive," says Ben Hall. In *Trading TV Formats*, Fey advises, "originality can be expressed in:

1. the contents of dramatic action, comprising such elements as plot devices, story lines, story characters, role of the presenter, role of the contestants, games, competitions; and

2. the audiovisual presentation, comprising such elements as visual graphics, sound design, lighting design, filming and editing work; and

3. the combination of both the contents of dramatic action and the audiovisual presentation."

Fey notes a number of cases where producers and broadcasters have been taken to court for copyright infringement.

* Castaway TV (Charlie Parsons, Lord Waheed Alli, and Sir Bob Geldof), the UK owners of the *Survivor* format, accused the producers of *Big Brother* of stealing their format (rejected by the court).

* Endemol, the producers of *Big Brother*, accused the Brazilian makers of *Casa dos Artistas* of ripping off their format (upheld by the court).

* CBS, the channel that shows *Survivor* in the US, tried to get an injunction against ABC to stop them showing *I'm a Celebrity Get Me Out of Here* (rejected).

* CBS took Fox to court alleging that *Boot Camp* was a rip-off of the *Survivor* format (upheld, and an undisclosed agreement settled the dispute).

* RDF Media took Fox Broadcasting to court claiming that its *Trading Spouses* format infringed the copyright of *Wife Swap* (upheld).

If you want to avoid falling foul of the old adage "where there's a hit, there's a writ," make sure your idea is sufficiently different from any other, which is where hybrid formats can come in useful.

> *If you steal from one author, it's plagiarism. If you steal for many it's research.*
>
> —Wilson Mizner, US screenwriter

The best way of illustrating the issue is by looking at the comparisons the judge made the between the disputed elements in the *Survivor* vs. *I'm a Celebrity Get Me Out of Here* court case, which led to the verdict that *Celebrity* hadn't infringed *Survivor*'s copyright.

Fey records that "the court determined the characteristic elements in the

Survivor and *Celebrity* programs based on the programs and the report and compared them as illustrated in the following chart":

Expressed Elements	Survivor	I'm a Celebrity Get Me Out of Here
Mood	Drama	Comedy
Participant selection	Very dramatic decision-making among the contestants (the Tribal Council)	Contestants are selected by the viewers. Decisions are passed on in a relaxed manner
Production value	Artistic takes, high level of professionalism	Home-video look
Interaction	None. Viewers watch an adventure, which takes place in the past with no ability to influence events	Viewers can follow events live (sometimes with a twenty-four-hour delay) and decide live what happens next, selection of participants by the viewers
Setting	Dry Australian Outback	Australian rainforest (jungle)
Contestants	Normal people	Celebrities
Presenters	One presenter (Jeff Probst), serious manner, tasks: judge and interviewer, appears twice per episode	Two presenters (Ant & Dec, comedy duo from the UK), humorous entertainers with sarcastic elements, appear constantly throughout the show
Goal of the show	$1 million in prize money	King/Queen of the Jungle prize money for charity organization
Teams	Two teams, leads to strategic alliances	No teams
Tasks/contests	Necessary, prize money is the motivation	Participation is voluntary
Music	Deep, chanting, tribal music	Upbeat and kicky
Animals	Dangerous situations and animals (crocodiles and snakes)	Harmless animals, entertaining
Task difficulty	Contests are physically strenuous	Contests are not physically strenuous, contestants have to overcome revulsion
Contestants' meals	Contestants have to find their own food, quantity of food is limited	Contestants' meals are provided, contestants can complete tasks in return for better-quality meals

What's to Stop Someone Stealing My Idea?

Nothing is more dangerous than an idea, when you only have one idea.

—Alain (Emile-Auguste Chartier), French philosopher

The only guaranteed way to ensure that your idea doesn't get stolen is to tell no one about it. Unfortunately, that's not an option if you want to sell your idea. "You do what you have to do in order to get your idea off the ground and in order to do that you have to rely on other people's goodwill and that doesn't always happen in TV," says Peter Rees. But it's a gamble you have to take because, "otherwise how do you get a show up and running and how do you get experience if you don't put yourself forward?"

A disgruntled documentary producer once posted a complaint on a message board for filmmakers that claimed the "theme" of a successful fiction movie was stolen from him; a belief that is as naïve as it is absurd. As we've seen, themes and subject areas are not copyrightable; only the particular combination of approach, talent, set design, and plot points in the finished program can be protected by copyright.

As there are a limited number of subject areas, themes, story lines, and approaches, and as everyone is attuned to the same zeitgeist, it is inevitable that similar ideas arise at around the same time, originated by different people.

Don't be paranoid. Most development people learn that it's all about the timing when two people have similar ideas, and which one gets through is about luck. *Deadliest Catch* came about by chance, as a result of another program that was in production. But it wasn't the first time someone had thought about doing something like that. "One of [Thom Beers's] most successful shows is called *Deadliest Catch*. I pitched that exact same show to Discovery a year before," says Chuck Braverman. "It was called something else, but it was about dangerous fishing up in the same area; it was the right idea, but it was the wrong timing." A development producer agrees, "I know people who have said, 'That's my idea' when they've seen it on TV, and I can honestly hand on heart say everybody had that idea. Saying 'We should do something on travel with a team of archeologists' does not make you the inventor of *Time Team*." However, by being as specific as possible about your format in your written proposal you can go some way to proving that you did come up with an original idea.

Another way to protect your idea is to start filming it. "If it's a great idea, chances are someone else will be having the same idea," says filmmaker Barry Gibb. "The difference between you and the other person is that you might have the camera and the contacts to actually start making that film and turning it into something real. If it's a great idea and you can film it, just film it."

Most people starting out in the business fear that "*they*" will steal their ideas. Forget stranger danger: it's probably more common for someone you know to take credit for, borrow, or steal your ideas.

"A junior researcher I worked with years ago was foolish enough to steal an idea, but it wasn't just an idea, it was a presenter's idea," says one producer/ director. "He pitched it and it got commissioned, but I have to say he made himself extraordinarily unpopular, with that presenter, and with all the other presenters as well. In the end nobody wanted to work with him, because nobody trusted him."

And it's not unknown for channels to take an idea from one producer and give it to another. "I got a call from a commissioning editor the other day who passed on an idea and said he'd commissioned, 'the identical show from someone else but their timing was better'; it was six weeks later," says Ed Crick. "However, he said, they didn't have an ending to the show, could he give them mine? So what do I say? I said, 'Yes, of course you can.' What are you going to do?"

"I was working on an idea with a company for three months and the broadcaster took it from us and gave it to another company," said one develop-ment producer. "They said that the other company had a track record in making those types of shows—and they did, but I'd developed the format points and cast it. It's gone on to be such a hit; so much so that whenever I'm in a briefing they always refer to this series and say that's what we want, we want another one of those; I feel sick every time I hear that."

"I once walked into the middle of a pitch meeting to hear the channel controller, commissioner, and another production team 'spontaneously' brain-storming an idea I'd previously pitched to the same commissioner!" recalls a producer. "The controller said it was, 'a perfect example of how creative people sitting round a table can come up with a great idea on the spur of the moment' and I sat there with my mouth open, but I couldn't say anything as I was the most junior person in the room."

However, many experienced producers take the view that if you have enough ideas, and are confident in your ability to generate more, the benefit of getting it out there and in front of the right people outweighs the risks.

When you have lots of ideas, losing one idea to an unscrupulous operator doesn't hurt as much as when you only have one idea to sell. "I can probably count on the fingers of more than one hand the number of meetings I've sat in under the guise of a meeting to help me out and I've never heard from those people again, and I suspect it was just to listen to someone else's ideas," says Barry Gibb. "You know what, fine. You'll never just have five ideas and if you do there's something wrong. If you like thinking about things you will continue to have good ideas. It doesn't matter if someone steals them. You can't be too precious; otherwise you will become a hermit."

Unfortunately, the misappropriation of ideas, whether deliberate or inadvertent, is an occupational hazard. Fortunately, it's one in which no one dies; so it's important to keep things in perspective.

Protecting Your Idea

In *Trading TV Formats*, Christoph Fey describes the case of an allegedly stolen idea. In 2005, a Texan man called Harry Keane (who wasn't a TV producer) sued the producers of *American Idol* and Fox, claiming that they had stolen the idea for a show he'd had in 1994, which he'd planned to call *American Idol* (or *Ultimate Starsearch* or *American Superstars*). He was claiming damages of $300 million. However the court dismissed his claims: "Because Keane sent out unsolicited letters, which detailed the specifics of his idea, to several different production companies and advertised his idea on the Internet, the district court correctly found that he cannot demonstrate that he had a trade secret that was unknown outside of his business or that he took measures to guard the secrecy of the information."

So, although it is impossible to fully protect your idea, there are some basic things you can do to mitigate the risk and prove ownership of a format or concept in case of a dispute; the main advice being that you shouldn't post your idea on the Internet.

1) In order for you to successfully claim that someone has stolen your idea, you must first prove that your idea is an "original work" and that you own the

copyright. If you work for a production company, chances are that you don't have any personal ownership over the ideas you generate for them anyway. "If you look at your contract you will notice that they stipulate that any idea you come up with during employment with them belongs to them," says Peter Rees. "It is a Faustian pact. You take the regular wage that they provide for working on shows, and they own your ideas."

2) Include as much detail as possible in your proposal, emphasizing its unique points: there must be enough detail that a reader can "see" the program as it would be on screen (more on this in Chapter Seven). It does sometimes happen that two or more proposals are submitted for the same idea at the same time by different sources; a detailed proposal will help differentiate yours from the rest and help the channel executive decide on their preferred approach.

3) Ensure you mark it clearly with your name and contact details.

4) The Alliance for the Protection of Copyright (UK) advises that additional protection can be obtained by registering the proposal with a legal representative; BECTU offers a script registration service (which covers proposals and concepts) for its union members; the US Copyright Office in the Library of Congress, and the Writers' Guild of America also offer a registration service.

5) Place the copyright © symbol and year in the footer of your proposal along with the name of the copyright holder (which might be you or your production company if you are working for an indie).

6) Include registration number if you have registered your idea with a registration service or entertainment lawyer.

7) If you are a member of a professional body, such as BECTU or the Writers' Guild, include your membership number.

8) Pitch your ideas only to established production companies or via the established procedures at TV channels.

9) Don't send unsolicited proposals to a production company or broadcaster.

10) Once they've invited you to send in your idea, state (preferably) in writing that you are submitting the idea in confidence.

11) Keep a record, or "paper trail" of all your correspondence with an independent production company or channel: a copy of the dated proposal, along with a record of whom you sent it to, and on what date; any emails received or sent in relation to your idea; and a written record of meetings and telephone conversations. Follow up any meetings with an email to confirm what was discussed.

12) Avoid inadvertently give away your secrets to your rivals. "I've been sent emails that are essentially an update on a series that's actually in development at another channel that I never even knew existed, until I saw that email," says one US channel executive.

Here is a paragraph you can use in the footer of your proposal:

When you register your proposal, you are registering your proposal as a "finished" work; any changes mean that you should reregister it. This obviously poses a problem as most ideas do change as they are developed and it is therefore hard to register an evolving concept. Keep dated copies of all versions of your idea so you have a paper trail.

Some producers like to ask the person they are pitching to, to sign a non-disclosure agreement (NDA) or confidentiality agreement. However, it might mean that the development producer at the production company or channel you are pitching to refuses to read your proposal. Chances are high that they have already heard a similar idea to yours, or they might have something similar in development themselves, but they have no way of knowing that until you've told them your idea. If they sign an NDA it could make things much more complicated for them as it means they are putting themselves at risk of being sued by you even though they are innocent of any wrongdoing. "We don't accept unsolicited ideas," says Dan Hall. "We can't read them because we might be developing something similar. We don't want you coming back and saying it was your idea."

Creative caution works both ways; most production companies and channels won't accept unsolicited program ideas, as they fear being sued by someone who claims they had their idea "stolen." So it is likely that you will be asked to sign a submission release form, which protects them from such claims, before they will accept your proposal. "We don't take pitches from people just off the street," says Tim Duffy, VP development, Spike TV. "They have to get to us through someone that we trust. It's usually through an agent or an entertainment lawyer, because ultimately, you are exposed. Even though I've been pitched a show a thousand times before, there might be a slight tweak that someone will come in with next week that this person doesn't have. So I'm thinking: is this person going to sue me if I buy it from the next person? Because, even though I work for a big company, our jobs are at stake, especially in this very litigious society."

"We get unsolicited pitches all the time and we have a process for dealing with them—if you don't have an agent or you're not from a company I'm familiar with, you'll have to sign a submission release before we will consider it," says another US cable exec. "Once you've signed the release we review everything. We won't necessarily set up an hour pitch meeting with you, I might say, 'Send me the tape,' I'll take a look at it and if I like it we'll set up a meeting or a phone call to discuss further. If I set up a meeting for every unsolicited pitch that would be a full-time job."

If you want to get your ideas out there so they can be made, it's probably best to be sanguine about the risks. "Don't worry about people stealing your ideas," advised Howard H. Aiken, a US computer engineer and mathematician. "If your ideas are any good, you'll have to ram them down people's throats."

Before you write your proposal, there is another element to consider: would your idea benefit from some multiplatform content?

Development Master Class 5

Creating, Shaping, and Protecting Your Format

1. Take a look at How to Turn One Subject Area into Ten Program Ideas: http://tiny.cc/1into10. Try it with your subject area.

2. Sign up for a free account at Bubbl.us for access to an online brainstorming/mind-mapping tool, which is useful to capture ideas as you can access it from anywhere. You can share your mind map with your colleagues online, via email, or you can save it as a picture and print it out http://bubbl.us/.

3. Create a Word.doc template with a storytelling grid containing the following points down the left side:
   a. What is this story about?
   b. Who is this story about?
   c. What happens to kick-start the narrative?
   d. What do your characters want or need?
   e. What's standing in their way? What obstacles must your characters overcome?
   f. How do the characters overcome the obstacles?
   g. What's the climax?

   Print it off and fill it in for your idea to see if it helps you troubleshoot your story.

4. Photocopy the Reality Check grid on pages 116–19. Print it off and pin it on your notice board where you can see it. Run every idea through the reality check before you start writing the proposal.

5. Explore some of the FAQ sections in the copyright websites listed below to familiarize yourself with the issues surrounding format protection in your own territory.

Explore More

David J. Bodycombe: *How to Devise a Game Show*
Game shows are specialized but you might be called upon to develop one, or to include game show elements in your format. This excellent e-book describes the development process, including all the legal considerations, in great detail. I read this as a crash course in game show development over one weekend and managed to secure a spot in a competitive pitch situation against more established game show producers with the resulting proposal http://tiny.cc/gameshow.

Research

HARO—Help a Reporter Out: free online US-based resource that puts journalists in touch with experts and PR people. They have more than 100,000 sources and you can send a request for an expert, information, or stories to be included in their email newsletter, which goes out three times a day. Good for research, gathering background information and finding potential experts (as the sources are unvetted you need to do your own due diligence) http://www.helpareporter.com.

ProfNet: US-based database that lists approximately 27,000 academic and corporate experts willing to talk to the media. Free to journalists, but experts must pay a fee https://profnet.prnewswire.com/PRNJ.aspx.

Storytelling

Robert McKee: *Story*
Classic storytelling bible based on the three-act structure. Aimed at screenwriters, but McKee has influenced documentary makers too: BBC2's *Horizon* embraced the three-act structure for its science documentaries.

Christopher Vogler: *Writer's Journey: Mythic Structure for Writers*
A book aimed at screenwriters but helpful for anyone trying to structure a story: Mark Burnett's programs, such as *Survivor*, make use of mythical storytelling techniques.

Budgeting

Donna Michelle Anderson: *The ShowStarter: Ten Steps to Creating and Pitching a Sellable Reality Show*
A book focused on the US market that has an overview of how to work out a ballpark budget for your program idea.

DocumentaryTelevision.com: details program budget information for channels such as Science Channel, A&E, Planet Green, Military, Animal Planet, and more http://documentarytelevision.com.

Copyright Issues

Chrisoph Fey: *Trading TV Formats*
Published by the European Broadcasting Union, this book discusses the issues around the copyright of program formats and how to protect your ideas. Although it's a complex area, the book does an admirable job of explaining it in plain English with lots of case studies and advice http://www.ebu.ch/en/eurovisiontv/formats/formats_handbook.php.

Writers' Guild of America West: WGA provide a script registration service that you can use for your program proposal/treatment. You don't have to be a member and you don't have to live in the US. WGA suggests registering drafts and works-in-progress with them and registering the final draft with the US Copyright Office at the Library of Congress in Washington, DC. The WGAW registration fee for non-members is currently $20 http://www.wgawregistry.org/webrss/index.html.

Writers' Guild of America East: the WGA also has an east coast office. Registration currently costs $22 for non-members https://www.wgaeast.org/index.php?id=238.

US Copyright Office at the Library of Congress, Washington DC: offers various services that register and record the authorship of an original work http://www.copyright.gov/.

BECTU: UK's media and entertainment union offer a registration service to its members for "proposals, concepts, ideas, formats and outlines, as long as they are written down in detail" http://www.bectu.org.uk/advice-resources/script-registration.

The Script Vault: approved by the Writers' Guild of Great Britain, the Script Vault offers a script, format or treatment registration service for £10 http://www.thescriptvault.com/home.html. They also offer a useful paragraph you can include when sending your idea to third parties: http://www.thescriptvault.com/apc-cofp.html.

Own-It: provides a free intellectual property advice service for creative professionals in the UK http://www.own-it.org/advice.

6

Considering Multiplatform Content

Anyone who isn't confused doesn't understand the situation.

—Edward R. Murrow, American journalist

A Californian supply teacher taps into an extensive global network of informers— government officials, travel agents, and tourism directors—to get commercially sensitive information. A US fridge magnet manufacturer gets aerial photos of a location within an African no-fly zone, using a remote-sensing satellite to take high-resolution photographs from space. A man, who goes by the name of ChillOne, travels into the Amazon looking for an abandoned tribal campsite.

What do all these people have in common? They are all fans of CBS's *Survivor* and are part of an online community called spoilers. Their aim is to find out every-thing they can about a forthcoming *Survivor* series before anyone else does. In his book *Convergence Culture*, Henry Jenkins describes how there are three parts to *Survivor* spoiling: finding the location of the series; identifying the contestants before they are officially announced; and predicting the order in which the con-testants are booted off the show, along with the identity of the eventual winner.

Once they've confirmed the location of the new series, the spoiler network sets about identifying the cast. During the production of *Survivor: Pearl Island* a woman booked into the hotel where the production team were holding cast interviews and refused to move out when the producers asked for a block booking, enabling her to take photographs of the contenders. The photos were shared online so that the spoilers could check their photos against any potential names they had in the frame.

On one series, the Ellipsis Brain Trust (a brain trust, according to Henry Jenkins, is "an elite group of spoilers who work within a closed list and make their findings available to the larger community") obtained the names of the sixteen competitors by hacking into the email account of the *Survivor* website designer, where they found sixteen web addresses that contained names. The group checked out the names, weeding out all candidates who were too young, old, or infirm to be a *Survivor* applicant, and were able to confirm all the contenders before CBS released their names.

After the contestants are identified, the spoilers try to determine the order of evictions before they're revealed on air. Quartzeye visited the car lot where Brian Heidik from *Survivor: Thailand* worked and took his photograph, which was then compared with pre-series publicity shots to work out how much weight he had lost: the skinnier the contestants are after the series, the longer they are deemed to have survived on camp rations. Brian appeared much thinner than he did in the publicity shots and was indeed the winner of that series. The spoilers also knew before time that there would be an accident on *Survivor: The Australian Outback*, as Brian Skulpin was photographed with a bandaged arm between filming and transmission. During the series it was revealed that he had fallen into a fire and had to be medivaced out.

Another *Survivor* fan, Mario Lanza, interacts with the show in a different way. He has written three fictional 'series' of *Survivor*, which feature a cast drawn from the real-life contestants; so those booted out early in the TV series get to star in an alternative series, where they are pitted against an 'all-star' cast of contestants drawn from across all seasons. He sets his shows in places where the real show is unlikely to go: Alaska, Greece, and Hawaii. Each *All Star* 'episode' is between forty and seventy pages long and he uploads installments to his website a couple of times a week when the CBS show is on downtime. He's received fan mail from the contestants he's featured in his online serialization, and they've praised him for capturing their personalities or pointed out where he's got them wrong. Some episodes have been co-authored by the real "Survivors" and some of the dialogue is taken from interviews Mario has done with his real-life "Survivors."

These fans are extremely engaged, and interact with the content of *Survivor* in a number of ways: community building, game playing, and creating and uploading their own content. But *Survivor* doesn't exist just on television and the Internet. As well as the official CBS *Survivor* website, there is:

* SurvivorSucks.com—a spoiler site that was visited by an average of 3,400 people per day in the year up to July 29, 2009; they visited an average of three times per day;

* an eBay auction at the end of each series to sell the props;

* online games, board games, and computer games;

* *Survivor* merchandise such as mugs, tribal-themed jewelry, beach towels, dog tags, magnets, multifunction tools, *Survivor* Host Jeff Probst Wacky Wobbler Doll;

* *Survivor* soundtrack CDs;

* *Survivor* DVDs;

* *Survivor* party kits;

* insider books, and academic books analyzing the *Survivor* phenomenon;

* *Survivor: The Ride* thrill ride at Great America in Santa Clara, California;

* *Survivor: Live*—at three US theme parks where fans "take part" in *Survivor*-style challenges.

Online, Survivor has an active presence on

* Facebook page (with 58,000 fans);

* Twitter;

* iTunes.

In other words, *Survivor* is a highly successful *multi*platform brand.

In a 360° Spin: What *Is* Multiplatform?

"Multiplatform is the current phrase used mainly by broadcasters to describe projects that essentially exist on more than one platform, one of them being television, and the other one normally being the web, but it can also include mobile phones, games, consoles, books, events etc.," explains Mike Dicks, Director, BleedinEdge Ltd.

Channels increasingly expect TV producers to include multiplatform content in their TV program proposals. "Multiplatform will become more and more important," says Lucy Pilkington. "That's an advantage for producers, because we don't have the ideas for multiplatform." Whereas channel executives usually come from a TV program-making background, there are few who have any multiplatform experience, so channel executives are looking for producers to be proactive and lead the way. "I think over the next eighteen months to two years, we will more and more be saying, 'Well, that's just a TV idea, we're less interested, we want the idea plus ...' And I suspect it will be the same with everybody," forecasts Lucy.

Seth Lawrence, an agent at Rebel Entertainment Partners, LA, agrees that you should consider all the ways that an idea could evolve: "What's the 360-degree programming? How does this work? Are there spin-offs? Is there a concert component? Is there a tour component?"

In *How to Get a Job in Television,* Elsa Sharp says that multiplatform is becoming part of the normal development process. "I worked in development at CBBC Factual, developing factual entertainment formats for the channel and for BBC1. When devising and writing formats the shows had to fulfill a number of criteria outlined on the commissioning forms: as well as being innovative, interesting, original, and engaging to watch, they also had to work on several different platforms—the Internet, on mobile phones, overseas—and satisfy audience research. We had different meetings with various BBC departments, including Interactive, to create spin-off ideas for the CBBC website, creating interactive games for six- to twelve-year-olds, the channel's audience."

CASE STUDY

Greenlit: *How to Start Your Own Country* (6 x 60´ BBC2)

Leafstorm

"We commissioned Danny Wallace to do *How to Start Your Own Country*," remembers Tom Archer. "It bombed on air but it did fantastically well online and helped make Danny Wallace quite a big star.

"Actually that was the second time we'd brought him in to pitch to a channel controller, with basically the same idea, with about a year between the two attempts.

"Whereas they weren't prepared to take the risk the first time, the second time they were, possibly because of the online application."

Start Your Own Country had a website with forums, message boards, and voting, BBCi (later renamed BBC Red Button) with exclusive footage and live phone-in. It won a BAFTA and has been nominated for several other awards.

Multiplatform is so new that there is a lot of confusion about the terms used to describe it. "Last year everybody was calling things 360-degree content and in the past it's had various different names, interactive or cross-platform," says Mike Dicks. "Every two or three years, the two sides of the business, the digital [also known as interactive or online] side and the television side, keep trying to invent words that explain what it is that they are doing, [but it] normally boils down to the same thing," he says: "your content is designed for a number of platforms from the beginning."

There is a tendency, when thinking about multiplatform content, to forget the basics; you still need to have a good idea. But not every idea deserves to be a multiplatform idea nor should every TV program have an online element. "The primary thing is that you have to make sure that you have a compelling story or piece of content, whatever it is," stresses Mick Dicks. "It doesn't matter if you are a TV person or a digital person. You need to get that core story right and test that with various people. Early on you need to test your idea to see what would happen if you did that on the web, what would happen if you did that on mobile phones? Is this a television show at all or is it something that is better as a game? And that thinking needs to be done early in the process so you can adapt your content to work across all those platforms." Until the multiplatform industry matures, TV programs will still drive the content, and therefore should still come first for most of your propositions.

Multiplatform shouldn't be treated as a last-chance saloon for your TV ideas. "I get pitched a lot of multiplatform ideas that didn't make it as TV ideas, and you see that especially in the entertainment world," says Martin Trickey, BBC multiplatform commissioning executive. "I've seen an idea pitched to controllers and TV execs, and then they come for a meeting and they say, 'I've got some interesting multiplatform ideas,' and you say, 'No, you pitched that as a half-hour TV show for BBC2.' There's no passion or belief in it, it doesn't fit, it just feels like, 'Well, I've tried everywhere else …'"

To be taken seriously, you need to do more than tack the suggestion of a program website on to your proposal. "That you can have a website accompanying the program, or you can upload clips online is a given these days," says Martin Trickey. If you are proposing multiplatform content you have to ask yourself if having that content will add real value to the viewers' experience or just add more noise. For example, *Test the Nation*, which was a live studio-based nationwide IQ test, wouldn't have worked without the audience playing along at home via Internet and interactive red button on their remote controls: their scores were needed so people could compare their IQ score with that of the rest of Britain. Therefore the multiplatform elements—online and onscreen red button— were integral to the format and added value for the viewers.

Television producers and digital producers see their audiences differently. Television producers have creative control of their content, which is consumed passively by the audience at a scheduled time, and the producers don't get any feedback from the audience until the overnight viewing figures are published. Digital producers, on the other hand, deal with an active audience who consume their content whenever and wherever they want to, and who give constant feedback, which means the digital producer can tweak the content over time to make it better for the users.

It is useful to team up with a digital producer (or TV producer if you are a digital producer) when you are contemplating adding multiplatform content to your proposal to ensure you generate the best ideas and don't make elementary mistakes. "In the past, I've been most successful when I've got someone from the TV world and someone from the digital world, and put them together and let them clash creatively," says Mike Dicks. "That little bit of friction that you get between the two worlds is the important thing, as each person brings a knowledge of their platform to the conversation."

There are three elements to consider when you are thinking about developing multiplatform projects: type of content, platform, and user interaction.

Types of Multiplatform Content

Content is the material you use to tell the story or give the audience information about the story. It could be:

* archive footage;

* highlights clips;

* unseen footage from the series;

* interviews with behind-scenes team;

* video diaries;

* streamed online footage (as in *Big Brother*);

* live webcam footage (as in *Springwatch*, which followed the progress of young nestlings);

* blogs of characters or talent;

* mobisodes—short, online episodes;

* games;

* podcasts;

* email newsletters;

* web conferences;

* Mp3 downloads such as audio tours;

* photo uploads;

* webchats with presenters;

* SMS text messages;

* user-generated content;

* geo-tagged content;

* Google maps.

Different Platforms

Think of the platforms as you would TV channels—each one is essentially a place where you can "transmit" your content. Examples include:

Social Networking Sites

Social networks allow people to interact with friends, keep in touch with contacts, and grow their network of acquaintances.

* *Facebook*
  Users upload their status updates and share photos, play games, and join fan groups. You can relay information about your upcoming program to people on your program's fan page.

* *Twitter*
  A "micro-blogging" site that allows people to update their status or share information in 140 characters. Many celebrities, such as Stephen Fry and Ashton Kutcher, are avid tweeters.

* *MySpace*
  Particularly popular with musicians.

* *Fan sites and groups*
  A website dedicated to a band, program, or group, which shares information and news and allows fans to chat to each other via message boards.

User-generated Content Aggregators

Content aggregators allow people to upload and share their own content with other people.

* *YouTube*
  A website that allows anyone to upload videos, leave comments, share or embed the videos in their own blog or website. Registered users can create channels; broadcasters such as the BBC use these channels to show clips from their shows.

* *Flickr*
  A photo and video sharing website.

Content Distribution

Distribution sites offer an alternative way to consume TV or radio content at a time that suits the consumer, on a device that is convenient to them.

* *Program website*
  Classic multiplatform add-on to a TV program: can contain behind-the-scenes information, clips, cast blogs, and interviews and games.

* *iPlayer*
  The BBC's program "catch-up" service, which streams programs for seven days after TV transmission. Channel 4, Five, and ITV have their own catch-up services.

* *Hulu*
  A free online video streaming service where you can watch your favorite TV show; currently available only in the US, but there are plans to roll out in the UK.

* *iTunes*
  Online music and video store where you can also subscribe to podcasts of your favorite radio shows.

* *BBC big screens*
  Twenty cities across the UK host 25m. sq. digital video screens, with more planned in the run-up to the 2012 Olympics. The screens deliver news, sport, music, event coverage, and documentaries twenty-four hours a day. Content is tailored to the location.

User Interaction

While it's enough for TV viewers to sit back and watch programs, multiplatform content is designed to encourage the audience to interact with it. Here are some of the things you might want the audience to do with your multiplatform content:

* share;

* play;

* find information;

* vote contestants off or voting for favorites;

* bet on outcomes;

* learn skills;

* respond to a call to action;

* campaign;

* influence a plot line;

* build a community;

* give feedback;

* get "insider" information;

* choose which version they want to watch (via red button technology);

* upload their own content.

CASE STUDY

Greenlit: *Facebook vs. Twitter*

Current TV

"We did a brilliant live stunt called *Facebook vs. Twitter*," says Emily Renshaw-Smith, "where we sent out two teams, one representing Twitter and one representing Facebook and pitted them against each other in a number of daily challenges. They had to use their online communities to help them complete the tasks and that was a real experiment for us. They were doing outreach for about a month before they left and the Twitter girls got eight hundred-plus followers and the Facebook boys got about seven hundred fans.

"During the stunt, we had a live link-up every day to the daily TV show via Skype and then we put out an hour-long show, which was the story of the whole week, on the Sunday night.

"Interestingly, the communities engaged in different ways: the Twitter community was incredibly supportive but the Facebook community were able to do more to help them—it was easier for them to upload photos or movies—it was the platform that made it slightly easier.

"But on Twitter they managed to get Matt Damon [to respond to] some of the stuff they'd posted. And we'd recently done a film with Mark Borkowski, author of *The Fame Formula*, and he was tweeting about what we were doing so suddenly their followers shot up. Twitter won."

What's Online Tonight?

There are so many different forms of multiplatform content it can be hard to imagine what elements an idea might include. The best way of beginning to think about how to expand your ideas on to a number of platforms is to explore what has been done in the past:

Dragons' Den Online http://www.bbc.co.uk/dragonsden/about/online.shtml
Dragons' Den (*Shark Tank* in the US) is a hugely popular television series where we watch budding entrepreneurs pitching their business ideas in the hope of

securing investment from one of the millionaire "dragons" on the panel. It has a website where viewers can learn more about the dragons, watch highlights of upcoming programs, and apply to take part. Viewers can sign up to receive texts about the latest news and upcoming highlights on the show.

An online version of the show features two new dragons who take pitches from people who are looking for up to £50K investment. Viewers upload their three-minute pitches and online users judge their viability before the successful applicants face the online dragons and get their verdicts. The success of the online content led to the creation of a new 30' TV series based on the online version.

Elements: TV, website, video clips, text messaging, original online content, viewer voting.

Deadliest Warrior: The Aftermath—Spike TV (9 x 60')
Deadliest Warrior's première season on Spike in April 2009 drew the channel's best ever audiences for an original series. Within three weeks they had capitalized on the buzz around the show by launching a round-table web discussion after each show called *Deadliest Warrior: The Aftermath*. The comments boards went wild with fans suggesting themes and combatants for future series, and requesting a *Deadliest Warrior* video game. The series was the top-selling show on Xbox, PlayStation, and iTunes, and was sold to Virgin Media in the UK where it was transmitted on Bravo.

Elements: TV, complementary original online web series, message boards.

Take One Museum—BBC4 (6 x 30')
First-time presenter, polar explorer, and expedition guide Paul Rose took viewers of the television series on a non-stop tour of some of Britain's most interesting museums revealing the stories behind the treasures. Filming in one take over thirty minutes (inspired by the ninety-minute one-take *Russian Ark* documentary), it was based on the premise that you can still get a lot out of a short trip to a museum. Viewers could download an audio tour narrated by Paul Rose to take them on their own trip around the museums or watch the programs as interactive online videos, which allowed the viewer to interrupt the program in order to take a detour to view extra content related to the show.

Elements: TV, MP3 downloads, interactive online video. Read the original program proposal on page 153.

Four Weddings—Living (10 x 60') and TLC

Each episode of the TV show features four brides who compete to have the best wedding. They each attend the others' weddings and rate their choice of venue, reception, dress, and overall presentation. As the show airs, viewers upload their own ratings online and interact via Twitter and other social media sites. An online wedding planner takes viewers to a Living TV shopping site where they can buy white satin shoes, bridal corsets, and wedding rings.

Elements: fan forums, live chat board, and voting during TV transmission, live Twitter feed, Facebook fan page, and merchandising.

Wimbledon BBC

Every year, tennis fans can choose which matches they want to watch by pressing the "red button" on their remote control. For example, during the Wimbledon tennis tournament, viewers choose which of four matches they want to watch, and can flip between courts as they wish.

Red-button technology is also used during broadcasts of the Glastonbury Festival, allowing viewers to choose which music stage they watch.

Elements: TV, website, BBCi Red Button.

Where's the Audience?!

Not all viewers want to interact with multiplatform content. Some TV program fans—such as older followers of a drama series—will never go online because their TV show satisfies all their needs. Others, such as fans of *Strictly Come Dancing, Big Brother*, and *Survivor*, are already active online and hungry for extra content related to their shows, but they expect to be able to interact with it on their favorite platforms, which means that you have to go to them rather than expecting them to come and find your content.

Martin Trickey describes the life cycle of multiplatform content as having four stages:

Pre-TV Transmission

For big competition reality shows, the online presence builds the buzz a long time before the transmission of the first episode and the week prior to the first episode will see the heaviest online traffic. "Everyone desperately wants to know who is going to be in it. And they want to go in and get themselves tooled up with all the information they need to be able to go and enjoy the show," says Martin Trickey.

During Transmission

Once the show is on air, make sure that any extra content you offer is better than the TV show. If you are just showing niche interviews or behind-the-scenes footage, it won't appeal to the people who are engaged in the TV show, except for a small number of *über* fans.

After Transmission

This is the period of cool down and post mortem. It is "the wallow stage where you can just hang around and chat and discuss the program." Martin says that, "The *Strictly Come Dancing* message boards are full of people who congregate to discuss what's been going on in their lives over the past year." In 2008, portly political correspondent John Sergeant won over the audience despite his leaden footwork, and he kept being saved from expulsion by the public vote. When it looked as though he might go on to win the show, John withdrew from the competition, scandalizing viewers and sending the message boards into overdrive.

Between Series

In terms of the life cycle the TV show—assuming the television show is transmitted in two 6 x 30′ blocks—the audience engagement is shaped something like this:

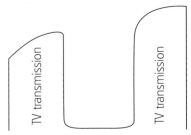

An online element can make the audience profile more "hammock-shaped" as fans are kept engaged with the series through the online content, which keeps the brand alive between series.

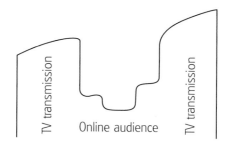

How to Develop Multiplatform Content

Although some multiplatform content is commissioned purely for online consumption, most multiplatform development is still based around a TV concept.

Step One: Work out your television proposition. (Ignore this step if you are developing a purely multiplatform project such as a game that doesn't need a TV element.)

Step Two: Decide if a multiplatform approach is appropriate to your audience—are they already active online?

Step Three: Research where your audience hangs out online.

Just as you would research TV channels and their audiences before pitching your ideas to them, so too should you know which audience you are aiming for and which multiplatform "channel" they favor, so you can put your content where your audience is rather than expecting them to come and find you (they won't). "It's important to have a look at what's available rather than trying to reinvent the wheel," says Martin Trickey.

Step Four: Think about how you will attract these users to your content.

Will you place it on Facebook or YouTube? Or will you set up your own fan pages that encourage people to share your content? Will there be a call to action from the TV program? Can they embed your content in their blogs? "With multiplatform you seldom get marketing," says Martin Trickey. "If you put something on BBC1 you will get an audience in millions, but if you put something on a website, you can get nobody. So one of the key things is: what is it and why on earth are people going to come to it? How will it generate interest around itself? And because it's interactive, how are people going to interact or consume it?"

You can start using social networking sites to test your ideas before you pitch them. "The thing I absolutely encourage in the development process is to make use of Facebook to help you promote your idea, because most broadcasters are on Facebook," says Mike Dicks. "You can start to build an interested audience— if you can build 1,000 fans from a Facebook group for something you are working on, or if you have built a little game on Facebook, and you've got 500 people playing it, that's a good demonstration of how popular your subject might be."

Step Five: Bearing in mind the above, develop your multiplatform content ideas, making best use of existing applications.

Using established resources means that you are not trying to invent something that already exists and has a built-in user base. It is too costly in terms of money and time to build a social network from scratch; it is much better to partner with Facebook or another existing site and spend your money on creative content. "The way web 2.0 works is that you use YouTube to show your video rather than building your own video server, because YouTube already does it well," says Mike Dicks. "You might want to build a social network, but why would you do that when other people have already done it?" These third parties will generally be extremely happy for you to use their platforms, because it helps their brand too. For example, "Google maps make money from advertising and what they want is traffic, so if you have something that generates 100,000 hits on a Friday, they are quite happy," points out Mike Dicks.

Step Six: Consider whether you have chosen ideas that best suit the available platforms and your intended audience.

"A multiplatform project has something about it that is specific to the platform that you are putting it on," says Martin Trickey. "So why would you do that idea online rather than on telly? Or how does it work with online and telly and red button working together, and what added value do you get from doing it on these different platforms?"

Step Seven: Interrogate your ideas.

"My biggest bugbear," says Martin Trickey, "is that 90 percent of the ideas I get pitched have huge gaping logical holes in the interactive part of it because producers made massive assumptions about what people would do." Walk it through in your head and try to see how each element of a game will work.

Don't assume that 50,000 people will use your content if you haven't thought about how you are going to attract all those people to your site. Think about how you are going to monitor message boards (which is expensive if you have to use moderators), how long the site will need to be maintained, and data protection issues around social networking sites. Remember that as a TV producer you have total control of your program content, but online anyone can join in, which potentially opens you up to a lot of editorial/legal risk. "Thrash it out and try to pick holes in your idea," says Martin. "Nobody seems to do that as much as they ought to. Really pick at it because that's what the commissioner will do." If you are unsure about all the issues, talk to a digital expert and get advice.

"Partnering up with a digital agency [a company that specializes in producing interactive, online content] beforehand is a great idea," says Martin Trickey. "So if you've got a great idea, talk to a digital agency, or vice versa—because I also get pitched a lot of ropey television ideas by digital agencies." Try to make sure that the agency you partner with is a good fit for your idea and think about how you are going to retain or share the intellectual property rights of any ideas you develop together. "If you are going to go with a digital agency I would pay them to consult," says Mike Dicks. "Or bring in individual digital producers who work on a freelance basis, as it makes you more independent," suggests Mike Dicks. "Digital agencies tend to specialize in a particular area such as software development. As you develop your idea, it might [turn into] a brilliant mobile phone idea but the agency you are working with don't have any experience of building mobile phone applications but [by then] you are stuck with them. You are better, I think, to have an independent digital mind working on it."

If you are a digital producer looking to work with a TV production company on a multiplatform idea that includes a TV element, Mike suggests that "you try to cut a deal with the production company, because sometimes it's better to do a revenue deal and take a bit of a risk yourself. I would start at 50/50 ownership, because these days you aren't going to get a big commission without a multiplatform angle on it and therefore you might as well go in sharing the format, otherwise how are they going to exploit it globally without a digital partner? It doesn't make any sense. It's becoming an equal playing field these days."

Other Issues to Consider

Production Timeline

If you get a commission, make sure that your TV production schedule and multiplatform production schedule work in tandem, as you may need to schedule in extra filming days to capture material for the website.

The most intensive effort on a TV production tends to be from the middle to the end of the production schedule. In the early days you are doing your research, crewing up etc., while later on you are filming and editing.

In multiplatform production all the effort is at the front of the schedule when applications are being built. Later on, just when the TV production team is busy, the multiplatform producer is testing and tweaking the content.

These two different styles of working can cause a problem if the multiplatform team need rushes that have not yet been shot, or the production team expects them to conjure up a fan base two weeks before transmission of the TV program. Online content takes time to build its audience, often over many months, and gets adjusted in response to user feedback. Understanding the peculiarities of each other's schedules will keep last-minute stress to a minimum.

Budget

TV producers can get caught out when thinking about the budget for multi-platform content. "Television costs pretty much the same to make with a few variables each time," says Mike Dicks. You know that an idea that has A-list celebrities is going to be expensive, but you might not be aware that building a social network could cost millions of pounds. Which is a greater incentive to use what's already available. "The way it works with Facebook and MySpace is that you can build software that works in all those sites without having to pay anything to any of them," says Mike Dicks. "MySpace will quite often get involved in promoting what you are doing and even fund part of it. Using their model is like using a free television channel."

You should also start thinking about how you might monetize your content via premium telephone line, sponsorship deals, or product placement, but don't get too caught up in this. "Your job as a content creator is to come up with a brilliant story that brings the audience in and then it's up to someone else to work out how to monetize that," says Mike Dicks.

Maintenance of the Content

While a TV program or series has a limited lifespan (although many series are licensed to allow the channels to repeat the programs a number of times over a set period), you should assume that any content you put online will be there forever, and that poses a problem: who is going to look after it? Some types of content are more labor-intensive than others; for example if you have message boards, someone needs to moderate them to make sure that nothing offensive is posted, so a message board is best avoided unless you have thought about how you will manage and pay for this over the long term.

A broadcaster might be willing to pay for the project over a period of twelve months, say, but if the TV show is no longer airing and unlikely to be recommissioned, they will want to hand over the running of the site to someone else. "It can be a burden to continue running a site for more than twelve months, and that's quite often the point at which someone like the BBC will pull out and leave you with a problem," says Mike Dicks. "I suggest thinking about outside relationships with other funding partners like Microsoft or advertising revenue," to support the content on an on-going basis.

Other options are to create content on a site such as YouTube or Flickr that will look after your content indefinitely. Matt Locke, new media commissioner at Channel 4, told the *Guardian* that he had partnered with MySpace so that discussions around a program could continue when the project had wrapped. It's important, he said, that "our projects can degrade gracefully back into the web."

How to Pitch a Multiplatform Idea

Writing a multiplatform proposal is like writing a TV proposal. "Your opening paragraph is, what's the story, who are the characters, and so on," says Mike Dicks. "You then need to explain exactly what the TV show is, and how that pans out— as a series or a one-off—then go into a description of how it pans out on each platform."

But there is extra information that you need to include that you won't find on a normal TV proposal:

* Who is the intended audience?

* What will motivate the intended audience to come to, and use your content?

* How will you promote the multiplatform elements of your idea? Through the TV show, marketing, or virally?

* How will users be able to share your content with their friends?

* Who will design and build the content? Do you have the expertise or are you working in a digital partnership? What is their track record?

* What's the budget and how long will the project take to build?

Channel 4 Education has a detailed page on its 4 Producers website that describes the perfect pitch. They favor using the NABC format for the proposal:

Need: Why does the audience need this content?
Approach: How does your project address the audience's need?
Benefits: What are the benefits to the user?
Competition: What other projects are addressing the audience need?

In May 2005, when I pitched *Take One Museum*, multiplatform programming was still in its early infancy (YouTube was yet to launch), but we were using a version of the NABC approach: you can see the original proposal on page 153.

Once you've got your proposal ready, you can arrange to see the channel executive and present a verbal pitch. According to Martin Trickey, a good multiplatform pitch is like *Star Wars'* R2-D2: "It's smart, it's intelligent, it's versatile, and it's short." Unfortunately, he says, most people, when pitching their idea, "can't actually describe it or haven't thought through how to describe it or what they are going to say: try to get it down to one or two sentences."

"You've got to tell your story in a way the commissioning editor will like," says Mike Dicks. Specialist multiplatform commissioners like to be involved in the early stages of development, but you still need to have enough of a grasp of the idea to be able to articulate it clearly. "I would do a PowerPoint pitch, with lots of visuals, to a broadcaster early on to gauge their interest," says Mike Dicks. If they are interested you can put more development effort into working out all the elements before you pitch again. You should at this stage also be thinking about whom else, beside TV channel executives, you might need to pitch to. For example, you might pitch the mobile phone part of the application to a telecoms company, Microsoft with another part of the project, and a broadcaster for another part, which is the multiplatform equivalent of international co-production for TV projects. You have to juggle the needs of several clients in order to raise the money to fund your project—with all the diplomatic challenges that can bring.

While it's good to sound out various funding options, it's usually the TV commission that will get everyone else on board, because that's the easiest way to attract a big audience to your content. "When you've got the interest of a broadcaster, it becomes much easier to get the deals from the telecoms companies, games companies, and web companies," says Mike Dicks.

If you are pitching a multiplatform project that starts or exists solely on the web, you'll pitch your idea to a multiplatform channel executive. If your proposal is mainly TV-focused, you should write the multiplatform elements into your TV proposal and pitch it to the usual TV channel channel executives.

In the next chapter we discuss proposal writing in more detail.

BBC SF Science   **Take One Museum**   8x30′

Budget: Net £ xxx per ep, Gross £xxx per ep.   Delivery: Week 36 2006.
Cost Drivers: Presenter costs (and availability); location fees, UK filming, one take, steadicam shoot with little or no editing; Access costs.

Idea: In an interactive series, Paul Rose explores Britain's museums and institutions, showing us the artefacts that you mustn't miss if you have only thirty minutes to spare. Each stand-alone program builds across the series into a unique compendium of Britain's scientific and cultural heritage.

Support:
* 80 percent of people are keen to learn, gather knowledge and immerse themselves in new experiences—but don't have the time.
* There are 2,500 museums in the UK. Four out of five of the UK's top tourist attractions are museums.
* Visitor numbers at UK's museums are rising.
* The average length of visit to a museum is 2–4 hours.
* Silver surfers are increasingly turned on by technology and are keen to use the Internet and for life-long learning.
* More people admit to being bored in their spare time than at work.
* Most people feel they don't fully exploit the cultural opportunities around them.

* *Around the World in 80 Treasures* has been a hit on BBC2 and attracts an AI of 82 percent.

Tonality: Dynamic format charmingly delivered, with integral interactive content.

Approach: In each 30′ presenter-led program, Paul Rose visits a labyrinthine British museum or institution and takes us on a **whistle-stop tour of the objects** that must be seen if you are in the area and don't have much time to spare. His brief is to give the audience a **must-see guide to each museum**, adding value with insights that people might not get when visiting themselves. He will have chosen and researched the objects before filming, but he has to take us on the tour **in real-time** (30 minutes) and—as far as possible—**in one take**. As well as choosing a number of **key objects**, he will tell the **story of the building and of any key characters** connected with the collections.

As he wanders the galleries, his **visual narrative style brings to life people and objects** from different eras and continents, ranging from the tree stump that marked the spot where Livingstone died, to the 7′8″ skeleton of Charles Byrne, the Irish Giant. As he stops to admire objects, he tells their story and directs the camera operator to film this object or that. This **intimate style** draws the viewers in, giving the feeling that Paul is talking directly to them.

Interactivity:
* Museum visitors will be able to take Paul's **extended mobile phone guided tour** to the objects featured, plus other objects not seen in the series.
* iPod owners will be able to download mp3 files of the tour, for a "podcast" which can be divided into sections to provide a "play list."
* Viewers at home will be able to examine the **objects in more detail interactively via red button and website**.
* **Printable tour guides/activity sheets** will be available online for people to take with them.

* **User-generated museum tours**—people pick their favorite local museum and film/photograph their own tour. They write a report online, which other users can read, rank and choose "top 20" lists of other people's tours.
* **Web-links into Where I Live** (websites) and **nations and regions** (programming) for variations and additional information.

Institutions will range from the grand to the quirky, representing a wide range of specialties and locations, for example:

* **Royal Geographical Society, London** (geography/exploration)
* **Hunterian Museum, Royal College of Surgeons, London** (anatomy)
* **The Oxford Museum of the History of Science** (mathematics)
* **Pitt Rivers Museum, Oxford** (anthropology)
* **Maritime Museum, London/Liverpool** (maritime)

Benefits: A low-cost, repeatable, long-running series that engages with viewers across the nations and regions. The audience will benefit from activity/interactivity opportunities beyond the TV series. BBC Four raises its profile, reaching young families and tourists with the interactive mobile/iPod/web services. Viewers could nominate their favorite institution and must-see objects for future series. OU [the Open University] are interested in co-funding.

Competition: People's number-one preoccupation is that they spend too much time staying at home and watching television. *Take One Museum* is a television proposition that complements and enhances the cultural experiences viewers can enjoy outside the home. Web broadcaster current.tv is leading the way with user-generated content.

Development Master Class 6

Live Like a Digital Native

1. Explore the following websites to familiarize yourself with the different ways that content can be delivered and consumed:

   a. *Addicted to Beauty*—Oxygen

      TV, online videos, original web series, merchandise, game, forums, and blogs http://addicted-to-beauty.oxygen.com/.

   b. *Battlefront*—Channel 4

      TV, video reports, blogs, campaign tools, partnership with Bebo http://battlefront.co.uk/.

   c. *Britain from Above*—BBC 360° project

      TV (BBC1, BBC2, and BBC4), geo-tagged original online videos, photographs, "making of" videos, archive clips on YouTube, embedded Google maps, Google Earth, embeddable content http://tinyurl.com/britainabove.

   d. *Shark Runners Game*—Discovery USA

      TV (*Shark Week*), website, online game, email, text messaging http://tinyurl.com/sharkrunners.

   e. *Springwatch*—BBC2

      TV series; website with blogs, message boards and webcam footage; official Flickr group with geotagged photos; book http://www.bbc.co.uk/springwatch/.

2. Subscribe to Cynopsis Digital's daily email newsletter to keep up to date with the latest (mainly US) multiplatform commissions.

3. Create an account at twitter.com

   a. Start following @mikedicks and @matlock (Commissioning Editor Channel 4 Education).

   b. Use http://search.twitter.com/ to search for keywords related to TV commissioning and find more people to follow (follow one or two people at a time or you might get blocked as a potential spammer).

   c. Start tweeting on a regular basis and get involved in conversations.

Explore More

Channel 4 Education Multiplatform Commissioning Website: clear and detailed information about developing and pitching a multiplatform project http://www. channel4.com/corporate/4producers/commissioning/education.html.

Cynopsis.com: Cynopsis Digital has a useful glossary of digital terms http://www.cynopsis.com/content/view/2271/80/.

Henry Jenkins: *Convergence Culture: Where Old and New Media Collide*
An entertaining introduction to the ways that audiences respond to, interact with, and repurpose old media content on new media platforms.

New Media Age: weekly magazine dedicated to interactive media with a range of free email newsletters http://www.nma.co.uk/.

7 Writing a Killer Proposal

Anybody can have ideas—the difficulty is to express them without squandering a quire of paper on an idea that ought to be reduced to one glittering paragraph.

—Mark Twain

"Get More Action" is the motto of US cable channel Spike TV, which if you hadn't guessed, is aimed squarely at "young adult men." If you send them a program proposal, it needs to hit them between the eyes. "I got pitched a show, called *Deadliest Warrior*," says Tim Duffy, Spike's vice president of original programming. "In its original form, the logline was: '*Ninjas vs. Spartans.*'

"It was clean enough in the logline [a single sentence that sums up the idea] to get me through to the next sentences. I was like, that's cool—give me more: '*We pit history's greatest warriors in a battle to the death. Using science, cinematic re-creation and a final choreographed battle, based on all the information we've just gained, we will determine who is the deadliest warrior.*'

"Then those three to five sentences were broad enough to get me further interested and specific enough to paint the picture. All of a sudden, I'm beginning to conjure up the visuals. I'm like, OK, this could be like a *MythBusters*-type show meets something that's re-creation-driven on History Channel. And it enticed me to ask further questions. Every step along the way, you are enticed to develop the project further or not waste your time."

Deadliest Warrior premièred in April 2009, pulling in 1.7 million viewers (95 percent of them were men), which was 50 percent more than Spike's average primetime audience.

Although some channel executives prefer to see something on tape, you will still be required to write your idea down at some stage of the development process, whether it's in an email, on a channel's e-commissioning website or as a full treatment, so it's important you can write a proposal that entices the channel executive to engage with your idea.

Overwhelmingly, when asked, channel executives said that in terms of a written proposal, less is more. "I prefer shorter rather than longer," confirms Martin Morgan. "I get fifty to one hundred proposals a week and I read them all; and you have to remember that that's not all I have to do." A proposal should be no more than a page long: small but perfectly formed. There's no point writing pages and pages, because they won't be read. "I'll read the first page," said a US cable exec. "I might flip through the rest of the treatment to see how they've structured it, but I've mentally decided pretty quickly that a show is not right for us."

Don't be fooled into thinking that a short proposal is something you can dash off in a few minutes. One cable channel executive said that he often had to rewrite proposals before submitting them to the head of the channel because they were so badly written. Another complained, "I'm pretty consistently amazed at the quality of the writing: grammar, spelling, that sort of thing. People are shockingly lazy. There are lots of producers who are great writers but if I get a treatment, especially an unsolicited treatment, and the person can't write, and hasn't spellchecked it, that's a huge strike. And you have to have an amazing tape to overcome that initial hurdle."

Writing your idea down is a key part of the development process: something that seems wildly exciting in your head can be revealed as having no substance once you try to pin it down on paper. Writing it down "irons the wrinkles out of the storytelling before you go into production," says Nick Emmerson. And before you pitch you'll need to boil your idea down into a couple of simple sentences and you can do that only by writing and rewriting and editing your proposal.

"On the whole, the world of development can be loads of work going no-where," admits Nick Shearman. So a good compromise, in terms of time management, is to write a rough draft of your proposal to help you order your thoughts and make sure you have all the elements in place, and then condense it into a paragraph that you can pitch by email. Once a channel executive has invited you to send a proposal, all you need to do is tweak your draft proposal to include their input and polish the grammar and spelling before sending it off to them.

Gathering Your Materials

Before you start writing your first draft, you must get all your information together. This might include research articles, notes from meetings, feedback from your executive producer, transcriptions of telephone conversations, or a list of potential talent. If you have all this close at hand you will find it easier to get into the flow of writing.

If you have reams of research it is important that you don't let the volume of material overwhelm you. It is helpful to use an editing analogy to help you prepare for writing your proposal. Go through your material, and make your "selects," that is, pull out any key facts, interesting quotes, ideas about program structure, locations, and presenter. String the information together in a "rough cut," then keep cutting and pasting until you find the best order, making sure your most important material is at the top.

Structuring a Seductive Proposal

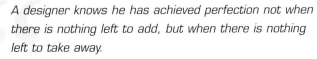

A designer knows he has achieved perfection not when there is nothing left to add, but when there is nothing left to take away.

—Antoine de Saint-Exupéry, French aviator

There is no "industry standard" format for a proposal, but there is a general consensus on how it should be structured, and what information it should contain.

Everything, including the title, the tagline, and the first few paragraphs should make your reader want to read more. Rather like a newspaper article, it has the most important, headline, information at the top, with more detail as the article goes on. It is, says Iikka Vehkalahti, Commissioning Editor YLE TV 2 Documentaries, Finland, "like a pyramid. You have a strong title. A clear and attractive one-liner opening the film, then you have one paragraph giving a compact description of the film's topic, genre, style, tone, structure, protagonist, dilemma, or conflict. Next you have a synopsis that expands on what you've written before without repeating it; this is where I should be able to 'see' the film. All this on one page only." Tim Duffy explains the synopsis further: "It could be information about the cast, it could be information about the format, it could be information about the world itself."

A common mistake is to hide the most important information within the body of the text, a tendency journalists call "burying the lede." I am guilty of this; I usually find the best paragraph is the last one. It happens so often, I now accept that's the process I go through, and now automatically cut and paste my final paragraph to the top of the page.

Use bullet points, subheadings or emboldened words, to break up the text and draw the eye down the page. You can also add a picture to help illustrate the story. Make sure your font is no smaller than eleven-point, otherwise it is hard to read.

Titillating Titles

The title is an extremely important part of your proposal—and could be the most important part. "The title can be the hardest thing; you shouldn't underestimate the importance of it," says Tom Archer. "BBC3 has commissioned several shows on the strength of the title, which have been quite brilliant," such as *Dog Borstal*.* Daisy Goodwin was leaving a meeting with Ben Frow, then commissioner at Channel 4, when she asked him "How clean is your house?" Ben was intrigued by the question and commissioned *How Clean Is Your House?* on the title alone.

Equally, an unappealing title can stall a commission. Producers spent six months trying to sell a show called *Pro-Celebrity Dancing* to Lorraine Heggessey, who was then controller of BBC1. They were insistent that "celebrity" should be in the title, but Lorraine resisted. Eventually they came up with *Strictly Come Dancing,* which she thought was much better and she commissioned the show (which is known internationally as *Dancing with the Stars*).

A title should be short because "it needs to look great on the EPG," says Nick Shearman. Electronic Program Guides (which you flick through on your television screen to find your programs) allow around forty characters for a movie title, fewer for a shorter program. For thirty-minute programs only the first ten or twelve characters will be displayed, so the casual EPG surfer needs to be hooked by the title to make them stop and take a closer look.

One US development executive said, "My favorite title is a 'this is what this is,' literal title, so you don't have to give a logline, like *Dirty Jobs.*" So for example, *Jurassic Fight Club* (History Channel), *Iron Chef America* (Food Network), *Dirty Jobs*

*Borstal is an old-fashioned British term for a correctional facility for young offenders.

(Discovery US), *Deadliest Warrior* (Spike), and *Supernanny* (Channel 4) successfully convey the content and the tone of each of the programs. Someone coming to *Dragons' Den* (BBC2; known as *Shark Tank* on ABC in the US) for the first time might be forgiven for being surprised to see a business program.

American channel executives like powerful, energetic words in their titles. Reess Kennedy, writer for CableU, collated a list of "signature titles" from the top thirty US cable networks, and found the following words dominated: *JACKED, PARANORMAL, OUTRAGEOUS, BIG, WILD, EXTRAORDINARY, FUNNIEST, GRIZZLY, PREY, KILLING, EXTREME, MONSTERS, RAW, UNTAMED, UNCUT, DEADLIEST, DESTROYED, DIRTY, DANGEROUS, WEIRD, FREAKY, BUSTERS, WARP, QUEST, ATTACK, DARK, EDEN, HAUNTED, GHOST, BIZARRE.*

"It's not," he notes, "'*Moderately Difficult Engineering*' or '*Slightly Haunted*', it's *EXTREME ENGINEERING* and *MOST HAUNTED*, respectively. It's not '*Sometimes, Somewhat Dangerous Catch,*' it's '*DEADLIEST CATCH*' ..."

It is possible to agonize for days or weeks over the right title. A killer title can certainly get you a commission, but don't delay pitching if you can't come up with something right away—while you are thinking about it there is probably someone out there pitching a show similar to yours and you don't want to get beaten to it. Channel executives know what kind of titles work best for them, so your lovingly crafted title might never make it through to transmission anyway. One US channel executive said that he was wary of a great title in the early stages of a pitch, as he thought a great title can mask a lack of real content. So if you can't come up with the perfect title, give it the best working title you can, and change it later.

Hook, (Log)line, and Sinker

The logline (also known as the strapline or tagline) is a short sentence that sums up the show that you are proposing: it's the line that should be designed to seduce your buyer into reading on. There's a lot riding on that one sentence because, says Tim Duffy, "Once we hear the logline, 95 percent of the pitches get weeded out." The logline comes directly after the title, for example (in bold):

* *4th and Long:* **It takes a legend to find a star** (Spike)—American footballer Michael Irvin oversees twelve hopefuls as they compete to make the Dallas Cowboys squad.

* *Bridezillas*: **Engaged. Enraged. About to be committed** (WE tv)—Busy brides-to-be go crazy as they try to plan their perfect weddings.

* *Ice Road Truckers*: **It's a job … to die fo**r (History)—On the road with the world's most fearless truckers who risk their lives driving their eighteen-wheelers across Canada's frozen lakes.

* *Snog, Marry, Avoid?*: **Perhaps the world's first make-UNDER show** (BBC3)—Jenny Frost uses a Personal Overhaul Device to strip women of their fake tans, heavy make-up, and skimpy clothing to turn them into natural beauties.

* *Supervolcano*: **It's under Yellowstone. And it's overdue** (BBC1)—A sleeping volcano under Yellowstone Park erupts violently with devastating results for America—and the world.

* *Survivor*: **Outwit. Outplay. Outlast** (CBS)—Sixteen fierce rivals are pitted against each other in a competition that will test their endurance and allegiance. One by one they are voted off: the last one to survive wins $1million.

Some people call the emboldened sentences "taglines" (similar to those used on posters advertising movies). They suggest that the logline is in fact one or two sentences that outline the premise of the show (i.e. the sentence that comes after the channel in the examples above). Whichever way you do it, each element—title and logline—tells a story and compels the reader to find out more.

Continue this principle of unfurling the story as you continue writing your proposal.

First Paragraph

Use the first paragraph to explain the Who, What, Where, Why of your idea. For example,

Dino Younge runs a high-end events company in Los Angeles catering to Hollywood's stars. Each episode of *Starry Nights* focuses on a different event and takes us behind the scenes as Dino and his team deal with the stress of putting on high-profile events week after week.

Libby Overton won the opportunity to pitch her idea to a panel of channel executives in London with the following description of her film, *A Tale of Two Carnival Floats*:

Following two feuding carnival associations as they prepare to compete against each other, this quirky film about small-town life ponders the importance of beauty, success, popularity, and escapism … and that's just the organizers.

For a more content-driven film, such as a science or history program, you could start with a hook: an insight or interesting fact that makes you want to know more, before outlining the narrative.

Robert Cialdini, a social scientist at Arizona State University, studied the way that scientists communicated with a non-specialist audience and discovered the most effective passages posed a question. One astronomer wrote:

How can we account for what is perhaps the most spectacular planetary feature in our solar system, the rings of Saturn? There's nothing else like them. What are the rings of Saturn made of anyway? … How could three internationally acclaimed groups of scientists come to wholly different conclusions on the answer? One, at Cambridge University, proclaimed they were gas; another group, at MIT, was convinced they were made up of dust particles; while the third, at Cal Tech, insisted they were comprised of ice crystals. How could this be, after all, each group was looking at the same thing, right?

This passage could easily be the opening paragraph of a proposal for a documentary about Saturn: it tells you the what, who, where, and why of the story. Add a sentence, such as, "this documentary unravels the mystery and reveals which of the scientists was right," and it explains the content of your program, along with the conflict-laden narrative arc. This paragraph also explains why the audience will want to watch: to find out the answer to the mystery.

Body of Proposal = Anatomy of Program

Next, explain how you will shoot it, for example: "using interviews, actuality of the scientists facing each other down at a prestigious conference, and NASA footage, we …" There is no need to reveal the answer to the question if you posed one—save that nugget of information and reveal it in your pitch. Nor do you have to go into the scientific details, they're not necessary; at this stage, the channel executive needs to know the story in as few words as possible. They will be in the market for a documentary about astronomy or they won't.

If your series is character-driven, describe your characters, what they want and what's standing in their way. In the *Starry Nights* example, after telling us that each episode follows the story of one event, the outline might continue:

Each event is different—an Oscars after-party, a bar mitzvah, a sweet sixteen or an intimate dinner for a famous movie star and his new girlfriend—and each one brings unexpected challenges. We follow Dino and his team of part-time models and actors as they juggle the demands of their high-maintenance clients with trying to progress their careers. Dino—an ex-chef and father of sextuplets—has his patience tested as he attempts to get his team to focus on the job in hand.

Starry Nights follows the lives of the waitstaff: aspiring model Amarika, who spends her wages on plastic surgery; Rashid, a thirty-two-year-old failed actor who is devoted to his six Chihuahuas; and Ellis, Dino's right-hand woman who has to pick up the slack when people fail to turn up for work.

If it's a format, explain what happens each week, and the narrative turning points, but there's no need to go into great detail. "I don't want a running order: I want to know what this show is going to make me feel at the beginning, in the middle and at the end, what journey it's going to take me on, how it's going to work for the viewer and keep them interested with all the twists and turns," says Lucy Pilkington.

Finally, if there have been other programs similar in tone and content to your proposal, explain what makes yours different, and if appropriate say why you are the right team to make this program.

Don't waste space telling them *why* they should commission it. One of Lucy Pilkington's biggest complaints about proposals is when the first page tells her "it's in the air; it's topical; it's important; it's a must see." She says, "Don't tell me why I should commission it, that's my job to know that. It's your job to tell me what the show is and how it's going to work." If your channel executive is interested and they want more detail, you can submit an expanded proposal, with any extended narrative or episode breakdowns added as an appendix.

Drugged Culture

It's the early twenty-first century and we're completely dependent on drugs. Not recreational drugs, not hard drugs, but the steady march of pharmaceuticals from vast research corporations. Pills for pain, pills for depression, pills to keep us awake, pills to help us sleep, pills for blood pressure, obesity, or even intellectual boosts. We are a nation of pill-poppers.

But while we reach for those clinically white, plastic bottles, how many of us ever question the validity of the pills we're consuming, flooding our blood and brain with body- and mind-altering chemicals? Why, when, and how did we become so accepting of drugs?

Drugged Culture is an unflinching, investigative examination of how synthetic chemicals became such an accepted part of contemporary culture while scrutinizing how much good—or harm—they actually do. Mixing archive material with interviews and a contemporary feel, we'll look at the history, present, and future of pharmaceuticals covering major landmarks—such as the discovery of lithium to treat psychosis.

As part of this journey, psychologists, medical historians, and artists will examine our fascination with "pills as cures" while everyday people relate their good, and bad, experiences of legitimate drug use. Ultimately, we're asking how many of these powerfully marketed pills we really need and are we in danger of losing an important aspect of our humanity as we become increasingly reliant on chemicals to get us through the day?

Dr Barry J. Gibb, brief biography: A former biomedical researcher, Barry now explores science via writing and filmmaking. The former culminating in his book, *The Rough Guide to the Brain* (Rough Guide books, Penguin Publishing), due for release first quarter 2007. Through his use of film, Barry aims to go beyond the more traditional approaches to "science communication," an approach often rooted in the belief that understanding

---

science "is good for people." Instead, Barry's darker, unconventional style attempts to hook people in by sharing the wonder he himself feels at the machinations of this universe.

Examples of his work can be seen here:
http://www.channel4.com/fourdocs/film/film-detail.jsp?id=18344
http://www.channel4.com/fourdocs/film/film-detail.jsp?id=12221

Contact Details:
Dr Barry J. Gibb, digitalis media
Email: barry@digitalismedia.net

© Barry J Gibb

Getting in the Writer's Zone

Writing is easy: all you do is sit staring at a blank sheet of paper until the drops of blood form on your forehead.

—Gene Fowler, American journalist

When starting a fresh proposal, just write something. If you think about it too much you will become paralyzed with self-doubt and never write a word. No one except you will see your first draft, so it's OK to write a bad one. In fact, it's necessary. Once you've written it and slept on it, the flaws will become obvious and you will immediately be able to improve on your first effort.

It is helpful, before beginning to write a new proposal, to immerse yourself in writing that is similar in tone to the channel you are targeting and the proposal you need to write. Spend some time reading channel websites, blogs, and fan sites to help you get a feel for the channel and their audience. Sometimes you'll find a quote to inspire a great tagline or title. Flick through the magazines that appeal to your target audience. Notice the kind of words they use, the sentence structure, and tone. This kind of exercise is like a mental warm-up, stretching your creative muscles before you launch into your writing sprint (or marathon).

It is helpful to break the white expanse of screen with a picture or quote that conveys the attitude and/or themes of your program. Flickr.com is a good source of inspirational photographs. Looking for a picture can help you ease into the relaxed mental state that is necessary for writing; but don't spend too long—that's simply procrastination.

Sometimes you can find yourself genuinely stuck. If you are working at a desk full of papers and tottering piles of books and old coffee cups, spend a couple of hours going through your paperwork and filing or binning every piece of paper on your desk. Chances are you'll come across a useful article or piece of research that you'd forgotten about that will help your proposal. At the very least, you will sit down to a clear desk, which will help you to focus.

Find out what gets you into a creative state of mind. When working in an open office environment I put on headphones when I'm ready to write a proposal. This has two benefits: it signals to people that I am concentrating and not available to chat, and it blocks out disruptive noise such as loud telephone conversations. I usually listen to the same CD on repeat for weeks on end, barely aware that it's playing. When coming back to rewrite or edit a proposal, all I need to do to get back in "the zone" is to put on the CD I've been playing and I'm instantly tuned into where I left off. Some people can only work in silence, others in busy environments. Find out what works for you.

With practice, and a few tried and tested techniques, you should be able to switch in and out of your "writing mode." In busy periods, I can easily write two or three drafts a day, as the words flow automatically. I find the hardest proposal to write is the one that comes after a period of no writing activity, when it can take me a week of effort to finish a draft proposal. This is like a runner who performs at their peak during an intense period of training, but soon loses their speed and stamina if they stop training.

But what if you get to the end of five hours and still haven't managed to produce the roughest of drafts? As a creative director in advertising once advised Harry Beckwith, who had been struggling to write an ad for three days: "If it's this hard to write the ad, the product is flawed."

Take a good look at your idea and ask if you are trying to write a proposal for a flawed concept. If so, go back to the previous chapter and run it through the reality check, ask your colleagues to interrogate the idea and find out if you are trying to sell a dud. If so, change it or kill it and move on to the next idea.

Polishing Your Proposal

Once you've got the content of your program idea down on paper, it's time to polish it so it looks professional.

Mind Your Language

Aim to make your proposal as easy to read as possible, as the channel executive is likely to scan it at speed. There are a number of ways to achieve this:

* *Use simple, easy to understand language.* A good rule of thumb is to write as if writing for a twelve-year-old, which is the level to which advertisers pitch.

* *Use a conversational voice with short sentences and paragraphs.*

* *Don't assume your channel executive will understand specialist terms and phrases.* This is especially important if you have a PhD in the subject you are pitching. Don't force your channel executive to ask you what jargon means, it will make them feel stupid and that's not good for your relationship.

* *Avoid clichés "like the plague."* Leave the "edgy," "noisy," "powerful," "compelling" words to the channel executives' briefs.

* *Don't oversell.* Don't say that this is a "unique program" or that the host is going on "an incredible journey" or that it's an "extraordinary story." Use the classic drama principle of "show don't tell" in your writing and those things should be self-evident and your proposal will be more convincing.

* *Be confident in your use of language.* Say what *will* happen, not what might happen. Use active verbs in the present tense to make your proposal punchy. Make every sentence count—each one must move the narrative on. Every word must be necessary and appropriate.

* *Be as specific as possible about your program's elements, but don't promise something you can't guarantee.* So, for example, rather than say "we put sixteen people together in a house to compete for a job," say "sixteen

ruthlessly ambitious businesspeople compete for a $250,000 apprenticeship with Donald Trump." If you haven't secured access to Trump, say "sixteen ruthlessly ambitious businesspeople compete for a six-figure apprenticeship with a world-famous business magnate," and be prepared to discuss a short-list of potential candidates.

* *Keep it flexible.* A proposal is an opening salvo, the starting point of your discussion. It's likely that your channel executive will want to have some creative input and you are more likely to win the business if you can accommodate their suggestions. For example, say that the host "will be someone like Mike Rowe or Bear Grylls" to give an indication of your vision, but to leave it open to other suggestions.

Tone of Voice

Is your target channel cultured and intellectual, homey and down-to-earth or macho and provocative? Take your cues from the channel website and publicity material and use a similar style of writing in your proposal—it proves you understand the channel's character. Don't be po-faced if you are pitching a satirical program.

Spelling and Grammar

Once you've edited your proposal to your satisfaction, print it off to proofread it, as mistakes are easier to spot on the printed page than on a computer screen.

* Double-check your spelling, especially the names of onscreen talent and place names.

* Have you been consistent with your use of the present tense?

* Can you split any long sentences into two shorter sentences?

* Is every word, and every sentence, absolutely necessary?

Once you are happy, ask someone else to read the proposal to see if it makes sense to them. Rewrite as necessary, correcting all errors.

If you are pitching the same idea to more than one channel, check and tweak your proposal so it is tailored specifically to each channel's brief.

Proposal Checklist

You should now have a strong proposal containing all the following elements:

1. **Title**—"Fairly early on, it's quite a good warning sign if the title is TBA—those gaps are quite illuminating," says Tom Archer. If you haven't got a final title use a working title (w/t).

2. **Channel**—"You might get a pitch document at the BBC and it says this will work well for Channel 4," says Martin Trickey. "You think: you could have at least changed the name on it!"

3. **Your contact details**—"Sometimes there are some basic things that people miss off, like company logos and who it's come from," says Nick Shearman.

4. **Episode length and number**—"My favorite was one that came in that said '6 x 1 hour for some lucky fucker,'" recalled Martin Morgan.

5. **Logline**—If you haven't done your development thinking, this will be the most difficult part of your proposal to write.

6. **Outline**—This is the what, who, where, when, why of your idea, with the most important information at the top, and supporting detail further down the page.

7. **Price**—Many producers leave the price off the proposal, as this can be seen as sensitive information; and they don't want to pitch it at a lower price point than the channel might be willing to pay. However, have a ballpark figure in mind if you go to pitch your idea verbally, as you are likely to be asked. Suggesting a budget that is too high for the channel or too low for the ambition of your pitch will ring alarm bells for the channel executive. Ballpark channel budgets can be found in the Appendix, but enlist the help of an experienced production manager if you don't have any experience of drawing up a budget.

8. **Delivery**—This means the date by which the program will be finished and available for physical delivery to the channel. Take into account how long it will take to produce and any other factors that will influence production, such as an event that takes place only once a year or filming that can take place only in a particular season (such as in a program about beach holidays).

CASE STUDY

Greenlit: *Rick Stein's French Odyssey* (10x30´ BBC2)

Denham Productions

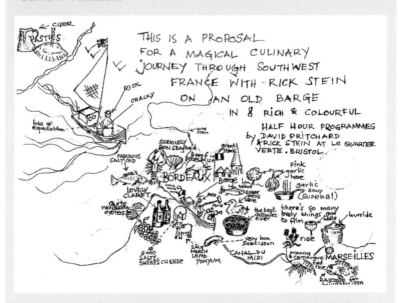

"We'd just finished a series called *Food Heroes* where Rick Stein went around the country looking at people who produced some wonderful food, like salt marsh lamb or cheeses or cider," says producer David Pritchard. "It came to an end as all good things do, and we were wondering what to do next. We felt at the time we knew every blade of grass in the country and we wanted a change.

"Rick and I were in a restaurant and we'd had a few glasses of wine and a jolly nice lunch of organic lamb. A few weeks previously, I mentioned to the BBC's features and documentaries commissioner, Tom Archer, that we fancied doing a barge trip to France, and he thought it was a lovely idea. Rick had heard of the Canal du Midi in southwest France and thought, what a wonderful idea to sail from Plymouth across the channel to Bordeaux and then go all the way down to Toulouse and then get on the Canal du Midi.

"We pushed everything to one side, and there among the breadcrumbs and the [cigarette] ash, we drew a map with a felt-tip pen and thought this is how it could be. We put: 'great cassoulet here'; and 'great goose here'; 'good beans here'; 'wonderful wine'; 'great cheese'; we thought the ultimate would be bouillabaisse in Marseille. So we did little drawings along the way like a children's storybook, and we were so proud of it we gave it to Tom Archer."

"It was," says Tom Archer, "a good way of showing travel and food together as a narrative—the journey would begin with Rick cooking shellfish on the beach on the Atlantic side of France and end up completely differently with the heat of Marseille and a bouillabaisse. It was a coherent proposal; it didn't need pages and pages. I just had to flash the tablecloth at Jane Root, then controller of BBC2, and we got the commission. It was just an issue of how many episodes we would make."

"All I had to do was to break that cartoon drawing down to ten half-hour programs, which is quite easy," recalls Pritchard.

Development Master Class 7

Write the Right Stuff

1. Write a one-page proposal based on the "tablecloth proposal" (above); use your imagination to fill in any gaps in the information.

2. Write a draft proposal for your own idea.

3. Take a look at the proposal for *Fifties Showgirls* (overleaf). How many mistakes can you spot? Turn to page 176 to find out and score one point for every one you identified.

4. Go back and edit your proposal, making sure you've flushed out any of the problems highlighted in *Fifties Showgirls*.

Fifties Showgirls

Channel: DIY Network

In this extraordinary, rollercoaster of an emotional journey we go to Las Vegas, which is known for gambling, wedding chapels and showgirls. Approximately 40 million people visit Las Vegas every year. In 2005 a shrimp cocktail cost 99c; the same price as it cost in 1959. Two years earlier, Las Vegas staged its first topless show. Today, eleven Vegas shows feature topless dancers.

Novice show producer Sal Sagev wants to turn back the clock and revive a classic Las Vegas show. Les Folies Bergère started in 1959 at the Tropicana hotel and was one of the longest-running shows in Las Vegas before it closed in 2009. We will follow Sal as he auditions hopeful show-girls; he has something different in mind—to be eligible they must have been born in 1959. As well as finding the dancers, Sal will have to find a stage manager, a set designer, make-up artists, and costume designers. Sal wants to make his show as authentic as possible, so he will do some research and he will discover old archive film and photographs of the original stage set. He will also find out that showgirls of that era had to be 5´4", weigh 116lbs and measure 34–24–34. Sal will have his work cut out.

We will follow the hopefuls who are auditioning for a spot in the spotlight in this new show. All of them are bigger (much bigger) than Sal's idea and they don't know that they will be required to dance topless. Something's going to have to give … Once the cast has been selected we will follow them through rehearsals and costume fittings as they also juggle their personal lives and adjust to living in Las Vegas. Each week there will be a new challenged to overcome and one of the dancers will be sent home.

Each episode will be a self-contained narrative, but over the course of the series, the tension and excitement will build, as Sals' ever-expanding entourage attempt to produce a hit show. With guaranteed high drama onstage and backstage, *1959 Showgirls* will probably be a real showstopper.

Pitiful Productions specialize in making low-budget documentaries about the outdoors.

Explore More

Brush up your writing skills with the following books:

Lynne Truss: *Eats, Shoots and Leaves: The Zero Tolerance Approach to Punctuation*
The slightly irritable guide to commas and semicolons.

William Strunk Jr. and E. B. White: *The Elements of Style*
The much-loved classic guide to grammar, composition, and style (Chapter V offers excellent advice that is particularly applicable to proposal writing).

David Marsh and Nikki Marshall: *The Guardian Stylebook*
An A–Z guide to tricky spellings, apostrophes, and foreign accents.

Fifties Showgirls

Channel: DIY Network

In this extraordinary, rollercoaster of an emotional journey we go to Las Vegas, which is known for gambling, wedding chapels and showgirls. Approximately 40 million people visit Las Vegas every year. In 2005 a shrimp cocktail cost 99c; the same price as it cost in 1959. Two years earlier, Las Vegas staged its first topless show. Today, eleven Vegas shows feature topless dancers.

Novice show producer Sal Sagev wants to turn back the clock and revive a classic Las Vegas show. Les Folies Bergère started in 1959 at the Tropicana hotel and was one of the longest-running shows in Las Vegas before it closed in 2009. We will follow Sal as he auditions hopeful showgirls; he has something different in mind—to be eligible they must have been born in 1959. As well as finding the dancers, Sal will have to find a stage manager, a set designer, make-up artists, and costume designers. Sal wants to make his show as authentic as possible, so he will do some research and he will discover old archive film and photographs of the original stage set. He will also find out that showgirls of that era had to be 5′4″, weigh 116lbs and measure 34–24–34. Sal will have his work cut out.

We will follow the hopefuls who are auditioning for a spot in the spotlight in this new show. All of them are bigger (much bigger) than Sal's idea and they don't know that they will be required to dance topless. Something's going to have to give … Once the cast has been selected we will follow them through rehearsals and costume fittings as they also juggle their personal lives and adjust to living in Las Vegas. Each week there will be a new challenged to overcome and one of the dancers will be sent home.

Each episode will be a self-contained narrative, but over the course of the series, the tension and excitement will build, as Sals' ever-expanding entourage attempt to produce a hit show. With guaranteed high drama onstage and backstage, *1959 Showgirls* will probably be a real showstopper.

Pitiful Productions specialize in making low-budget documentaries about the outdoors.

Annotations:
- No episodes or duration
- Inappropriate channel
- No tagline
- Clichéd: show, don't tell
- Irrelevant paragraph
- Paragraph too dense
- Future tense
- No indication of the type of characters we might see
- Typo
- Irrelevant production experience
- Unclear format —is it a competition reality show or ob doc?
- No name or contact details
- Punctuation error
- Lack of confidence in the idea

Score

0–5	Hopeless	Go back and read the chapter again.
6–10	Could do better	Write a proposal for your favorite TV program, paying attention to your weak areas.
11–13	Good effort	Don't let the little things trip you up.
14+	Professional	Move swiftly along to the next chapter.

8 Finding and Keeping Talent

*Talent without discipline is like an octopus on roller
skates. There's plenty of movement, but you never know
if it's going to be forward, backwards, or sideways.*

—H. Jackson Brown, Jr., author

In February 2003, Mark Burnett was in the back of a cab, on his way from La
Guardia airport to Manhattan, NYC, where he was to stay a few days while he
dealt with some *Survivor* business. He also hoped to set up a meeting with
Donald Trump to pitch him an idea he'd had while in the jungle filming *Survivor:
Amazon*. In the meantime he planned to polish his pitch so he would be word-
perfect. He put in a call to Trump's office, and was taken aback when he was
put straight through to Trump, who told Burnett to divert the car to his office: he'd
take the meeting right away. Stunned, Burnett had twenty minutes to prepare his
pitch as his driver zigzagged through the honking horns and sirens of the city
traffic.

Once in Trump's office, Burnett outlined the series idea, emphasizing the
drama and commercial potential. Trump's meetings happen at breakneck speed
and attendees feel like they need a hit of oxygen after being grilled by "The
Donald"; Burnett was no different. Forty-five exhausting minutes after walking
into Trump's office, Trump and Burnett shook on a deal: Donald Trump would
take part in Burnett's new show, which was tentatively titled *The Apprentice* after
The Sorcerer's Apprentice, with Trump playing the part of the sorcerer.

Trump told Burnett that his agent at William Morris would sort out the details.
Burnett stepped out of Trump's office to call the agent. But when he pitched the

idea the agent put the brakes on the deal saying, "I don't think that will work." Burnett, horrified that the deal might fall through, went on the attack, told the agent that *he* was wrong and promptly called the chairman of William Morris, Jim Wiatt. Having been assured that Wiatt would look into it, Burnett went back into Trump's office to tell him his agent didn't like the idea. Trump was unconcerned; all he was interested in was getting a fair deal. Burnett suggested that Trump could share in the profits of the show and they shook hands again. Deal done.

Within two weeks, Burnett's business manager, Conrad Riggs, had formalized the contract with Trump so they could begin approaching the networks with the idea. ABC had been chasing Trump to do a reality show for some time, but he'd always turned them down, even though the president of ABC, Lloyd Braun, had personally approached Trump. On a sunny, breezy Burbank day, Burnett walked into Braun's office and said, "I have exclusive rights to a reality show starring Donald Trump." Braun immediately said he wanted it; Burnett suggested he tell him the idea first. He also told him he was going to pitch the idea to CBS and NBC too. If Braun wanted it he'd have to come back with the best offer.

CBS came back with an offer of six episodes instead of thirteen and two-thirds of the licensing fee Burnett had asked for. NBC and CBS offered equal deals: thirteen episodes and ratings bonuses if the show did well, but CBS put a cap on the bonus payments. NBC agreed to all Burnett's terms, including a satisfactory ratings bonus structure. NBC won *The Apprentice*.

All the channels want big names to front their shows to pull people in to their network; a famous name guarantees newspaper coverage and saves on the marketing budget. "We are always looking for faces that are recognizable," says Lucy Pilkington. "We need people who are going to bring people to us on the EPG, rather than people we've got to build up." Having the right talent attached to your show can open doors at the channels—and if you are lucky, start a bidding war—but it's not easy to do.

Talent spotting poses something of a "chicken and egg" dilemma. Do you develop your idea and try to find talent to match or do you find the talent first and build a program idea around them? If you take the former approach, you risk putting a lot of effort into a show that you later find impossible to cast. Conversely, you can build a whole series around a celebrity only to find that they're unwilling or unavailable, or they've fallen out of favor. If that happens, you are stuck with a redundant idea that you must kill or try to recast, which means you're back to square one. In reality, you will use both methods of casting and development.

Sometimes you set out to find a certain type of host and end up with someone completely different than you expected. When Mark Burnett was casting the host for *Survivor*, he viewed more than one hundred talent tapes, before reacting instinctively to one of them. "The minute I viewed Jeff Probst's, I knew he was perfect for *Survivor*," Burnett said. "He wasn't famous, nor an expert adventurer, but my gut told me he was the one." And, of course, sometimes someone perfect comes along but isn't recognized. "A long time ago I saw a talent tape of Bear Grylls and he was doing naked wing-walking on a biplane," recalls Tom Archer. "I binned it because I just thought he was another posh, wannabe presenter and how desperate is this as a way of trying to get your attention … of course, he's done very well!"

Every factual genre requires a different type of onscreen talent. At the more serious content-driven end of the factual genre, the talent is absent (in the case of narrated documentaries) or relatively unobtrusive—there to illuminate the landscape not obscure the view. In entertainment-focused shows, the talent *is* the view.

If you are proposing a show hosted by an expert, say an Italian cookery series, and you fail to attach talent to your proposal, the channel is unlikely to take it seriously as there is no guarantee you would be able to find the perfect person—it makes it a risky proposition. Attach a fabulous, big-name Italian chef and you have a commission. If your talent is strong, but the channel execs don't like your program idea, they will be prepared to work with you on developing an alternative format around the talent.

With an entertainment-driven program, it's enough to suggest names of some well-known hosts/presenters to start a discussion with the channel. If the program is commissioned, the production team will agree a short-list of talent with the channel and begin negotiations with potential hosts' agents. Although it is possible for you to approach the presenters in advance and ask if they might be interested (this can add weight to your proposal), in practice it's difficult to get agents interested in an idea before you have a commission and production dates.

Some channels want A-list celebrities but can't afford their fees, and Z-listers may be off brand for them. In this instance the ideal solution is for you to find someone that the channel can grow and call their own. This used to mean finding a completely new face, but increasingly it means someone who is recognizable to the audience, such as a journalist or actor, but who's not necessarily a seasoned presenter. In the case of specialist factual programs, you might be tasked with finding a charismatic, telegenic academic, who doesn't mind risking his or her career and reputation by appearing on TV.

It is notoriously hard to find new presenters and is extremely time-consuming, but if you manage to find someone that works for a channel, your next four or five commissions suddenly become easier, as you have established talent on which to hang your pitch.

Depending on the genre in which they will work, presenters need different skills and attributes. And, of course, each channel has its own view on what makes ideal talent. Take note of the kind of people on your target channel and work out what it is that makes them successful. Is it an intellectual rigor, a hands-on approach, or an ability to empathize with interviewees? Make a note and add those qualities to your talent wishlist.

Entertainment presenters are professional television hosts, trained to read from autocue, and styled to add glamor to a show. But factual entertainment presenters must be deemed "authentic." That is, that they have experience outside of television, and that they have specialist knowledge they can share to inform and educate the audience. There is the sense that factual hosts are dipping into television rather than making it their whole lives (although some inevitably do), and could go back to doing whatever it was they were doing before they were talent spotted.

We're asking the audience to spend a lot of time in their company; so onscreen talent needs to be interesting and engaging. That doesn't mean that they should be cookie cutter clones; Duane "Dog" Chapman of *Dog the Bounty Hunter* and Tim Gunn of *Project Runway* each have a unique style and manner congruent with their respective shows. Dog is a muscular, sun-tanned, long-haired, wraparound-sunglasses-wearing tough guy who dresses in biker boots and studded leather waistcoats. Tim Gunn is a lithe, white-haired, bespectacled metrosexual who dresses in sharp suits. Some presenters have a "love them or loathe them" personality, that attracts faithful fans and stirs debate among their detractors, but they do need to be reasonably photogenic—you want to be listening to what they are saying, not distracted by an ill-fitting toupee or tombstone teeth.

Onscreen talent needs to be comfortable in front of the camera, able to memorize a script or running order and able to "walk and talk," that is behave naturally while talking to camera. They may be required to interact with, or interview other people, which involves being able to listen to what someone is saying and responding as appropriate, rather than plowing through a list of pre-prepared questions. They also need enough self-awareness not to talk over or interrupt the person to whom they're talking, so as not to make the interview difficult to edit.

Recognizing Talent

It's useful to think about the type of talent you need for your program. Disregarding the talent that will be cast by production (usually the hosts of big entertainment programs), there are five main types of talent you could be asked to find in development:

1. the intellectual expert;

2. the professional expert;

3. the everyman/experiential talent;

4. the interventionist specialist;

5. ordinary people as observational documentary characters;

6. celebrities as characters in their own shows.

Intellectual Experts—Recognized by their peers as experts, but may be unknown outside their field. "What you are looking for all the time are enthusiastic experts. People who know what they are talking about and are really enthusiastic and passionate about it," says Emma Swain.

Experts can come to the attention of TV producers after publishing a book or controversial new thesis. They are intellectual, and often opinionated and thesis-driven. Their approach can be polemical or objective. For example, Simon Schama, professor of history and art at Columbia University, and former cultural critic for *The New Yorker*, wrote and presented *Simon Schama's Power of Art* (BBC2/PBS).

Women seem to have a much harder time being accepted as intellectual, especially if they are young or attractive, although anatomist Dr. Alice Roberts is making some headway on the BBC. Conversely, older women often find it hard to make it on to (or stay on) the screen, while there are many examples of men presenting TV shows into their seventies and beyond. Find the right woman to front your show and you could set an industry-changing precedent.

An expert who explores a subject on behalf of the audience—rather than telling the audience what he knows—an approach common in history programs —needs to be comfortable with asking basic questions of other experts so the audience can follow the story. Many academics are uncomfortable asking what they deem to be "stupid" questions as they worry that their academic colleagues will think they are "dumbing down." Skilled presenters are able to put their egos to one side and play the part of the lay audience. They are able to explain complex ideas in a clear and visual manner without having to hide behind impenetrable jargon. When talking to an academic, pre-research an area of his specialty then ask him to explain it in a sentence or two. If he waffles or insists on using technical terms, he is probably not ideal television presenter material.

Academic experts can find the production process difficult. As a world authority on his subject, a professor is used to deferential treatment in the corridors of academe. Suddenly he experiences an unsettling loss of autonomy: "He must kowtow to the director's will, stand shriveling in the baking sun, speak to the camera in unholy hubbubs of traffic and the human race, tolerate a cameraman who angles his fish-eye lens as though it is essential to count every nostril hair, and be unfailingly benign when the sound-man's battery goes flat," complained Brian Sewell, art critic and presenter of *The Naked Pilgrim* (Five). Add resilience to your list of ideal qualities.

Professional Experts—Expertise gained through practical experience; they show us something new by demonstrating it rather than telling us about it. Bear Grylls was the youngest Briton to climb Mount Everest and served time in the British Special Air Service before appearing on *Escape to the Legion* and *Born Survivor* on Channel 4. Despite his accomplishments, he was reluctant at first: "I said no to TV three times, because I didn't have the confidence to do it. I'd always taken the piss out of TV presenters, and it didn't feel good-looking and slick and smiley enough." In the factual field a lack of ambition to be on TV is seen as a positive asset, because it means presenters' passion lies elsewhere, and it's that we're trying to capture. People who are desperate to be on screen, beyond all else, raise a red flag in the producer's mind, as they may not have enough life experience to bring to a show.

CASE STUDY

Greenlit: *Mythbusters* (3x60′ Discovery US)

Producer: Beyond Television Productions
Executive Producer: Peter Rees

"*Mythbusters* was inspired by two shows," says Peter Rees. "One was a brilliant Channel 4 show, *The Secret Life of Machines*, and our other inspiration was *Jackass*. We wrote one proposal in about 2001 and it had a component of experimentation in it but it was really just an urban legend show. Discovery rejected it the first time and said, 'We've already got a show like this on one of our networks, and it's not anything that interesting.' At that point it wasn't called *Mythbusters*, it was called *Tall Tales and True* or something along those lines. It had no hosts, no locations and almost no stories in it.

"Then something came into my head: We Don't Retell the Legends, We Put Them to the Test. That went back to Discovery and it was sold purely on that one line.

"And the difference was, rather than doing the classic re-enactment and interviews and talking heads, we would do scientific experiments that validated key aspects of these stories.

"Discovery commissioned a short 3x60′ series. At that time we were suggesting we would have one experimenter and one folklorist; someone doing the experiments and someone out in the field interviewing people who claimed this had happened.

"After the commission, we had a three-month period of development so we developed the initial stories and we also looked for hosts. We were looking for people with a workspace, because we couldn't afford a location; we were looking for people who had the tools to build anything, because we couldn't afford to fit out an entire workshop; and we also were looking for people who could build things from a variety of different sources. And finally, we were looking for someone who got the concept.

"I knew Jamie Hyneman because about five or six years before, I'd been working on a magazine series called *Science 2000* and I had done a show about *Robot Wars* in San Francisco. Jamie was one of the people that we profiled. He'd built this robot that ended up getting disqualified from the competition because it was so destructive—it was throwing metal into the audience. So it was clear that Jamie had the building skills, so he was one of the first people who came to mind when it came to doing the screen tests. The trouble is Jamie is completely monosyllabic. So when we spoke to him, he said, 'Umm, you know, I'm not that good at talking, but I've got a friend who is.'

"We asked everyone to shoot a video of themselves talking through the Larry Lawn Chair story [in which a LA man (inadvertently) ascended to 16,000 feet with the help of a Sears lawn chair and forty-two helium balloons]. There was another group that looked really promising: another odd couple. In their video they fired each other across a parking lot at the back of their shop with one of them inside a refrigerator. Jamie and Adam's video wasn't as spectacular as the other, but what they did do was display an understanding of what the show might be about. They stood in front of a white board and discussed how they would approach the balloon lawn chair problem. The video also displayed the basic dynamics of their relationship: even back then Adam was on at Jamie about being boring.

"We submitted the videotapes, of which we probably had ten at the most, with our recommendation that we preferred Jamie and Adam. Subsequently, I've spoken to Steve Burns, who I believe was Discovery's VP of Production, and he said he didn't actually see the original casting video when it came in but he said if he had seen it he would have commissioned a ten-part series straight away."

Mythbusters has been transmitted in twelve countries and nominated for an Outstanding Reality Program Emmy (in 2009) and won the Silver Dragon at the Beijing Science Festival, 2005.

Everyman Host—Has no specialist knowledge, but has an abundance of curiosity, a practical, can-do attitude, and a willingness to get their hands dirty. They take us on a journey and we learn about the world as they discover it for themselves. Examples include Bruce Parry on *Tribe* (BBC2)/*Going Tribal* (Discovery), Mike Rowe on *Dirty Jobs* (Discovery US) and Jimmy Doherty on *Jimmy's Farm* (BBC2).

Sometimes this kind of presenter is perceived to have an affinity to a subject. For example, Ross Kemp played a hard man in *EastEnders*, so it seems appropriate for him to hang out with hard men in *Ross Kemp on Gangs*. Likewise, Danny Dyer was an actor in *The Football Factory*, a film about football hooligans, so it wasn't a great leap for him to present *The Real Football Factories*, a documentary series about football hooligans, which wouldn't have been commissioned without Dyer's involvement.

"Originally, we were offered a series about the history of football hooligans coming up to the contemporary story, but we couldn't find the talent," says Lucy Pilkington at Virgin Media. "Eventually, the producer said, 'What about Danny Dyer, because he did *The Real Football Factories*.' Without Danny Dyer, that subject is too dark and out there, even for Bravo, but suddenly, when married with the right talent, that show suddenly came alive."

Rugged middle-aged men tend to dominate the kind of programs where a host is required to discover something by going on a journey, and it can be an advantage if it looks like life has kicked them in the ass. They need to be engaging communicators, and not take themselves too seriously. Women are attracted to them, and men want to go for a beer with them. They must immerse themselves in an experience without forgetting to explain to the audience what they're thinking or feeling, and must be comfortable talking about their emotional reaction to a situation on camera. The audience needs to feel that they are there in the moment with the host, experiencing it as they do.

Ordinary People as Characters—Larger-than-life characters, living in an extraordinary situation or doing an unusual job, such as *Dog the Bounty Hunter*, or *Ax Men* (History/Five) or *Little People, Big World* (TLC). These people would be doing their jobs and going about their lives regardless of the presence of TV cameras. While observational documentary characters are not hosts in the traditional sense, they need to be co-operative and comfortable in front of the camera, not mind the intrusion into their lives and willing to articulate their thoughts and feelings.

If the focus of the series is broad, for example you've secured access to film airside at JFK Airport, the production team would cast the key characters, but a pitch tape that contains one or two great potential characters can help to secure the commission. For programs that feature a particular character or family, such as *16 Children and Moving In* (TLC) you should find the contributors, secure access, and make a pitch tape before formally pitching the idea.

Specialist Interventionists—Intervene into ordinary people's lives in an effort to improve them, such Gillian McKeith on *You Are What You Eat*. "If you look at the classics in this genre from *Jamie's School Dinners* to *Supernanny* to *Mary Queen of Shops* and *The Restaurant*, they're all essentially built around one individual; they're fresh expertise with conceits built around them, and I think that's a much simpler thing for the audience to grasp," said Andrew Mackenzie, speaking at the Intelligent Factual festival. They can also work in pairs or teams, as on *Queer Eye* and *What Not to Wear*.

Interventionist hosts need a background in whatever kind of makeover they're undertaking. A host of this type may have an empathetic demeanor and be able to interact with ordinary members of the public, or could be bossy and opinionated. In UK shows this type of host is often cast in a caricatured role, such as the no-nonsense Jo Frost in *Supernanny*, the bossy Kim and Aggie in *How Clean Is Your House?* and "gay best friend" Gok Wan in *How to Look Good Naked*.

CASE STUDY

Greenlit: *Supernanny* (11x60′ Channel 4)

Ricochet

"We did a big nationwide casting: we thought it should be a woman, because it would be easier for parents, kids, and viewers to handle," says Nick Emmerson, president of Shed Media US.

"We spoke on the phone to nursery nurses, nannies, and care workers and brought one hundred women into our offices in Brighton. We were right into the screen tests and we had a middle-aged, matronly lady but none of us were convinced that she was right.

"Then on the last day of casting, Jo Frost walked in. She had star presence. You notice it as soon as someone walks in the room, there's a confidence bordering on arrogance—in a good way—and Jo had that. We were talking of filming for two weeks and Jo said, 'No fucking way; I only need a week!' Danny [Cohen, the then Head of Factual Entertainment, Channel 4] loved her.

"We did a mini-test, with Jo working on some of the issues for a day, and that was it."

Ordinary People in a Format—Cast exclusively for a time-limited participation in a reality show, such as *Wife Swap* or *Survivor*. They generally appear in only one show or series and then go back to their ordinary lives. Some, however, go on to become minor celebrities in their own right, like cleaner Maureen Rees who appeared on *Driving School*, and assorted *Big Brother* housemates. Others go on to have their own shows, like Laura Bennett who was a finalist in the third season of Bravo's *Project Runway* and the late Jade Goody, who after her appearance on *Big Brother*, had her life and subsequent death from cervical cancer documented on Living TV.

A casting producer will normally cast these characters once production is underway, so it is sufficient to outline the character types you expect to cast to give the channel a sense of the potential story lines and conflict.

Famous People as Characters—People already in the public eye, who become the star of their own series, as in *The Osbournes* or Janice Dickinson's *Modelling Agency*. These kind of shows are heavily constructed around the celebrity and continue for several series or produce spin-offs. Without the celebrity, there would be no show, so they need to be approached and access secured before you develop the show around them.

Professional Judges—Successful entrepreneurs or people with practical hands-on skills that can be transferred to television, who sit in judgment over others. For example, Bruno Tonioli in *Dancing with the Stars/Strictly Come Dancing* and Simon Cowell on *X-Factor*. A television career is secondary to their other business interests. They need to be comfortable expressing strong, and possibly unpopular opinions, and have the time and motivation to commit to a period of filming.

Judging panels are generally comprised of a mix of personalities, and casting them is beyond the scope of development. It is sufficient to say in the proposal that your panel consists of a bad-tempered mogul, a soft-hearted life coach, and a bitchy journalist, etc. with some suggested names, so the channel executive gets a feel for the proposed group dynamics.

Professional Hosts—Professional hosts, such as Ant and Dec, Cat Deeley, or Ryan Seacrest, who front a show, linking different segments and performing interviews. They are generally not known for anything other than television hosting, and are most commonly found on entertainment shows. Again, they will usually be cast once the program is in production, so are not a concern for development. It is enough to give an indication of people you would like to approach to host the show.

These are all generalizations, born out of what has worked for past programs. Of course, there are exceptions to every rule, and that is where the interesting shows emerge. Observe the rules, then see if you can break them. If you stray from the casting norm, you have a harder sell, but you could make a break-through show and attract a completely new audience to serious documentary; on the other hand, you might alienate your core audience. It's that risk and reward conundrum again.

Talent Spotting: Where to Hunt for Hosts

By far the best, and easiest way to find new talent is not to go looking for them against a deadline. If you are doing your daily development homework and keeping your eyes and ears open you will happen across all kinds of interesting people who might be right to host a show. Keep a notebook with you at all times to jot down the names of people, and a folder of articles and references to potential experts. Ideally, when you need to find someone specific all you have to do is pull out your talent folder to find someone who could be perfect.

This is where you need to employ talent triage. If you need specific talent for a show in active development, and you find someone with potential, they should be listed on your "hot talent" database, with photograph, contact details, website, and some background information, along with details of any correspondence.

If you find people who look like they could carry a series, for example, a family with sixteen children, whose names all begin with J, and are about to build their own house (*16 Children and Moving In*, TLC), get them on to your active development slate, make contact with them pronto, before someone else does.

Articles or book reviews that suggest academics, nonfiction authors, or other interesting people that might be worth future contact, should also be kept in your talent folder. Review this file periodically to see if a new commissioning fad has made one of your experts a potential hot property, or if there is someone in there who could be perfect for a proposal you have in development.

Sometimes, young and inexperienced people who are desperate to break into television will approach you; there are numerous training schools that encourage people to spend their money on producing a showreel. While these courses might prepare someone for general "rent-a-host" positions, it is unlikely that they would have the necessary life experience or intellectual weight to provide the authenticity that specialist factual audiences seek in their hosts. Therefore factual development producers must go looking for unsuspecting potential new talent in some or all of the following places:

On Screen—Look for people with some television experience, probably on cable and perhaps as part of a team, who have the potential to carry a show. For example:

* Ty Pennington, host of *Extreme Makeover: Home Edition* (ABC) was previously a carpenter on *Trading Spaces* (TLC).

* Mike Rowe started out selling items on QVC, before working his way up to *Dirty Jobs* (Discovery).

* Carson Kressley started out as one of five lifestyle experts on *Queer Eye*, before hosting the US version of *How to Look Good Naked* (Lifetime).

* *Tim Gunn's Guide to Style* was commissioned after Tim Gunn established his own fan base on *Project Runway* (Bravo US).

Also look for people with proven hosting skills that could be used in a different context. Andrew Marr, a BBC news political commentator, became a hit history presenter with *Andrew Marr's History of Modern Britain* (BBC2).

On Location—Ask your production colleagues if they've filmed anyone interesting. Sometimes, experts who appear as interviewees in documentaries can make fine presenters in their own right. For example:

* Professor Iain Stewart appeared on BBC2's *Horizon* as an interviewee before he was commissioned to present the geology series *Journeys from the Centre of the Earth*, and *Journeys into the Ring of Fire* and *Earth: Power of the Planet*.

* Jimmy Doherty was an entomologist who was being interviewed for BBC2's *BodySnatchers* when producers spotted his potential. He's since appeared in several of his own series, including *Jimmy's Farm*, *Jimmy's Farming Heroes* and *Horizon: Jimmy's GM Food Fight* (BBC2).

* Pat Llewellyn spotted Jamie Oliver when she was filming *An Italian Christmas at the River Café*. When he burst on to BBC2 with *The Naked Chef* (and *Oliver's Twist* internationally) he revolutionized the cookery show. With stylish scooter, a cool group of friends, and a potty mouth, he made cooking appeal to an audience beyond bored housewives tethered to their daytime TV; subsequently he launched a number of series, which are now shown in forty countries.

In the Office—You might have to look no further than the next desk to find the perfect person to front your next show:

* Kate Humble was a BBC researcher before presenting *Rough Science* and *Springwatch* on the BBC.

* David Attenborough was Controller of BBC2 before embarking on his long career as a presenter of the BBC's wildlife programs.

* Andy Cohen, Senior Vice President of Original Programming and Development at Bravo in the US, also hosts *Watch What Happens: Live* on the channel.

* Natasha Wood was a BBC production manager before co-presenting Channel 4's *How to Look Good Naked*.

* Mike Loades worked as a fight-arranger for TV and film productions before hosting *Weapon Masters* (Discovery Military).

On the Red Carpet—Are there any celebrities who could be reinvented? For instance:

* Alan Alda (*M*A*S*H*) fronted *Scientific American Frontiers*, a science series for PBS.

* Dr. Travis Stork (*The Bachelor*) is lead host on a US syndicated daytime medical talk show, *The Doctors*.

* British actor Stephen Fry, who famously absconded from a West End show with mental health issues, later presented an Emmy-winning documentary, *The Secret Life of the Manic Depressive* (BBC2) among many others.

At the Talent Agent's—Establish good relationships with talent agents so you can call them when you need a new face. But dealing with agents can be frustrating: many won't enter into a conversation about a celebrity client unless you already have a show commissioned; other agents will desperately send you the details of wholly inappropriate people. "Just because someone's got an agent doesn't mean they're any good," notes a weary development producer.

In Your Network—Cultivate relationships with publishers, PR people, and journalists so you're the first person they call with an interesting new client or contact. If you work in arts programming make it your business to know the most charismatic museum curators, art collectors, and antiques experts. If you work in history or science development know who's who in the academic world.

Professional Organizations—To find an as-yet-undiscovered presenter with expert knowledge, call the appropriate professional bodies, who should be able to suggest some names. Use this as a starting point only: the people they suggest will be suitably qualified, but not all will be good on TV. Do some phone bashing, and talk to as many people as you can; never put the phone down on someone without asking if they can recommend anyone else in that field.

Specialist Newsletters—Good for spotting young entrepreneurs and other experts who are well known within their industries but haven't yet been picked up by the media. For example, a producer looking to recruit an expert for a series about money could subscribe to hereisthecity.com (a website about London's Square Mile financial district) for names of financial experts and insider gossip about who might be "available" for other work.

Cultural Events—Go to book readings, museum talks, and comedy nights. It's much better to spot potential hosts in their natural environment when they're not self-conscious about being "talent-spotted." Note how they deal with their audience and how the people respond to them.

Newspaper and Magazine Articles—Look out for stories of ordinary people in extraordinary situations or who are extraordinary in their own right, such as the Roloff family featured in TLC's *Little People, Big World* (Mom and Dad and one of their twin sons have dwarfism while their other two children are of average height). If you spot someone, move fast, as every other production company is likely to be on to them too.

Online—Keep your eyes open for people who are blogging or uploading YouTube videos on specific subjects, such as cookery, urban gardening, or parenting. Log on to conference websites for edited video highlights of speeches: online videos are a great way to assess someone's presenting style.

From Casting Couch to Screen Test

Once you've identified someone interesting, invite him or her out for coffee, if geographically feasible. Keep the reason for the meeting vague; don't at this stage tell them you are going to make them a star. Get to know them first, find out what makes them tick and what they're passionate about. Can they express themselves? Do they have social skills? Are they as interested in you as you are in them? Are they curious and engaging or can they talk only about their own subject in a dull or unintelligible manner?

If you still like them, suggest that you'd like to think about proposing them for inclusion in a program. Explain what the proposed role entails but don't make promises, keep it casual. Ask them to send their résumé, references, and a list of any other supporting material such as articles they've written or books they've published. If their credentials stand up, the next step is to do a screen test.

Before committing to the expense of filming (especially if they live a long distance from your base) it is a good idea to ask them to get a friend to film them on a home video camera and send you the tape. Be clear about what you are expecting to see, as some people can get completely carried away, sending several tapes of them at a succession of family events. One interior designer sent several tapes of her husband's drunken birthday party; entertaining though it was, it didn't showcase her design talents. Generally, it's enough for them to introduce themselves, and then to do something (relevant to their expertise) while explaining it. From this you should get a good idea about whether they are photogenic, articulate, and engaging.

Next, draw up a short-list of candidates. Decide whether to go to their home or office to film them individually, or run a casting session where you pay travel expenses for all the candidates to come to a central location. If you have no money, Peter Rees has discovered that he can use the video function on Skype to do his casting: "Basically you ask them to have a camera on their end; you can do a certain amount of directing and you can record the video and audio stream."

During the session, emphasize that you are seeing lots of people. Don't make a big deal of the filming, as people can get starry-eyed and nervous, over-thinking what they're saying and "performing" to camera. Build their trust and get them used to you and the camera.

If they are uncomfortable on camera, or if you decide they're not right for you, let them down gently. If they aren't going to hear from you again, don't tell them you will call and then don't. Just contact them a few days later to say that unfortunately they didn't make it on to the short-list and thank them for their time. If you think you might want to contact them again in the future, be clear that you'd like to keep in touch, but that you have nothing in development that is right for them at present.

If they're great on camera, it's time to discuss the idea of their being formally pitched as talent for your program. Make sure they're happy with the role you've cast them in. For example, it would be pointless to pitch Bruce Parry as host of *Tribe/Going Tribal* if he was the kind of guy who would only stay in five-star hotels. If that were the case you'd need to find someone else. Discuss their personal boundaries with them and tailor the proposal to suit them, but don't allow them to dictate how the show is made. If an academic is writing his own script, he will need to be guided by experienced producers about how the narrative is best portrayed on screen. Make this clear from the outset, so there are no misunderstandings: don't give your host editorial control.

Before you formally pitch your new talent to a channel, it's likely that you will want to produce a more polished talent tape (which we'll explore in more detail in the next chapter).

Keeping Onscreen Talent Sweet

TV producers have a maxim about new onscreen talent: however likable, rational, and co-operative a new host is, within two years they will turn into a monster. For some programs, particularly culinary shows with fiery chefs such as Mario Batali or Gordon Ramsay, the host's enormous ego is their *raison d'être*; Simon Cowell's irritability is an indispensable part of his branding. This kind of larger-than-life host tends to be found at the entertainment end of the factual spectrum, and their antics are part of their appeal.

But even the most mild-mannered and co-operative people can become difficult to work with after a couple of years. Cornell University Professor of Psychiatry, Robert B. Millman, has described this phenomenon as Acquired Situational Narcissism, which erupts when a person with a predisposition to narcissism—arguably anyone who would consider appearing on TV—is subjected to filtered, positive feedback, reinforcing their belief that they are superior to others. When ordinary people are plucked from obscurity to appear on TV they receive a lot of flattering attention from producers eking out their best performance; channel executives hoping they've found a channel-defining star; and agents wanting to represent them. If their show is successful, they become the subject of breathless critical reviews or vitriolic blog posts. It's hard not to be seduced and unsettled by that kind of attention and that's how egotistical, insecure monsters are born. "They like the concept of fame, driving the pace car at the Indianapolis 500 or being on the Leno show, they love it," says Thom Beers of the *Deadliest Catch* crab-fishing crews, but "We never let the sea captains or crew get too 'Hollywood'—we threaten to recast."

You might be the first television professional your host or contributor has ever met, so build your relationship with them carefully. How you treat potential presenters will color their whole view of the industry and influence how they behave on all future productions; you have a responsibility to treat them with consideration, respect, and integrity.

It is important to manage the expectations of new talent and be honest with them about the process. Many producers make a fuss over someone, tell them how fantastic they are, and then suddenly disappear for apparently no reason, leaving the poor person wondering what they did wrong. Explain that the development process is convoluted and frustrating and that there are never any guarantees. Be brutally realistic about the chances of the idea being commissioned, and err on the side of pessimism. It's always easier to give someone good news than break bad news.

If you say you'll keep in touch, do. Send them an email during the holiday season or have a coffee every six months or so to keep up with what they're doing, and encourage them to drop you a line to keep you up to date with any developments at their end. For people on your hot talent list, put in a recurring date in your calendar to remind you to drop them a line. One development producer advises keeping "your contacts in a personal relationship with you rather than with your company because they are your currency when you move on."

Casting Stars and Talent Czars

An experienced casting producer can be a huge asset to a development team as they can draw the team's attention to potential hosts and help to develop ideas around new talent on a daily basis, making talent finding central to the development process. If your team can't afford a full-time casting producer, you can hire them in to work on specific projects.

CASE STUDY

The UK Talent Producer

"The thing about finding talent is that no one likes to do it, but I absolutely love it. I am always on the lookout, I could be on the bus or the train, I could be reading the *London Lite*, I could be at an event ... anything. If I see anyone that's got the X factor then I'm up to them: Can I get your number? Can I get your email address?

"But I always make it clear from the beginning: 'I'm not promising you anything, I haven't got a program to slot you into.' Then I say tell me about yourself: what do you do? Where are you from? What's your background? I try to understand who they are and what they are about. I'm always thinking is there a journey that they're going on? Or are they doing something over the next six months that you could film, or something going on next year that would be interesting to make into a single narrative film? On the other hand, if they aren't saying the right things, I think OK, could they be a personality on an entertainment program? Say their specialism is music, is there some kind of music show they could front?

"They are flattered that you've approached them, and they'll tell you everything you want to know, and I'll take notes and I'll go away and I think what can I do with this person?

"Nothing might come of it, but I'll get in touch with them and say, 'Thank you, I'll keep you in mind.' And then you never know, two months or two years down the line, I might think, she'd be great for this, and then I've already got the relationship with her.

"I ask them to send me a CV and a biog—two paragraphs about yourself, why should I be interested in you, what makes you special, what makes you stand out? I set them a test because you can ascertain whether or not they are serious: if they can't be bothered to do it then they're not going to be bothered to get up and go to a shoot on time.

"So the next stage would be shooting a taster tape with them. Usually I would shoot on a Z1 or whatever camera I can get. I like to do an interview with them, and maybe do a walk and talk, a little piece to camera, but mainly just get them doing something they like doing. The most important thing is you see their personality. That twinkle in the eye, a nice smile, a nice face. It's not about being good-looking, but I've got to want to look at them.

"The thing about talent finding is that it isn't a scientific process, it is quite a clumsy process, just calling someone up and asking if you can meet them. Sometimes it works, sometimes it doesn't. I love looking for new talent."

Behind the Camera: Production Talent

When we talk about "talent" we normally mean onscreen talent, but the talent behind the lens is as important. "Part of the appeal of the project is: who is the storyteller?" says Rudy Buttignol. It's the production talent that will reassure the channel executive that you can make the show that you are proposing. If you attach the wrong executive producer your show might never be commissioned, even if it's a great idea. "Bad reputations live for a long time," notes one US cable channel exec. Once an executive producer has fallen out of favor, there is little they can do, "unless there is a change at the top at the channel and memories are wiped."

Most producer/directors toil away their whole careers without as much as a mention in the *Fired!* column of the industry press. But occasionally someone will make a program that creates a stir, whether because of its innovative approach to filming or unique access to a subject, and they become household names in the broadcast world, suddenly welcomed into commissioning executives' offices. Adam Curtis acknowledges that he has an advantage when pitching his ideas. "I'm in a position where I can go in and talk to a channel controller because I make programs that get their channels talked about. I get them press." But not everyone is in that fortunate position: senior producers will have their track records examined closely, and some channels insist on approval of the director or executive producer before greenlighting a series.

CASE STUDY

Greenlit: *Deadliest Warrior* (9x60´ Spike TV)

Morningstar Entertainment

"When Gary Tarpinian, the president of Morningstar Entertainment, pitched *Deadliest Warrior*, I'd never met him before, but he had done re-creation-based shows and he had done a lot of History and Discovery Channel-type stuff, so I knew going into the room what he was about," says Tim Duffy, vice president of original series, Spike TV. "His shows hadn't gotten a ton of big ratings, but I knew them and I knew his production company enough to respect who he was.

"I knew he wasn't pitching beyond his means. He wasn't coming in and pitching me a formatted, elimination-based reality show never having done one. He was pitching me a show that was on brand for Spike and was still in the sweet spot for him creatively."

"To me, the most important person is the showrunner—the person who is actually going to make the show—because they are the one who is going to make or break it in terms of success," says Peter Rees. Discovery Channel "is looking back through the ratings of people who have made shows in the past, and who are being proposed for new series, and they are making their selections based on ratings history." Be strategic about getting to know the big-hitting executives—your job is much easier when the channel believes the proposal can be delivered. If it can be delivered by a known name, so much the better.

Now you have your polished proposal and your onscreen talent, and possibly a big-name director attached, you have to think about how to sell them to the channel executive.

Development Master Class 8

Start Star Spotting

1. Start a talent database. Make a note of anyone interesting you meet, see on TV or during your research. Record their expertise, contact details, and link to any online video.

2. Keep a note of interesting facts about celebrities or other people in the public eye: do they have an interesting degree, hobby, or passion that you could turn into a TV series?

3. Sign up to follow @redpages on twitter—http://twitter.com/redpages.

Explore More

123people: free people search engine. See where potential hosts have a presence on the web and get their contact details. Beware, as enquiries can throw up several different people with the same name http://www.123people.com.

Findatvexpert: free website featuring profiles, résumés, and contact details of UK experts who are interested in appearing on TV http://www.findatvexpert.com/.

Hollywood Representation Directory: book and online database that lists the contact details of more than 10,000 US talent agents, entertainment attorneys, and casting directors. Updated twice yearly in April and October. Online subscription is $19.95 per month http://tinyurl.com/hollywoodrep.

LinkedIn: check a potential expert's credentials and get introduced to interesting prospects via your connections http://www.linkedin.com.

Red Pages: subscription website that lists the agents, publicists, and managers for more than 20,000 international celebrities http://www.theredpages.co.uk/default.aspx.

Spotlight Presenters Directory: features profiles and agent contact details for more than 700 UK-based TV presenters. Cost: £20 http://www.spotlight.com/shop/product.asp?product=6.

TED Talks: non-profit organization dedicated to "ideas worth spreading," which holds annual conferences around the world where expert speakers from the worlds of art, business, science, and technology deliver inspiring eighteen-minute talks. Around 600 talks can be accessed online http://www.ted.com/talks.

CASE STUDY
Greenlit: _Tribe_ (6x60´ BBC2)
Producer: BBC Wales
Series Producer: Steve Robinson

"I'd worked with Bruce on a project called _Cannibals and Crampons_," recalls Steve Robinson. "I was the series producer for a strand called _Extreme Lives_, so I would acquire or buy finished films. Bruce, in the run-up to the millennium celebrations in 2000, decided that he wanted to be as far away from the celebrations as possible, and so ended up going on an expedition to New Guinea, Indonesia, and Irian Jaya to climb a very, very remote mountain. Along the way he bumped into some tribal people who he had been warned were still cannibals, and he filmed all this ... we ended up putting that out on BBC1.

"I did another couple of small projects with Bruce and kept in touch with him over the years. Bruce was an expedition leader and working in remote areas and the idea we—me, Bruce, and the development team at BBC Wales—came up with was quite a formatted popular approach to the question: what people live in the toughest environments on earth? What skills do they need to live there?

"It was going to be quite a _Ray Mears_-type making-bows-and-arrows-and-lighting-fires kind of instructional show, but what we didn't like on those shows was the way indigenous peoples and environments were used as props rather than as real people. It was never conceived as an anthropology show but we wanted to give these people a voice within a conventional survival-type format.

"We pitched it to Jane Root, channel controller at BBC2. We were quite bullish about it, about how it was going to be different. We didn't coin the word immersive at the time, but that was the general thrust of it: 'You haven't seen anything like this before.'

"The BBC gave us some development money, which led to me to flying out to Namibia, where Bruce was living in a cave in a remote game conservancy. He'd been working on the children's series _Extreme Desert_ as expedition leader and logistics manager when I texted him to say, 'Could I come out and film a little taster with you?' Luckily he was available.

"We filmed a taster of Bruce doing some horrid things like eating scorpions and drinking water out of pools filtered through wool that he found, showing the survival skills that he'd learned. He covered himself in mud from head to toe and squatted in a lake. It was also the home of the San bushmen, so we got their stories and we called it *The Naked Savage*.

"It was, visually, quite a striking taster tape. We took it back, pitched it, and showed the video and they loved it. It was commissioned on the strength of a good taster, no doubt. If you have got new talent, taster tapes are everything because it allows the controller to see exactly what it is they are going to be buying."

Tom Archer was the commissioner who took the idea to Jane Root: "I thought Bruce Parry was absolutely fantastic. It was funny, it was a little bit scary, and what I liked about him was his attitude—which comes through in all his programs—he felt natural. He wasn't an anthropologist, but he was a guy who was naturally curious and non-judgmental and not patronizing in the slightest, and he would also do things that most of us wouldn't.

"I must have seen three or four minutes and I was absolutely sure that this person would be a big star. What also excited me was that here was a way of doing anthropology, a subject that had disappeared completely; my feeling as a commissioner was that we'd got rid of anthropology by accident. The audience, I felt, had never fallen out of love with anthropology, so I was confident that if you got it right you would reconnect with an audience pretty easily, and I thought, this is the way to do it. I was desperately keen to get it away.

"In those days we were pitching in a room at the Hempel Hotel. At one end would sit myself, Jane Root, George Dixon who was then the scheduler, and some money people. About twenty groups of people would come and pitch one after the other. I suspect that I timetabled the pitches that day in a way that kind of slipped this idea through. We didn't say, 'We need to go back and do anthropology,' as that could have raised Jane Root's hackles. We focused on the presenter.

"Steve Robinson is an interesting pitcher, because he's a guy who's quite an alpha male and his pitch for Bruce Parry was almost monosyllabic; he was exactly the opposite of the flamboyant pitcher. There's a kind of honesty that I know channel controllers like. If I'm looking them in the eye and they're saying, 'This is going to be bloody good,' and that's about all they're prepared to say and you go with it. I've seen it again and again."

Steve takes up the story again: "The written proposal said things like '*Boy's Own* adventure meets anthropology.' 'An adventure format that makes Ray Meers look like a lardy-arsed Boy Scout in a Millets cagoule.' We didn't get as far as format points—the notion was who are the toughest people on the planet? What is the most extreme environment and how do people live there?

"It had been offered to Discovery before it was pitched to BBC2 and they didn't want it. They didn't like that it was small cameras and thought the production values may not be great—they just didn't get it at all. Then of course Jane ended up as General Manager of the Discovery Channel and saw the finished series and bought it [and renamed it *Going Tribal*]. They reversioned the first series and then co-produced the second and third series."

Tribe has been seen in more than fifteen countries, and Bruce Parry was awarded an RTS Award for Best On-Screen Presenter in 2008.

9 The Pitch Tape

A conversation that starts with a DVD is a damn sight easier than a conversation that starts with a piece of paper.

—Ben Hall, MD Shine Network

Imagine trying to verbally pitch a documentary about "the story of two wheelchair rugby teams, Canada and USA, who are battling it out to be world champions at the 2004 Paralympics. We get to know the characters and find out how they cope with life with a serious disability. It's an amazing story of triumph over adversity." Sounds kind of interesting … but maybe a little worthy? And sportsmen aren't that interesting to non-sports fans, are they?

Now picture this video clip: an indoor sports hall with USA Rugby banners and the Stars and Stripes on the wall. There are two teams of athletic young men, one side dressed in black vests with USA logos, the others in yellow and green, all of them in beaten up *Mad Max*-esque wheelchairs. It appears that a match of some sort has just finished. The losing team files past, congratulating the winners.

A middle-aged, grim-faced man, also in a wheelchair, mills about. A woman approaches him and says, "Joe, can you wait until we're done?" He sighs theatrically and says, "Yeah, I can but Kevin came over here during one of our games and you …" The woman walks away, and Joe yells after her, "Fuck you, bitch!" Frame freezes on a close-up of Joe's angry face laid over with a soundtrack of pounding, up-tempo, heavy metal music.

CAPTION: *Joe, Polio, 43 years ago.*

A glass-fronted cabinet displays two sports vests. One bears the name:

Soares. A fast-cut archive sequence of a younger Joe, in the thick of a violent game of wheelchair rugby. Intercut is news archive: "Joe Soares is arguably the best quad rugby player in the world. Childhood polio took Joe's ability to walk but not his drive to excel," says the newsreader.

MONTAGE: dozens of trophies. A young man sitting in a kitchen says, "My uncle Joe, if you go to his house, the wall of fame isn't just a small little shelf, it's huge." The newsreader continues, "Joe's just about the most competitive man I've ever been around, and it shows in his sports accomplishments and it shows in his efforts." A woman in a USA team shirt says: "In '96, Joe was the man. That gold medal: he was a huge part of that. Unfortunately, his speed started going down and he got older. So he got cut." She shrugs.

WIDE SHOT of sports hall with teams playing rugby, Joe looking on from the sidelines. VOICEOVER: "Joe got upset and angry he didn't make the team, he tried to take us to court." A man in dark shirt in wheelchair, captioned "*Team Leader*," says, "He pissed and cried and moaned over it, but he lost all of his protests."

Guy in kit room says, "Just because things didn't work out for *him*, he jumped ship and went up north, and now he's coach of Team Canada." Shots of Joe in a huddle leading an aggressive war cry before a game. "USA, learn a new way!" "He took some of our players with him," continues the interviewee.

MID SHOT of blond bare-chested guy with goatee in wheelchair. "If Joe was on the side of the road I wouldn't piss on him, to put it out." Shots of the blond guy in the midst of a violent game of rugby, and Joe taunting him, yelling loudly from the sidelines. The other players look on in amazement.

MID SHOT interview, blond guy. "He thought I should just respect him for who he was, well fuck you. I ain't gonna respect you for who you are, you've got to gain respect from me."

CAPTION: "After beating six countries, 5th-ranked Canada advances to the Finals."

WIDE SHOT of sports hall. Metal music crescendos. Low, fast tracking shot in to Team USA at one end of the hall, fronted by the blond guy, who stares down into the camera. WS of sports hall. Fast tracking shot in to Team Canada at the other end of the hall. Joe, in the center, stares defiantly ahead.

CLOSE-UP Joe, red-faced, yelling, "This is ours for the taking boys! This is ours! So tonight no drinking, and get ready for USA in the finals. Have you got that? All right boys, great job! Great job!"

Fast track into a golden trophy on a table flanked by two officials. Card captioned: "For the first time, Joe will face his former USA teammates."

That is a 2'51" sequence from the multi-award-winning, Oscar-nominated feature documentary *Murderball*, which was shown on A&E after a theatrical release.

If you were pitching this film and slipped this clip in the DVD player your buyer would be captivated: even if they don't want to buy it they will make that decision knowing exactly what it is you are trying to sell them.

This short sequence (which actually happens about six minutes into the finished film) sets up the whole story. Not just the main narrative of the two teams heading toward a showdown at the Paralympics, but shows:

* Joe and Mark Zupan (the blond guy) as main characters and arch rivals;

* Joe's anger and humiliation at no longer being "the man";

* jeopardy, physical and emotional intensity;

* excellent access to the characters;

* an unfamiliar world;

* the approach includes interviews, and observational documentary shot from their point of view (i.e. at wheelchair height);

* the pace and tone of the film—swearing, bone-crunching wheelchair clashes, fast editing and driving metal music. It's not going to be a violin-stringed look at living with a disability.

A pitch tape (they are still referred to as "tape," even though the format is now DVD) needs to hook the audience in straight away, starting with a fantastic sound-bite or surprising bit of action to "grab somebody by the balls and say 'Look at this!'" says a producer/director. "It's a visual device for showing the format or the cast of the show," explains Nick Emmerson, "it often sounds and feels like a series tease."

By Any Other Name: The Pitch Tape

Producers and channel executives use lots of different words for a pitch tape: mood tape, talent reel, screener, promo, trailer, showreel, format tape, sizzle reel, demo or taster tape, but they all do the same thing—sell your concept. "It gives you a much better flavor of what you are going to get," says Nick Shearman, "because it tells you something about the tone, which is difficult to capture on paper, and you'll get a sense of what that person's approach is to the subject because of the tone they've given it."

Chris Shaw, senior program controller for News, Current Affairs and Documentaries at Five, told *Broadcast* about a two-minute pitch tape made by Delissa Needham. The proposal was for a late-night documentary about people who have sex in cars, called *Sex on Wheels*. "Delissa had taken the trouble to shoot a scene of her friend sitting in a sports car describing a sexual escapade from her past ... it really helped sell the pitch because it encapsulated the whole tone and style of the program, which couldn't have been conveyed on paper. It was funny, had great background music and proved that the program would work, making it far easier for me to present the idea to my director of programs ... they got the deal just three days after we received the proposal."

A pitch tape can be specially shot, compiled from archive, or rostrum shots; be hosted or narrated; composed entirely of graphics or storyboard drawings. But one thing is certain: "Everybody wants to see a sizzle reel," says LA-based producer Chuck Braverman. It makes it easy for a channel executive to see what they're buying and make a quick decision. "It's like a date: you can go on a date with somebody and within the first two minutes you know," says Braverman.

But, as with everything, making a speculative pitch tape isn't without its risks, warns Rudy Buttignol. "A clip can do two things: it will immediately spark interest in your project or it will kill it. And then trying to work against that first impression is an uphill struggle."

Why Do You Need a Pitch Tape?

It is important to know what you are trying to achieve before you make your pitch tape. You might want to excite a channel executive about the idea; prove the competence of a new presenter; demonstrate format points; show off a cutting-edge graphics technique or introduce characters for a new observational documentary.

Whether you need a pitch tape at all depends on the idea you are pitching, your track record, and the person to whom you are pitching. Some channel executives, especially those with a production background, begin to visualize a show from an evocative title. Others cannot turn words on the page into an image and need to be physically shown what the program will look like in order for them to understand the content, tone, and dramatic arc. So yet again, it's helpful to know whom you are pitching to. "Who are you trying to reach? Who will it be shown to, and how will it be seen? If it's going to be seen by one or two people in an office that's different than if it's going to be seen by three hundred people on a big screen in a conference," says a UK producer/director.

However you present it, the aim is the same: you are trying to seduce your buyer into entering into a creative relationship with you. "If you make something that is exciting enough you begin to own that project in the channel executive's mind," says Dan Hall, "and so the point of a tape is to keep you in the race, get them to read your treatment and to get them to arrange a meeting with you."

Help Channel Executives Pitch Your Idea to Their Boss

Channel executives like to use a tape to help them sell your concept to their colleagues. It also helps to stop your ideas getting bent out of shape. "That's why sizzles are so important," says Thom Beers. "If you are pitching to a director of development you know that they are going to pitch to their head of development, who is going to pitch it to the VP of development, who is going to give it to their head of channel; so by the time your pitch gets up there you have no idea what they're pitching. If they can show a sizzle reel, the pitch message doesn't get changed on its way up the chain."

Showcase Your Directing/Shooting Skills

For the channel, buying a program from a paper proposal is like buying a house sight unseen. If you are pitching in a new genre or have never worked for the channel before, a pitch tape showcases your ability to make the program you are proposing. "If it's a domestic situation or some kind of a conflict, in which direction is the filmmaker pointing the camera? That's not a given: sometimes the most interesting action is happening somewhere else in the room," say Rudy

Buttignol. "You are looking for a spark of talent and an eye for a story or a character."

Entry-level channels also expect to see evidence of your competence, says Emily Renshaw-Smith at Current TV. "Most of our filmmakers shoot their films themselves, so it's nice to see something they've shot before. If they haven't got a showreel or haven't picked up a camera before, we are understandably cautious about what we send them off to do. We may send them away to shoot something to show us before we commit. If you've shot something and uploaded it to YouTube that's enough, you don't need to have had a previous commission or to have made a complete film."

Pitch Tape Pitfalls

There are a number of things to consider before you make your tape:

Cost—Making a tape costs money, and you will usually have to cover those costs yourself. "I would always get a sniff of interest before I committed money to making a taster," says Ed Crick. "If there was a real glimmer of interest, then I might make the decision to spend £2–3K, and then if I lost the money I lost the money."

Length—Two to three minutes is the optimum length for a TV pitch tape. "Controllers will turn it off after a couple of minutes, because they just want to get the basic idea, a sense of tone or a sense of the talent," says Nick Shearman. "If you can't hook a controller with a two-minute taster then you should probably give it a miss." Seth Lawrence agrees that longer tapes mean "you are going to lose your buyer's attention—they are going to be thinking about the meeting they're going to next, or some emails that they need to write. It's oftentimes better to leave them wanting more."

Tone—Another problem is that every channel has a different tone, and your tape needs to match that tone, says Nick Shearman, at the BBC. "People have made tapes that they've probably tried to flog to the commercial channels and I'll say, 'I like the idea, but I think you've got to give it a different tone.'" That's another good reason to wait to shoot your tape until a specific buyer has expressed interest in your idea, as then you can tailor it specifically to their channel.

Quality—Obviously, a poor pitch tape should not be shown. "A good tape is better than a written pitch, but if it's bad, withhold tape. It can't be mediocre," said a former US channel executive. "It must be good enough to provoke a reaction. One funny moment can sell the show if it encapsulates the show. One single reaction can do it."

When to Produce Your Tape

Competition is so fierce at the moment that big-name production companies produce a tape for every pitch. "We're getting pitch tapes most of the time now," says one US cable channel executive. "The level of producer that we're working with typically won't pitch something without tape." But it's not compulsory, he says: "I will absolutely look at something that doesn't have tape."

"It's always about judging, how much money is right to spend," says Ben Hall, "because what you are doing is trying to marry your belief in the idea with your buyer's expectations." Produce a glossy tape for a channel executive who doesn't like to see tapes, or for a documentary that can be successfully pitched on paper and you've wasted time and money. Lorraine Heggessey recalls seeing "taster tapes where people have wasted money on title sequences, which is irrelevant at this stage. If you're going to make a tape, spend your money wisely, use the tape to show that you've got a good character or good access."

One good reason for going ahead with a tape without channel interest is when you have an idea you are passionate about, and big-name talent who wants to be involved. Get them on tape as soon as you can, as Sod's Law says they will be on a protracted foreign filming trip when a channel does express interest. And having visual proof of commitment from a famous face increases your idea's appeal to the channel.

There are a number of pitch tape options available to the producer. From most risky for the channel to least risky, they are: "mood" tape (which gives an "artistic impression" of the program using archive footage or photographs); pitch tape; non-transmission pilot and pilot.

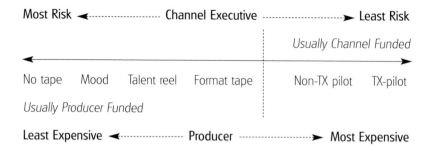

Most Risk ◄·····················— Channel Executive ·····················► Least Risk

Usually Channel Funded

No tape   Mood   Talent reel   Format tape   Non-TX pilot   TX-pilot

Usually Producer Funded

Least Expensive ◄·················· Producer ··················► Most Expensive

Most channels these days expect you to fund your own mood, talent, and even format tape. Decide which option offers the greatest reward for the least risk to you as the producer, and which type of tape is best suited to showcasing your program. This is a fine balancing act. The least expensive option in terms of time and money is at odds with what will impress the channel. If the channel executive likes your idea but isn't ready to commit to buying a full series, they might fund a non-transmission pilot or pilot program (a single program used to test audience reaction before committing to a full series); some big production companies will fund their own pilot program upfront if they believe passionately in their concept.

Judge the best moment in the development process to invest the time and effort in making a tape. A program "pitch" takes place over several meetings—the received wisdom being that you have to talk to a channel executive about an idea three times before they will be confident enough to commission it. Many development producers stage an escalating pitch, starting with the casual headline pitch: "Would you be interested in a series about turning a high-rise tower block into an urban farm?" If the answer is no, nothing has been lost. If it's yes, the producer can return with a fully researched proposal and present a verbal pitch, describing the format and dramatic potential in detail, and suggesting that they can do some filming with some of the characters. If the channel is keen, they might offer to fund the pitch tape, which is the ideal scenario for the development producer.

If the channel is only mildly interested, the two sides might engage in a game of chicken, where both sides want a pitch tape, but neither wants to pay for it. If the channel won't stump up the cash, the development producer must make a judgment call about whether a pitch tape would make a difference, or whether the channel is feigning interest to be polite. If the interest seems genuine, the production company will stump up the cost of making the tape. That's a good investment if the channel eventually buys the show, but a waste of money if they don't.

In some instances, a channel can reject a proposal in the early stages of discussion, but if the production company are particularly passionate about the project they will invest in some filming, and repitch the show supported by a pitch tape, and this can result in changing a channel executive's mind. "We just start doing the film," says Chuck Braverman, "so we can cut something together, because we are so committed to making that film." That is a good rule of thumb—if you feel strongly enough about the idea, you won't resent making a pitch tape upfront. If you aren't keen to produce a tape, ask yourself whether you are committed to the idea.

You should produce a pitch tape if:

* Your proposal features an unknown presenter.

* You are pitching an observational documentary series that hinges on the characters. You can say in your proposal that you will cast a compelling cast of characters. It is more convincing to show that you already have. And, as one cable channel executive points out, "It doesn't matter how dynamic your character is; on the paper they're still flat."

* You are proposing an access-driven series. A tape proves you have access and gives a tantalizing glimpse behind the scenes, whetting the channel executive's appetite for more. "If the characters are not interesting, or if the access isn't good, it doesn't work," says a cable channel exec.

* You can afford to produce it professionally to broadcast quality.

* The economy is bad: people are less inclined to take risks so a tape can help reassure them.

You shouldn't produce a pitch tape if:

* You are pitching a straightforward documentary that can be adequately pitched verbally and on paper.

* The content of the pitch tape adds nothing, confuses or detracts from the proposal.

* You can't produce a quality tape.

* You have an excellent track record and a good working relationship with the channel and they don't require tapes from you.

* You anticipate pitching the idea to several different channels. Each channel will need a different approach and this is time-consuming and generally not cost-effective.

Who Should Produce Your Pitch Tape?

Whatever type of tape you make, you must make it as good as you possibly can, and that means using a director who knows how to make the type of program you are proposing. They need to "get" the program idea and produce a tape that accurately reflects it. Ideally, you need someone who is as passionate about the idea as you are. But not all directors understand what a pitch tape is. "A taster tape only conveys what it needs to convey, it is not a half-hour pilot; it is not a complete story from beginning to end. It is a teaser, it is a pitch, it is not a piece of artwork," says one development producer. Dan Hall agrees: "A series producer shouldn't make it because they will want to start making the program."

Do not, as often happens, ask the most junior person on the team to make it because you can't spare the time or money to get someone else in, warns Nick Shearman. "It's a crucial part of the selling process and there's no point doing that cheaply by sending out someone inexperienced to do it because you are going to shoot yourself in the foot. When DV arrived there was a lemming-like rush to send researchers out shooting, who had no idea how to cut and who had never been in a cutting room; that creates problems down the line. I think people have sharpened up a lot since those early days but none the less only send out your researcher or assistant producer if they are a bright button who understands what is required."

This tape is an investment in future business, and some development teams have someone whose sole job is to make the pitch tapes. They know exactly what the channels need, and how to deliver what they need to get a commission. If you produce a fantastic tape, but don't get the commission, you'll still come away with an enhanced reputation. Produce a terrible reel and you could lose all credibility with that particular channel. "If I get a tape that looks like shit, but the character is great, it makes it more complicated going forward," explains a US cable channel exec, "because I'll need to pair this producer with someone who can compensate for their shortcomings."

If in doubt, or you have the choice of cobbling together a tape or not making one, don't make one. Wait until the channel are keen on your idea and get them to fund you so you can do the job properly.

What Kind of Pitch Tape Should You Make?

There are five main types of programs that require a pitch tape: the content-driven, format-driven, talent-driven, character-driven, and authored one-off documentaries. Each program type requires a different approach to the pitch tape in order to effectively highlight the program's unique selling point.

An additional type of tape showcases new technology, such as a new type of computer-generated graphic that will help visualize the inside of the human body, or a new camera that allows you to film in difficult circumstances for the first time. Showing the channel executive these techniques is always more effective than telling them about them.

There are no real rules about how you should structure your pitch tape—beyond starting with a bang or hook and keeping it short—but it can be helpful to think in terms of:

* *the proposed program's beginning, middle, and end*—most useful for explaining a format or competition series;

* *question set up*—good for setting up the premise for a content-rich documentary, character-based or observational series.

1) Promo/Sizzle Tape: Content-Driven Program

A promo, also known as a sizzle tape, is designed to give the channel executive a "feel" for what the proposed program would be like in terms of content and tone, rather than show exactly what the finished program will look like.

"Sometimes you can do a sizzle reel from stock, from other films that you have, and can put together," says Chuck Braverman. It's often used when pitching an expensive show to potential co-funding partners.

A promo/sizzle is designed to arouse excitement, intrigue, or aspiration in the buyer but television channel executives are wise to this. "Buyers are savvy and will say, 'Well, that's slick, but what exactly is the show?'" says Seth Lawrence. "I understand the promotion of it, and I understand I might be able to put it on a billboard, but people are still going to need to tune in for twenty-two minutes every week for a half-hour or forty-plus minutes [for an hour]."

If you decide to make a promo/sizzle tape, think carefully about what you are trying to say, and choose your material accordingly. Sometimes you have to use stock footage, but it's far better to shoot something original if you can.

CASE STUDY
Greenlit: *Hiroshima* (1 x 90′ BBC)
BBC Science

"The *Hiroshima* tape was quite a challenge because it's clearly a serious subject, but [that pitch tape] was one of my most successful," says Claudine King-Dabbs. "I understand that the commissioner didn't want the program. As a last-ditch attempt they showed her the tape and she commissioned it. I was thrilled by that.

"The tape was a combination of archive footage from when the bomb was dropped and tested, and bits of archive interviews with the people we wanted to feature, one of whom had flown the plane. We included a bit of him so the commissioner could see how articulate he was.

"It also had individuals' testimony, which was harrowing with some graphic descriptions of mothers and babies; it was so raw. I thought it was hard-hitting and effective but I was asked to take that out because it was too distressing, and I think that was probably a good call—you can actually turn people away by being too shocking, and I think that probably was too shocking.

"I used simple text to make people think and added a cracking piece of music that was exciting and driving. It had a minor key so it was emotionally quite edgy; I don't know if it was the music that did it or not, but I watched a lot of people watching it and they did seem to think, 'Whoa, what's this?' and be taken in by it."

Hiroshima, an Emmy- and BAFTA-winning docudrama, was broadcast on the sixtieth anniversary of the dropping of the bomb. It was a co-production between the BBC, ZDF in Germany, TF1 in France, and Discovery in the US. It was shown in thirty countries around the world.

2) Format Tape: Format-Driven Program

A format tape consists of specially shot footage that shows something tangible about your program that is part promo and part exposition.

If you were pitching *What Not to Wear*, for example, you'd want to film the key moments of the show: the secret filming footage, the "hit" where the hosts surprise the "victim"; the moment where the hosts put the woman in front of the 360-degree mirror to reveal the full horror of her fashion choices; the makeover; and the reveal. This takes an hour to play out in the show, but you have to fit it into a few minutes. The other risk is that if you can show the whole show in five minutes, the channel will wonder how you are going to sustain it for an hour. It might be more prudent to show a single killer moment, such as the 360-degree mirror, and describe the rest of the format verbally.

3) Talent Tape: Talent-Driven Program

A talent tape showcases the skills of new onscreen talent, usually someone you are hoping will host your show. It needs to prove that the potential presenter is photogenic, articulate, and knowledgeable, which is important in establishing their credibility.

When Jamie Oliver started out on *Naked Chef* (BBC2), he was uncomfortable talking directly to camera, so the shooting style was adapted so he could speak to the producer slightly off camera, making a virtue of a potential weakness. If you have a similar problem with talent, you put yourself in a stronger position if you've spotted any potential weaknesses and worked out a solution before you pitch. The talent tape is a good testing ground for this.

"I didn't spot Bruce as a talent as much as I should have done, or would like to claim," says Steve Robinson. "He's obviously very good but I'd never been particularly keen on working with presenters—I'd always liked making films about people and so I didn't clock Bruce as being a presenter. Equally, he's sort of an anti-presenter, anyway.

"We got to location and started doing some pieces to camera with him and it became pretty obvious that he wasn't very good at doing pieces to camera, so we came up with this style of it being much more observational so he was like a documentary subject that you could direct.

"It wasn't about scripted pieces to camera and walk-through shots, it was much more fluid and just stick him into the situation and he tells us what's going on and we experience it through him as he experiences it."

The making of the talent tape is a great opportunity to test the potential host's willingness to take direction. If someone lacks skills but is happy to take instruction from the director and you can see them improving, then it's worth taking a chance on them. If they point-blank refuse to do things your way, or can't seem to do what it is you need of them, it might be best to call it a day and thank them for their time and look for someone else.

Emma Swain says a talent tape has three elements: "You want to hear what they sound like when they are not in vision, as you can hear their voice more clearly. You can see what they look like when they are trying to communicate something and do something at the same time, because that's quite difficult; and you can see what they look like when they are trying to communicate something without moving, because that's also quite difficult. Any variety of those three things shot in any way is a good thing."

Depending on the format you are proposing, your talent needs to be able to interview or chat to other people, so a short segment of your tape should prove they can ask questions, listen and respond appropriately, ad lib, and refrain from talking at the same time as their interviewee.

If you are pitching the talent for a specific format, such as a cookery program, it helps to mock up part of the program, perhaps have them prepare and cook a dish, as they would in your finished program.

However, avoid using the type of showreels that agents send in. "I never look at those," says Tom Archer, "they're boring. I think when you are looking at talent you need to be looking at them doing something that is related to the proposal, to the proposition." Nick Shearman agrees that the agent reels "always look the same, they're always done in a standard way. In many ways that's a barrier to you taking anyone on because it automatically feels like every other one you've seen."

As a talent tape is a test of the talent's skills rather than your production skills, channels are more forgiving of less polished talent tapes. "You're not expecting a talent tape to be all bells and whistles," says Nick Shearman. "I don't mind if it's quite rough—all you want to do is get a sense of those people and you are not too bothered about the production values around it. You can have quite raw production values, but you can still get a sense of whether it's comic or tragic or serious or light and how they are going to deal with the subject matter, just by the choice of material they've cut together to show you." Emma Swain agrees. "A talent screener can be quite rough because you can tell quite quickly whether someone is able to speak to the camera as if there's only one person in the room."

Sometimes, you can find someone with potential, invest time, energy, and emotion in them and discover that they become wooden and inarticulate as soon as the camera is switched on. Don't be tempted to "fix it in post," that is get the editor to take out all the ums, ers, and repetition, to give an illusion of a polished performance. Some people are not natural performers in front of the camera and pretending that they are is just storing up a lot of misery and expense for the production team who will have to spend much longer than necessary in the field getting the talent to say their lines straight and then more time in the edit making them sound coherent. Admitting defeat at this stage is less trouble than having to fire the hapless host in a few months' time. It's not fair on them or the production.

CASE STUDY

Greenlit: *Journeys from the Centre of the Earth* (6x60′ BBC2)

BBC Science

"One of the [talent] tapes I produced was with Iain Stewart," remembers Claudine King-Dabbs. "It was pretty clear that he was a talented and a likable person when he'd been interviewed for *Horizon*. I don't know if the production team had thought he could do more or whether it was someone else who'd seen him on the program, but they wanted to see him a different context.

"I asked him to do a variety of different things; I was exploring what he could do, because there's no point if they don't have the range of skills they need to be an effective presenter.

"It was suggested that we do an interview with him but I didn't want to because they take a long time to set up, and you don't have much time or money to make taster tapes. So I had him doing vox pops [impromptu interviews with people on the street]. Vox pops are much maligned because they do look a bit rough and ready, but what you do get is a sense of whether that presenter can go and approach someone, and whether they can put their own shyness and self-consciousness to one side and engage totally with a member of the public. It's a useful skill to have—if they can do that they can do most types of interview (although perhaps not the prime minister).

"Vox pops also show a (potential) presenter's ability to think on their feet, in Iain's case, to take the active lead, rather than the passive role of a contributor. Yes, it is important for presenters to be able to interview some heavyweight contributors at times, but for the purposes of a test tape, I don't think it's ever fair to expose them to that kind of pressure— they might compromise themselves, as well as how they are perceived professionally in the future, and you need to think carefully about protecting your protégés!

"I also asked Iain to do a variety of different actions, for example, some digging, to see if he could do a variety of actions while talking to camera— he could. And I deliberately kept the laughter going; presenters are much more relaxed if they can have a bit of a laugh with you—you get a more natural and spontaneous result.

"You also need to see if they can take direction, for example, when you ask someone to do it, will they do it? Or will they say, 'No I'm not doing that,' for some reason? They might feel self-conscious or nervous or they just might not want to do it. If they can't or won't take direction you are going to have all sorts of problems."

Professor Iain Stewart was commissioned to present *Journeys from the Centre of the Earth*, and went on to present *Journeys into the Ring of Fire* and *Earth: Power of the Planet*.

4) Character/Casting Tape: Character-Driven Program

If you are pitching a character-based docuseries, you need to choose the most exciting, entertaining, or emotional sections of your footage to show the essence of their character and the potential for comedy or conflict; there's time for subtlety once you've secured the commission.

Your characters must be memorable and "jump off the screen." "You want to get a sense of their world and the people in their world, how it looks, how they communicate," says a US cable channel exec. "Most importantly, you want to be able to tell how open they are; get a sense of what access they are going to give you. You need to see if they are going to be guarded, if getting them to open up about their life is going to be like pulling teeth or whether they are exhibitionists and are going to show you everything." Agent Seth Lawrence agrees: "I'm a big fan of 'show me, don't tell me.' I don't need to hear them being interviewed saying that they are crazy and outrageous, I need to *see* it."

Peter Grimsdale (then commissioning editor for history, religion, and features at Channel 4), told *Broadcast* about the time he was pitched a documentary about a Muslim fundamentalist, but he was uninspired by the idea. He asked the producers to bring him more information, so they shot a taster tape over the course of a weekend. When he saw it he commissioned it immediately. "I told them that since they had started filming they had better keep going. It was one of the simplest decisions I've ever had to make ... Nothing was written down on that occasion, which demonstrates how a showreel can carry an awful lot of weight. Fundamentally, if you have a program idea that rests on a character or a presenter, then discussion is hypothetical until you've seen the person. Making a short tape of them counts for a lot, as it shows how they work onscreen."

Just as you need to hook the viewer in a mood tape, you have to start with a bang in your character-led tape too, says Chuck Braverman. "If you are doing something like *High School Boot Camp*, you would definitely have the kids getting off the bus and the instructors yelling at them, because here you have these big physically strong intimidating adults yelling at these thirteen-, fourteen-year-old kids who are suddenly in shock. That's dramatic, and it tells you right away what it's about." But it doesn't always have to be physically dramatic. "An explosive opening can be as subtle as a trying emotional moment between a husband and a wife with, perhaps, a confrontation, aftermath, and tease for a resolution; it doesn't need to be an explosion with trees falling, people running in a panic and all that," says Seth Lawrence, "just a catchy opening, a slick tape, good music, good graphics, real moments, and a cliff-hanger or a good conclusion."

5) Samples, Demos or Work-in-Progress for Grants and Film Markets: The Documentary Fundraising Trailer

If you are an independent producer raising funding for your one-off, authored documentary you'll need to produce a pitch tape that shows your film as a work-in-progress to show to potential buyers at festivals, grant foundations, or other funding bodies. This kind of tape is known as a demo, sample, or trailer.

According to Fernanda Rossi, Story Consultant and author of *Trailer Mechanics*, a fundraising trailer is a seven- to ten-minute audio-visual pitch of the film. In *The Art of Film Funding*, she tells Carole Lee Dean that a fundraising trailer "is a short [film] without an ending. People tend to think that a fundraising trailer for a documentary is like a music video. Nothing could be further from the truth. Grant foundations don't necessarily want to see something flashy. That only proves that you've got a skilled editor. It doesn't prove that you have a story or that you have access to a character or that you have a distinct voice and style for this film."

Instead of showing just the edited highlights of your rushes, in a fundraising trailer for an authored, one-off documentary, you construct complete scenes to prove that you can tell a story. "The scenes need to show who [your characters] are, what motivates them, if there is an opponent or something working against them," says Rossi.

And, importantly, you have to leave the buyer wanting more, by building in a cliff-hanger or hook at the end. "It is obligatory to have this element for every trailer," says Rossi, because "a fundraising trailer with a definite conclusion is doomed to fail. Any grantor or broadcaster who sees a wrapped-up story can say, 'Oh, thank you for sharing. Nice little story.' The story is complete. But if we have a short without an ending, then we want to know more. The cliff-hanger gives the promo the sense that there is something else that can be explored in the longer version of the film."

According to Rossi, a fundraising trailer is designed to be an authentic representation of the final film, and is assembled from specially shot footage that will also appear in the finished piece. One of the challenges for the independent filmmaker is in deciding which footage to show the buyers and which to leave out. Rossi advises that you don't get bogged down in logging all your rushes to find the best moments: use the material that you best remember. She says that filmmakers always worry that they haven't chosen the best sequences. "If a scene was that good it is very unlikely a filmmaker will forget it," she says. "If something was left out and you didn't remember it till the day of the [pitch], it probably wasn't worth keeping."

Polishing Your Pitch Tape

Once you've edited your tape, you need to make sure that it does what you want it to do and that it is presented professionally. Show your finished tape to a few people who aren't familiar with the idea and ask them to describe the proposed show to you. If they're wildly off the mark, work out what the problem is and fix it to convey the right message. In *Trailer Mechanics*, Fernanda Rossi outlines a checklist for analyzing the effectiveness of independent documentary fundraising trailers, which is helpful for troubleshooting TV pitch tapes too:

1. Is the content and narrative clear?

2. Is it clear throughout the trailer who, or what will carry this film?

3. Does each shot provide new, relevant or meaningful information?

4. Are there any shots you can do without?

5. Is the footage visually engaging?

6. Are interviews and voiceover repeating information we get from the images or adding to them? Every element of your trailer should add new information.

7. Is the narration necessary or excessive? You are working in an audio-visual medium, so the more you can show, the stronger your trailer will be.

8. Does the music enhance the material evoking an emotion or mood? Or does it distract the viewer? Music can pull a weak piece together; make sure your content stands up to scrutiny and you're not using music as a crutch.

9. Do you have a strong ending that leaves the audience wondering what will happen next? A weak ending can hurt an otherwise great trailer. Viewers remember clearest what they saw last. Pull them in with a hook and leave them with a cliff-hanger or revelation.

10. Does the overall style of the pitch tape accurately represent your production ability and the content and tone of your program idea?

Make sure that your executive producer signs off on the tape, especially if they are going to be pitching the idea. "I have two bosses, a business boss and a creative boss and I pass my cuts by them and they will always make suggestions that are annoyingly right," says Dan Hall. "The business guy will say, 'What is it you are trying to say? What's the point? Remember it's going to the Americans—so not so much intelligence, and more pace.' The creative guy will say, 'There's a lot of show, but I don't know what I'm being sold editorially.'"

Your tape needs to start with a dramatic bang, but it's prudent to put a few seconds of "buffer" material at the front of the reel. In a pitch situation, especially if you are pitching to a group, people will start talking among themselves and shuffling in their seats as you put the DVD in the player, and there will inevitably be a few seconds at the beginning when you need to adjust the volume. A title card, or set-up shot with some music, signals to the audience that something is about to happen and that they should pay attention. If you put your best shot right at the top of the piece they will miss it, but equally, don't meander into your piece with lots of leisurely wide establishing shots, or you'll lose your audience before you've started; get them to pay attention then sock 'em between the eyes.

When your tape is a polished as it can be editorially, check grammar and spelling on any titles, subtitles, or names and play it on a few different televisions to check that your sound levels are even. Get a few copies of a DVD made so you have one to leave with the channels and some spare for future pitches. And finally, label all the DVDs with a professional-looking label—not scrawled in illegible handwriting (label the master copy with red ink and keep it under lock and key; keep a spare master copy at home, in case the original goes missing).

Some producers are doing away with the DVD format entirely by uploading their footage to a password-restricted page on a video hosting site such as Vimeo, and sending the hyperlink to channel execs by email.

Now you have everything you need: idea, proposal, talent, and pitch tape. There's one more hurdle to cross before you (potentially) win that commission. And it's a big one: it's time to pitch.

Development Master Class 9

Visualize Your Idea

1. Explore the websites of various production companies and watch their trailers. Analyze what works and what doesn't.

2. Decide if your idea needs a pitch tape; if so write a short treatment for it.

3. Shoot and edit a two- to three-minute pitch tape and transfer to DVD (use inexpensive equipment such as a flip camera and Final Cut Express if you don't have access to professional equipment).

4. Show your pitch tape to someone who isn't familiar with your idea. Ask them:
   a. What is the idea about?
   b. Who are the main characters?

c. Are you engaged by the story?

d. What emotions did it evoke?

e. Did you tune out at any point?

f. Is there anything you don't understand?

g. Is the music overwhelming?

h. Do you want to see more?

5. Consider if there are any other visual aids you can use to illustrate your pitch if a tape isn't possible or appropriate.

Explore More

Fernanda Rossi: *Trailer Mechanics*

A short book, aimed at independent documentary makers, which explains the art of making a fundraising trailer. It's also useful for helping to crystallize your idea (and your motivation for making your film).

The Pitch

In 1995, two hundred people filed into a warehouse not far from the BBC's Television Centre, in West London. They thought they were going to see ten robots competing in a tournament, but in fact they were about to witness one of the most extravagant TV show pitches in television history.

The previous year, Tom Gutteridge, founder of Mentorn, had seen some home movie footage of a San Francisco-based event, organized by games designer Marc Thorpe, in which homemade radio-controlled robots battled it out gladiator-style. "It was hysterically funny and I thought it would make a great TV series," says Gutteridge. "It was all taken extremely seriously but it was really just tin boxes with axes on, which appealed to my sense of humor." Gutteridge acquired the rights and asked a conceptual artist to come up with some designs for some new robots, while he worked with Steve Carsey, a children's producer at Mentorn, to develop the format.

Gutteridge first took the idea to Dawn Airey at Channel 4, but she turned it down in a letter that said, "I'm afraid my colleagues and I don't seen any future in robots fighting on primetime television." He decided to try the BBC, and had a conversation with the BBC2 scheduler, Adam McDonald, who loved the idea, but couldn't imagine that the then controller of BBC2, Michael Jackson, would "get" it. Gutteridge suggested staging a run-through, and McDonald said that if he could arrange one he would do everything he could to get it in Jackson's diary.

Gutteridge didn't want to risk another rejection, so he decided to put everything he could into the pitch. He hired a warehouse, flew in the best six American robots to compete against the four specially built house robots, which included a funny, child-friendly robot called Mousebot. He enclosed the robots in a steel cage and surrounded them with tires to protect the specially invited audience, who were each given a glass of wine. On the day, McDonald told Jackson that the meeting wouldn't be taking place in his office, but was happening across the road instead.

The unsuspecting channel controller walked into the arena to see the robots fighting in front of a baying crowd, the air thick with smoke. Impressed, Jackson turned to Gutteridge and said, "Well, I guess we'd better do it then."

Gutteridge spent £95,000 of his own money to get Jackson's attention, but it took nearly four more years to get it on air. Soon after McDonald rang Gutteridge to say BBC2 would order six episodes, Michael Jackson left BBC2 to become controller of BBC1. Alan Yentob took over BBC2, and the project stalled.

When Mark Thompson took over a couple of years later, he decided that he should honour the commitment that Jackson had made to Gutteridge and ordered six episodes, even though he too was unsure of its appeal. Thompson scheduled the show in the "death slot"—6PM on a Friday, where BBC2 shows managed to attract only around 600,000 viewers, up against Channel 4's popular *TFI Friday*.

After the first transmission in 1998, Gutteridge received a call from Thompson, with the news that they'd got an audience of 2.5 million. "It's payback time. I want as many as you can make as soon as you can make them," Thompson said. They went into production the same day and made twenty-six episodes a year for the next six years. The show ran for nine series (including an *Extreme* edition) and was shown in twenty-six countries. Mentorn eventually made back the initial investment plus another £7 million; not a bad return.

Most pitches will be neither as elaborate nor as lucrative, but everything you have done so far rests on this moment. If you pitch your idea well, you might walk away with a commission. If you screw it up, you walk away with nothing. The face-to-face pitch is a vital part of the process.

There are many books and courses that purport to teach you the "right" way to pitch, but there is no failsafe technique. It all depends on the idea, the style and personality of the person pitching it and the receptiveness of the person they are pitching to. To be successful:

* pitch the right idea;

* to the right person;

* at the right channel;

* at the right time.

Whom to Pitch to?

If you are starting out in the industry, it is likely you will find it extremely challenging to get a meeting with a commissioning editor.

"Everybody in America watches television; and everybody wants to get rich quick," says Tim Duffy. "As soon as someone comes up with a game show or a reality show, they write it down at three o'clock in the morning, and they see dollar signs. I don't want to talk to those people, because they never have the next big idea. They might have the kernel that a production company or agent could craft for us, so it becomes a viable show to pitch. But we don't have the time to deal with every Tom, Dick, and Harry off the street that thinks they have a great idea."

There are also the logistical problems that come with being a lone operator. "In my experience, sole operators would be bankrupt within three months of working with any of the big US cable broadcasters," says Peter Rees. "It's the way the money works; I've done shoots where the first payment wasn't made until after principal photography. How many individuals can actually sustain that?"

For those reasons, "Smaller producers will often pair themselves with a larger company," says one US cable channel exec, "because they know the bigger company will have access to the different channels, and the pitch will make more noise that way. The alternative is for the smaller producer to come in on their own. If we love it then we'll work with them to find a producer that's mutually satisfying." Wherever you are working in the world, if you have already partnered with an established production company of your choice it makes the commissioning process smoother for the channel, and you have more control over whom you work with on the project.

How to Find a Compatible Production Company

If you have contacts at independent production companies, call them to see if they know what kind of ideas the company is currently looking for and ask if you could introduce you to the head of development. If you don't have insider contacts, the principles for pitching to production companies are the same as those for pitching to channel executives:

To find production companies that make programs similar to yours:

* Check the end credits of shows in the same genre as your idea to find out who made them.

* Search IMDB (internet movie database) to find the production details of past programs.

* Search industry databases such as Broadcast's Greenlight and tvmole.com for information on upcoming commissions and check which companies work in your genre.

* Once you've narrowed the field, go on to each individual company's website to see what shows they've got in production.

Once you've compiled a short-list of production companies that might be a good fit, find out what their submission policy is. Some won't accept any ideas from outside; some will accept your ideas if you've worked with them in the past and they know you; and some do accept unsolicited proposals.

Find out the correct person to contact—it will either be the head of the company or the development head. Make a quick call to check that the person listed on the website is still in that job before you send off an email to request a meeting.

Whom to Approach at the TV Channels

If you are working in a well-known independent production company, it is likely that you will pitch to your existing channel contacts. If not, do some research. Find out which channels transmit your genre of program and go to their websites. A search for "commissioning" or "producers" should take you to the channel's commissioning page (if they have one). There you will find all the briefs, contact names, and submission guidelines.

If there is no information available, call the channel and ask to speak to the channel executive in the genre you want to pitch to. "Some networks you can find out who the individual is who is doing development [commissioning], you can ring them personally and you might be able to build a rapport with them," says Peter Rees.

If you are a newly formed indie, and have credits, it's a good idea to approach the smaller, newer channels as they are more open to building new relationships. "There are people who just send me ideas, introduce themselves to me and then I will work with them," says Lucy Pilkington. "I try to have a balance between the ones I know and trust and refreshing a pool of new producers, so that I'm not dependent on a small group of people."

The Hollywood Creative Directory is published three times a year and lists telephone numbers, contact names, and addresses for US cable and network executives. In the US, most channels take pitches only from producers and production companies who are represented by an agent. *The Hollywood Representation Directory* provides contact information for agents, managers, and entertainment attorneys in New York and Los Angeles and is published twice a year.

Getting the First Meeting

Commissions come from dialog, so engineer a face-to-face meeting with a commissioning executive:

* Call the channel and ask for the assistant of the exec; you are unlikely to be put straight through to the channel executive, and it's good practice to get their assistant on your side as they can help smooth your path if they like you.

* Explain that you've got an idea that you think the channel executive would like, and ask the assistant how best to approach them.

* Get their email address.

* Send a short query pitch, which briefly outlines the subject of your idea and its format: e.g. observational documentary or competition reality series.

Don't send off your full proposal unless the channel executive has expressed some interest. If you don't know them well, you don't want to disclose your precious format too soon. If you do know them well, you don't want to sour the relationship by cluttering their desk with a proposal for a program they know they don't want; it means they have to formally respond to you and it adds to their workload.

The Email Query

The email query allows you to gauge if a channel executive is amenable to you sending a full proposal or to agreeing to a pitch meeting. "You can tell if someone has got the right tone and understands the channel from something quite brief," says Lucy Pilkington. "There is a very new indie who came and said they'd got some access and I thought a) they're thinking along exactly the right lines and b) they know the channel, and so that started a relationship." Simon Dickson says he "can tell straight away if I want to talk to them more about the idea."

The query email can also save you a lot of wasted time. "I would send through a paragraph by email to ask, 'Is this a waste of my time?'" says Dan Hall. "Ninety-nine percent of the time you get back, 'Yes it is.' But occasionally, you get 'No, it's not a waste of your time.'"

The trick to the email query is to give them enough information about the project to excite them, but not so much that you are putting your idea at risk of misappropriation. This is where your logline comes in useful.

Email Etiquette

The idea of an email is to seduce the channel executive into engaging with you, so make it easy for them:

* *Keep it brief.* A single paragraph should be enough to get your information across.

* *Put all the information in the body of the email.* Don't include pictures or attachments as they are harder to access, and useless if the channel executive is viewing their email on a PDA.

* *Put all the key information "above the fold."* "When you open your email, the area that you see without scrolling should contain the kernel of your

message," says Iikka Vehkalahti. "If it's interesting I will start to scroll down." If it's not interesting, they won't, so there's no point putting your best bits at the bottom, out of sight.

* *Don't hype your idea.* "A lot of people in their write-up will be unnecessarily boastful—'You've never heard anything like this …'—I get that all the time," said a US cable channel exec. "It's always the producers who don't have the credentials who are trying to get your attention and I find it off-putting. And it tends to be inaccurate; their idea is probably not the most original idea in the world. Just say, 'I have an idea I think is interesting …'"

* *Check links.* If you are sending a link to a clip, make sure you know that they will be able to access it. "One piece of advice is to find out from all of your channels what codecs they use and keep a sheet of paper that says 'Discovery hates Quicktime but will take Quicktime as long as it's in a Windows Media format codec,' because it saves twenty-four hours of wasted time."

* *Don't be weird.* A US cable executive recalls being sent a link in an email, "and it was a guy who had videotaped his pitch and had sent it to me. I clicked on it and it was like 'Hi, how are you? …' It was bizarre. It was like a private infomercial for me."

* *Don't relentlessly chase people.* "If you've sent a pitch to a commissioner by email don't send a 'did you get my email' next day; wait a week before you chase it up," says Emily Renshaw-Smith, "because when you are busy there's nothing more annoying than being reminded that you are not getting through all your work! If you need an answer quickly because you need to start filming straight away, state that in your email."

* *Make sure your idea is ready to pitch.* "Before you ping off an email with a few thoughts, make sure you've done the proper thinking," warns Ed Crick, "so that when they say, 'Yeah, that would be great, but what about this?' you don't end up saying, 'I hadn't thought about that.'"

Don't Telephone

Read any Hollywood pitching books and they will tell you to call the channel executive and deliver an "elevator pitch," a short one- or two-sentence description of your idea. The authors advise calling a potential buyer's office before or after working hours, as they might pick up the phone themselves if their assistant has not yet arrived or has left for the day. However, the consensus, from TV buyers at least, is that pitching by phone is a bad idea.

"If you don't know the commissioning editor, don't call," says Iikka Vehkalahti. "It is impossible to take the amount of calls and to concentrate when someone tells me who he is and describes his program. It is frustrating, I know, to contact via email, but in every case, someone is reading the emails. On the telephone I can't concentrate, it's no use."

"A phone call is the worst for a pitch," agrees Simon Dickson. "You can't pitch on the telephone, because at the end of the day I'm buying something from you. Would you buy something when people ring you up at home and try to get you to switch energy providers? It doesn't work. The commissioning process is based on trust and a belief that the person into whose eyes you are looking understands what you need and what you want and therefore you've got to meet them and you've got to spend time with them."

If you can't see a channel executive when you are talking to them, it's hard to properly gauge their reaction and tailor your pitch appropriately. It's much better to be in the room with the buyer so you can read and respond to their body language.

If your query email has provoked interest, you will be invited to attend a pitch meeting or send a detailed proposal. Ideally, you want to have the pitch meeting before you send your written proposal. The advantage of meeting first is that you can enter into a collaborative creative conversation with the channel executive and incorporate their thoughts into your written proposal before submission.

E-submission

Some broadcasters like producers to submit ideas via their e-commissioning system. Many producers hate the impersonality of e-commissioning, but there are some advantages, says Simon Dickson: "In order to assess ideas that come in, you can't be in a firefighting mode, you've got to be in a looking-out-the-window-smoking-your-pipe mode, and so if you go from one email that is about firefighting and the next is blue sky, and the next is firefighting, and the next is blue sky, you end up losing control of your head. So I have days when I firefight and days when I blue sky. eWorks [Channel 4's e-commissioning system] collects all the ideas into one place and I can work through them in a consistent frame of mind, and I can compare them, one against another, it feels more strategic, and I feel like I'm more in control, and it feels like I'm working more productively."

The BBC's Cassian Harrison (commissioning executive, specialist factual), explained the advantages of e-commissioning at the Intelligent Factual Festival: "We get so many ideas that it is important to log everything on to the e-commissioning system because it means it doesn't get lost, which is important. Flag it to me [in an email] that you have logged it and give me a one-line summary of what it is. And then, if it's an immediate thing that I think, 'Actually, yes, we're absolutely looking for something exactly like that,' then I'll be able to get back to you quickly. Otherwise, we're aware of it and we'll track it through the e-comm system as we are promised to do."

Different companies have different time frames, but they should all get back to you within a certain length of time (which is not likely to be less than twenty-eight days). If they are interested they will invite you for a meeting.

Prepare for Your Pitch

Before you meet your channel executive do some pre-pitch limbering up.

1. *Check the purpose of the meeting.* Have you been invited to a meet and greet session, or are they expecting you to pitch?

2. *Check the channel's schedule* and make sure you know where your program fits. Does it conform to the channel brief while offering them something new?

3. *Check the industry press.* Has the channel recently commissioned something similar, making your idea redundant?

4. *Fitness-check your idea.* Is it ready to pitch to this channel? Is the concept simple and clear? Does the format work? Does the content still feel new and exciting? Is the host credible and authentic? Do you still have access to your subject? Was it a topical idea that is no longer relevant? If you detect any weaknesses, fix them.

5. *Decide if you need to produce a pitch tape* if you haven't already done so. It's not always necessary or desirable, but make it a conscious decision not an act of omission.

Early Pitch Meeting

When you are first invited to meet with a channel executive, you might find yourself in an informal pitch meeting, and it's hard to judge what is expected. Be too casual and you might come across as unprofessional; launch into all-singing, all-dancing pitch and it might feel embarrassingly over the top, so be prepared for either and take your cue from them. Call their assistant to find out what kind of meeting they prefer.

"If you know someone well you can say, 'What do you think about this idea?'" says Ben Hall. "But if you are just coming into the business, make sure you produce a professional pitch, but constantly make it clear that it doesn't have to be done this way." The main thing, says Dan Edelstyn, is that, "you want to leave people with the feeling that this is a great project that you are passionate about."

Once you've had this initial conversation with a buyer, and they like your idea, you might need to do some more development to take into account any concerns, queries, or suggestions and ramp up the level of materials you present—a fuller treatment, a more polished talent tape, mock publicity materials, walk-through of game show format etc., before you go into a formal pitch situation, when you might be in front of the channel head.

Who Is the Best Person to Pitch the Idea?

Before entering into a formal pitch situation the first job is to decide who is going to pitch the idea. It needs to be someone who has good standing with the channel, and can demonstrate passion for the idea, and that might not be you. "You can have some people who are good filmmakers and have made some great stuff and they are terrible at pitching ideas," says Keith Scholey. "People who are good at pitching have an aura about them, they have a presence; when they start to talk you believe what they are going to say. They rarely look at notes, they look you in the eye and tell you how it's going to be. And they're good at thinking on their feet."

Different people have different styles, but whatever their style they must know your idea inside out and be passionate about it. It's no good drafting in someone who is a "good talker" if they have no interest in the idea they're pitching. "Sometimes the people who pitch the ideas are the least qualified to pitch them because they're not the ones with the passion for those ideas," acknowledges Adam Curtis.

If someone isn't comfortable with pitching, they shouldn't do it. "I don't care if they created it or not," says Ben Hall. "It's important to have the creator in the room so they can answer any questions, but they don't have to pitch the show."

Make sure that the person who is pitching understands production, so they have credibility when talking about potential production challenges. "I prefer the showrunner to pitch the show," says Emma Swain. "When a development person pitches it, you do worry that something is going to be lost in translation, or promises are going to be made that can't be kept; or, all of that works on paper, but actually you can't get permission to film in Zimbabwe, or whatever."

Preparing Your PowerPoint

Not everyone uses PowerPoint, but some producers swear by it. Its use seems particularly prevalent in entertainment and multiplatform pitches, but is rarely used in pitches for content-driven specialist factual documentaries. Some people use it as an *aide-mémoire*, others see it as a visual way to walk the buyer through a format that might be otherwise difficult to describe. "If you are pitching to a big group of people, it's a good way of telling a story," says Ben Hall. "They can't flick ahead, because you are actually going through it. It's a useful way of talking people through the format points, point by point. The great thing about PowerPoint is that if you're not interested I can stop it at any time."

Make sure you leave yourself plenty of time to prepare your PowerPoint and check that you will be able to hook it up to a screen in the meeting, or at least have it ready to go on your laptop. And be prepared with a contingency plan.

Dan Edelstyn traveled from London to Edinburgh to pitch his idea, *How to Re-establish a Vodka Empire*, about turning around the fortunes of an impoverished village in the Ukraine. "I spent the whole day before making a PowerPoint presentation with embedded video, but I heard at the last minute that I had only seven minutes to pitch and that had to include the trailer. My video went on for six minutes so I only had one minute to speak. So I made sure that I had all points that I wanted to hit in my PowerPoint presentation. And then at 11PM the night before, I spoke to a friend up there and she told me they didn't have facilities for PowerPoint so I printed copies out and handed them out on the day with a mini-bottle of vodka."

Anything that can help the channel executive visualize your concept can help the pitch. "Props help. It's more entertaining," says Dan Edelstyn. Particularly when it's vodka, it seems, as it helped him win some of the money he needed from the Edinburgh funders.

Props

According to a study conducted by the University of Pennsylvania, people remember 10 percent of the content of a verbal pitch, but 50 percent of a presentation that includes visual aids, so it is prudent to illustrate your pitch somehow. If filming a pitch tape is impractical, other methods of visualizing the content can be equally effective, and much cheaper. For example, former commissioning executive Peter Grimsdale once commissioned a program on trucks and combine harvesters based on a scrapbook of photos that illustrated the producer's ideas for the series.

"People hardly ever use props in the UK, but I think props are great," says Emma Swain. "I remember a producer bringing in a life-sized toy goose, and he started talking about how fantastic geese are because they mate for life and fly in formation. It was a simple prop, but made you more interested and made you think that he was somebody who was quite amusing and interesting. We didn't end up commissioning *Goose Watch*, but it did turn into some good telly because we did a *Super Goose* story line in *Springwatch*, which was about seeing who could spot the first goose to arrive from wherever they were flying in from."

If you need to enliven some potentially dry statistics you can use props to help visualize them. In *Made to Stick*, Chip and Dan Heath describe how Geoff Ainscow of the Beyond War movement used a metal bucket and ball bearings to raise awareness of the escalating arms race between the US and the Soviet Union during the 1980s.

He always carried a metal bucket to the gatherings. At the appropriate point in the presentation, he'd take a BB [ball bearing] out of his pocket and drop it into the empty bucket. The BB made a loud clatter as it ricocheted and settled. Ainscow would say, "This is the Hiroshima bomb." He then spent a few minutes describing the devastation of the Hiroshima bomb—the miles of flattened buildings, the tens of thousands killed immediately, the larger number of people with burns or other long-term health problems. Next, he'd drop ten BBs into the bucket. The clatter was louder and more chaotic. "This is the firepower of the missiles on one US or Soviet nuclear submarine," he'd say. Finally, he asked the attendees to close their eyes. He'd say, "This is the world's current arsenal of nuclear weapons." Then he poured 5,000 BBs into the bucket (one for every nuclear warhead in the world). The noise was startling, even terrifying. "The roar of the BBs went on and on," said Ainscow. "Afterward there was always dead silence."

If you have a show that is impossible to shoot a taster for—perhaps a foreign location or fantasy set—you could use a storyboard technique. "Animatics" (a kind of storyboard) were once common in advertising, but are now considered old-fashioned. As they're not often used in television, they retain some novelty value and can be useful to show something it isn't possible to film prior to commission. A storyboard artist outlines the narrative over a number of outline sketches that represent different scenes, format points, or key points of dramatic tension. An actor can voice the characters, if necessary, or a narrator explains the format. Simple animation can also be added to the sketches, to make a person's arm move, perhaps.

"We did something at BBC WW which I liked," says Ben Hall, "where we did computer animated promos. We decided to get a storyboard artist to map it out for three minutes. He drew us 120 stills and then we put it through an edit process so you could zoom in and out and pan and told the story in voiceover. It worked, looked great and didn't cost very much."

Ben Hall also describes seeing a tape of someone pitching their idea in front of a green screen. "It was almost as though they had video behind them; there were images flashing up behind them. It was very clever." Although, he notes, "you could have put those images on big boards and done it in the room."

Stunts

Although Tom Gutteridge's staging of *Robot Wars* made for an arresting pitch, it is beaten in terms of scale by a pitch described in *The Times*. Philip Jones, a TV sales executive, was trying to sell a documentary series called *Sea Power*, during the annual TV market in Cannes. In keeping with the theme of the series, he persuaded a Russian admiral to dock his warship in Cannes so that he could hold a launch party aboard ship for the buyers.

Stunts can be memorable for a number of reasons (not all of them good):

* A production company pitching an idea about emergencies invited the channel executive to a meeting at their office. Unbeknownst to her, they'd hired a stuntman to dress up as a works contractor, and had him fake an epileptic fit and fall off a trestle in front of her. As she panicked about what to do, the proposed show's presenter appeared and said, "In this situation, how would you deal with this emergency?"

* Lorraine Heggessey, former BBC1 channel controller, tells the story of being pitched an idea by a man in a business suit, which had a pair of fairy wings sticking out of the back. It made her laugh—and remember the pitch—but she didn't commission the idea as it was too expensive.

* A US cable executive remembers one "pitch where they wouldn't tell us the talent; they would only tell us it was a celebrity and it ended up being a puppet. I'd have been much more interested in the pitch if they'd said, 'A puppet's coming in.' But with all the big build-up and the mystery … and then a puppet shows up!"

* Another US executive had "a guy come to a pitch meeting in an amphibious vehicle."

* The same executive got to fly a B17 bomber as he was being pitched a series about WWII planes. "They flew me in this little plane to this airport in California and took me up in this big B17 that the guy owned, sitting in the co-pilot's seat and then he said, 'Go ahead, take the wheel.' We did a pilot but it did not go to series."

While stunts can be fun, they can be high-risk. The key, says Ben Hall, is to ask, "How can I be memorable—without being embarrassing—and make them want to see me again?"

Practice Your Pitch

Tailor your verbal pitch to the channel and the channel executives you are pitching to. "I think if you want to do a big pitch in entertainment," says Ed Crick, "that's all about trying to create the mood of the show you are going to deliver, which is all about entertainment, talent, big flashing lights, and fantastic technical knowledge and experience; whereas if you are pitching someone in specialist factual you'd best be buttoned up intellectually and factually and ethically."

Science or history producers are more likely to focus on the facts and the narrative. "I remember being in pitch meetings where I'd be pitching emotion instead of facts," says Dan Hall. "They would say to us, 'Where is the new fact?' And we'd say, 'It's going to be a very emotional journey.' But they would say, 'I don't give a shit about emotion, where are the facts?' It's fine if the emotion comes out of the facts, but not the other way round. I didn't realize that because I was too inexperienced. It's no good saying, 'We are going to show you what it feels like to be a drug addict.' You have to say, 'We are going to show you the chemical make-up of a drug addict's body, which is x percent methadone,' or whatever."

Here are a number of principles to help formulate a strong pitch, whatever your genre:

Hook them in with a story at the beginning that illustrates your concept, content, or theme then outline your program idea. "The way you pitch is to go to a commissioner or channel controller with a good story that they don't know about," says Adam Curtis. "Good pitchers are articulate, they can explain what it is, they can hook you," says Nick Shearman. "It could be a format point, it could be an anecdote, it could be a joke; there are a variety of ways that people do it."

It's tempting to use statistics to impress the channel executive but as Joseph Stalin noted: "One death is a tragedy; a million is a statistic." People are more likely to identify with an anecdote. Good lawyers solicit empathy from a jury by starting with an illustrative story that shows rather than tells of the distress and injustice suffered by their clients. Stories are more persuasive than adjectives.

If you feel you need to use statistics, make them surprising to get your audience's attention. For example, according to the Florida Museum of Natural History, you are more than three hundred times more likely to be killed by an encounter with a deer than with a shark.*

In one pitch, "Somebody was talking about farming in Brazil, which has become technologically driven," recalls Emma Swain. "They described these two crops planted in these massive fields and asked, 'What do you think is the fallow time between the crops?' The answer is half an hour! There was also this amazing image of a formation of combine harvesters going across a field

*Because a deer is more likely to run in front of your car than you are to swim in front of a shark.

harvesting the crop and right behind them another set of agricultural machines planting … it made me think there might be something in farming."

How to Run a Formal Pitch Meeting

Show your pitch tape early in the pitch. It's good to show your tape before launching into the main body of your verbal pitch. As it plays, watch the room. Are people engrossed or are they restless? If it's not holding their attention, stop it early and start your verbal pitch. If you pitch first, and they love your idea, your pitch tape can kill it if it doesn't live up to the vision they have conjured up in their minds.

Nick Emmerson always does "super-brief introductions and then [we] put the tape on so it gets a visceral reaction, gets the adrenaline going, and then we launch into the detail, or they may go straight into asking questions."

"I think it's quite good to show your pitch tape right at the top," agrees Emma Swain. "I think we're all a bit impatient and what we're interested in is what it is going to look like; if that's the first thing you communicate that's quite exciting."

A US channel executive agrees. "Come in, give a five-minute preamble, and then put in a well-produced tape that immediately sells me on the concept, and has a character that 'pops.' That pitch could be over in fifteen minutes and you could sell the show to me."

Be clear about the format. Make sure you tell the channel executives what it is you're proposing—they can sit through a pitch and by the end of it not have a clue whether they've been pitched a drama, a game show, or a documentary. No one will buy a product if they aren't sure what that product is, especially when you are asking them to spend hundreds of thousands of pounds or dollars.

Pitch with passion and confidence. If you don't believe in your idea, no one else will. "Confidence, enthusiasm and total belief in the idea for the time that they are pitching. You can think it's shit but you can't show that," says Ben Hall. "You have to be completely on top of it," says Emma Swain. "If someone asks, 'Who is going to present it?', you can never say, 'I don't know, we haven't thought about that yet.' Even if you don't know who is going to present/host it, you have to say, 'My absolutely number-one choice would be so-and-so, but if they are not available, my number-two choice would be so-and-so and if they are not available, I think we have to go back to the drawing board,' but be clear so that everyone can see the show with that number-one choice, so the whole thing comes to life a bit more."

Be authentic. How you actually deliver the pitch depends on your personal style, your relationship with the channel executive, their preferences and the type of idea you are pitching, whether it's a one-line pitch or a more intense formal pitch with pitch tape and props. Whatever the situation, be true to yourself. Some people are known for their flamboyance, others are much more low-key. Both work, but don't torture the channel executive with an excruciatingly self-conscious performance. If in doubt, tone it down.

Don't use jargon. Don't use any words that draw attention to the tools you're using for your pitch: it's like seeing the boom microphone dip into shot or the wires during an aerial ballet, it ruins the magic. You want the channel executive to be completely engaged in the story you are telling, not feeling hyper-aware of the need to make a decision at the end of your pitch. So, avoid movie industry jargon such as logline, third act, or inciting incident, even though you might have used all those tools to help you develop your narrative or format. Equally, if you are pitching a specialist program, about astrophysics or genetics, avoid using scientific jargon. At best, you'll lose your audience's attention as they cast around for the meaning of the word, or worse, you'll make them feel stupid.

Avoid hype. Just as you shouldn't use hyperbole in your written proposal, avoid telling the buyer how amazing your program is going to be. People much prefer to spot the potential in something themselves, and feel some ownership over it than be told something will be hilarious or exciting. Show, don't tell. "I like a person who will explain the kernel of the film, the essential reason to do the film and what makes the film unique and special," says Iikka Vehkalahti, "instead of telling me that it's very fine, fantastic, incredible. I want them to paint the film in front of me in a few sentences so I can start to see it. Is it an artistic film, a story-based narrative film, a strong conflict or dilemma, an issue-based TV documentary, or is it a feature documentary? Don't pretend to be passionate: *be* passionate about the film."

Don't read your proposal. "I've seen people sit and read the proposal to a controller," says Nick Shearman. "That's not much good, particularly if the controller's already read it. I think it's about summarizing the key points: what is the idea, how is it going to fit in to that controller's schedule, maybe the price if it's cheap and why it's an important story that should be told now." Don't be boring, says Rudy Buttignol, "Most often people don't pitch compelling stories; they pitch the research."

Make your pitch conversational and inclusive. Many channel executives (especially in the UK) hate being "pitched at"—it feels aggressive and noncollaborative. The trick is to find a way of pitching your idea that feels like a conversation, but allows you to get all your points across.

Make it about them. The channel executives are concerned about their schedule, their budget, their audience figures, and their jobs. The fact that you're passionate about airplanes and have always wanted to make a series on aviation is irrelevant to them unless that fits their programming needs. "Understanding your commissioner and their needs is crucial and being sympathetic to them and give them comfort," says Keith Scholey. "They are all about mitigating their risk of failure: your idea is not going to fail, it's going to succeed and this is why it's going to succeed and it's going to end up happily ever after. You have to believe that's the case and you've got to make them believe that."

Be concise and summarize. Provide a quick summary at the end of your pitch and include the title. "A good verbal pitch is about being absolutely clear what your idea is about, and how you are going to make it and deliver it," says Emma Swain. "Be clear about the different elements: this is what it's about, and this is how we are going to do it, and this is why it matters."

Know what you want. It is unlikely that your idea will be bought "in the room," so know what you want to walk away with. Are you asking for funding to make a taster tape, or are you ready to go into production and looking for the greenlight? Or are you hoping to open a creative dialog that can be developed over a number of meetings. You want to walk out of the room knowing what the next step will be and what action to take.

CASE STUDY

Greenlit: *The Bank of Mum and Dad* (6x60' BBC2)

BBC

"The first time I had to do a big formal pitch to Jane Root, it was for a show I had co-devised called *The Bank of Mum and Dad*," says Ed Crick.

"We'd made a taster, done a PowerPoint and me and a colleague, Michael Sutherland, did the pitch as a two-hander—we were like the Ant and Dec of TV pitching—which in hindsight was a bit embarrassing ... We rehearsed and rehearsed and rehearsed and drank too much coffee, and given that it's not an entertainment format, massively over-pitched the format elements.

"It was weird because we thought we'd done an amazing pitch at the time—in reality it was a good if somewhat over-keen pitch, but we'd rehearsed it to death and it had lost some of its spontaneity—nevertheless the people in the room liked it (my then boss, David Mortimer, had laid all the groundwork beforehand). To be honest, Jane could have stopped the pitch halfway through, like they would with a half-decent singer on *The X-Factor*, and said, 'Enough, you're through to the next round.'

"They commissioned it and I went on to make the pilot episode, which incidentally is where at least 50 percent of any format is laid down. The show was a success and did three seasons for BBC2 and sold as a format internationally."

Stacking the Odds in Your Favor

If you can influence the timing of your meeting try to avoid first thing in the morning when the caffeine has yet to kick in, or the post-lunch slot where the channel executive is likely to be entering an energy slump, or alternatively starving and irritable because they've not had time to eat. If you know you perform better at a certain time of day try to capitalize on that. And avoid the end of the day when everyone is tired and itching to get home or pick up the kids.

If you are taking part in a competitive pitch situation, that is, you are one of several companies pitching ideas against a particular brief, try to take advantage of the "recency and primacy" effect. People remember the last thing they heard better than anything that came before so, if you can, secure the last pitching slot. Failing that, people remember the first thing they heard better than anything that came in the middle, so the first appointment is the next best thing.

Make sure you call ahead to confirm that the meeting room has the necessary equipment. If at all possible, get into the room a few minutes early and test the audio-visual equipment. Ask (beg, or bribe) the channel executive's assistant to show you how to work the DVD player, television, retractable screen, and blinds. There's nothing worse than getting up to put in your pitch tape only to discover that there is no television, or that it's hidden behind a concealed door, or you can't work out how to switch the television on. It breaks the flow and gives people the opportunity to start chatting, at which point you need to work doubly hard at regaining their attention.

Know who's in the room. You might be pitching to one person, or you could be pitching to six or more, including executives from production, audience planners, the scheduler, and finance people. If possible, find out who will be there so you can anticipate their concerns. "Certain people have better attention spans than others, certain people are much quicker than others so you want to be cognizant of people's individual personality traits and quirks," says Seth Lawrence.

When pitching, make eye contact with everyone in the room. It is polite and makes them pay better attention if you engage with them. Not everyone will express an opinion in the room, but you can be sure they will once you've left, so get them all on your side. "When producers walk in the room, and you don't know them, I would look at this person and say do I want to spend the next six months with them?" recalls Thom Beers of his days as a buyer. "I would look at them and think is this motherfucker the one who is going to sink my career?"

Don't plan to pitch a "laundry list of ideas." Probably the worst thing is coming with a long list, which hasn't been quality controlled," says Tom Archer. "I have literally banged my head on the table in a meeting with an (unnamed) BBC production area, crying out 'No more! No more!' as we got on to page two of one-liners."

"If you are pitching me six ideas, I'm guessing you are not being that discriminating about what you are bringing to me; you are pitching everything in your briefcase and you are not thinking about what is right for this channel," says a US cable channel exec. "If you have three shows, maybe four shows that you think are relevant to me, that's fine. You don't have to just pitch me one show, but don't pitch me everything you've got because that gets awkward—you're going to make me pass five times."

Ideally, you should start by following up on an idea previously pitched: discuss an updated format, introduce new talent you've found or show a casting tape, with the aim of moving the idea toward the greenlight. This will warm you up and get a dialog going, before you move on to your new ideas.

Next, pitch your new idea. Then, before you leave, do a quick headline pitch of a potential future project. If they react positively, that's the idea you will bring back to the next meeting to pitch formally.

Anticipate objections to your proposal and respond to questions honestly. If there are challenges to be overcome, be honest about them. Don't promise what you can't deliver. "By the time you are pitching something formally, you should have thought about it a lot," says Emma Swain. "You should know what you want to say and why it's such a good idea. The person who is being pitched at is going to have loads of questions, but they should all be answerable:

* 'Do you think you can do this in sixteen weeks?' 'No, we definitely need to do it in twenty-four.'

* 'Do you really need to shoot this in Texas?' 'Yes, because this is the only place where this takes place.'

* 'Do you really have to shoot this in January?' 'Yes, because it only happens one time a year.'

Not, 'Oh, I'll have to look into it.' That sort of lack of confidence suddenly fills the room."

Don't undermine your colleagues while they're pitching. It's extraordinary the number of times I've seen executives yawn or roll their eyes when someone else is pitching. I once heard an executive producer tell the channel executive that he wouldn't be interested in an idea that someone was about to pitch. If you don't believe in the idea, keep your mouth shut.

Listen carefully to any comments. Many executives seem to develop selective hearing when a channel executive speaks, hearing only what they want to hear. If a channel executive says an idea is interesting, but their body language is defensive, they're probably just being polite. If they say it's interesting and they're engaging in an animated conversation about the possibilities, they're interested. Listen "around the edges" too. Do they make casual asides that suggest potential new program ideas?

If a channel executive is not responding with enthusiasm, don't push it. In this instance, it's good to have a couple of ideas up your sleeve that you can pitch if things fall flat. Failing that, use the rest of the meeting to find out what type of programs they are looking for—turn it from a pitching session into a briefing session so you will at least have something to work with when you get back to the office.

Know when to shut up. It is possible to win a commission and then talk yourself out of it, so say what you need to say, nothing more. Don't overrun your time.

If they like the idea and want to see a written proposal, have one handy that you can leave with them, if appropriate. However, if the idea has changed during your discussion, keep it and tell them you will send it to them. Revise your proposal to incorporate their suggestions and send it to them as soon as possible.

Ask one of your colleagues to take notes. When you are pitching, all your concentration is going into your performance (however restrained) and once you've left the room it's easy to forget what was said. Everyone hears something different. If you have an objective observer they can record everything that was said and by whom. These notes will be invaluable when you come to rework your idea and for briefing the eventual production team.

Targeting the US Market

America is top of most producers' pitching wishlists due to the size of the market and the potential financial returns on a hit format. However, it is daunting to head across the Atlantic for the first time, as you not only have the usual stress of pitching but also have to learn a whole new way of doing business.

"If you are getting into the international co-production business you have to build up an understanding of what those markets are," confirms Keith Scholey. "You do that by watching TV when you are in America at night in your hotel—sit and watch it in its own environment. You have to see it with the ad breaks and get a feel for the chaos it's broadcast in to get a feel for how a program has to cut through in a different way."

This difference in terminology is the first barrier to overcome when pitching internationally. A US channel commissioning executive is usually called a Development Executive, or Director/VP of program development. They are likely to ask you who your showrunner (series producer or executive producer) will be. When I started working as a development producer in the BBC's New York production office I signed up to attend the Realscreen conference in Washington DC and immediately started getting emails from North American producers trying to pitch me their documentary ideas. I was baffled until I realized (some time later) that they had assumed from my title on the conference attendees list— Development Producer, BBC—that I was a commissioning executive: in fact I was in competition with them.

In the UK, "reality" is used to mean a certain type of entertainment-skewed show; in the US the term is used for a broad swathe of factual programming. For example, *Ice Road Truckers, Deadliest Catch, Project Runway, American Idol, Little People, Big World* would all come under the reality banner; they might also be known as "alternative programming," a term not used in the UK.

Pitching to an American channel executive is much more like taking a meeting rather than "having a chat," as the UK commissioners are wont to do, so pitching requires a less casual, more business-like approach. Ed Crick, who spent time working as director of development for TLC, says "by and large, [the Americans] run their channels with a bit more of a business attitude, so at the start of the year what they want to be sure of is their bottom line, the break-even and profit; the easiest way to guarantee that is based on returning formats, reduced costs, and increase in sales. Advertisers buy known quantities, so channels market them, support them, build them and I think the UK has been moving much more toward the US system."

The best way to get your head around the cultural differences is to spend time reading the US TV industry press such as *The Hollywood Reporter, Realscreen Magazine*, and *Entertainment Weekly*. *Variety* is another industry bible, but has a whole language of its own: directors are "helmers," production companies are "shingles," and comedies are "laffers."

When developing an idea or preparing to pitch in the US remember that the scale of the country can affect your proposal in ways you might not anticipate.

For example:

- There are five time zones in US (including Hawaii and Alaska), with the west coast behind the east coast by three hours, which makes live voting shows difficult; this became a problem for *American Idol*, when they realized they couldn't have a results show on the same night. They solved the problem by screening the results show the next evening.

- Different states have different laws, so a registered building contractor in one state won't have a valid license to practice in another, which means your DIY expert might only be able to film in one state.

- Filming is more expensive if the crew have to fly to different locations around the country.

- Casting hosts and contributors becomes a massive logistical challenge. It's usual to ask them to submit tape of themselves before short-listed people are invited to a casting session in a central location, or at the production company offices. "It's harder for UK companies to sell us shows because it's all about characters and they don't have easy access to the characters," says a US channel exec. In other words, unless you are living and working in the US it can be hard to develop and pitch character-led shows.

- Sending DVDs and casting tapes to channels is much more time-consuming if you are used to the convenience of using bike couriers to transport packages across London; it's much faster to upload clips via an ftp server or send a link via email.

- Spelling and grammar are different. If you are trying to convince a US broad-caster that you can produce a program as well as any American producer, it can undermine your position if your proposal is riddled with British idiom and British spellings. Change your spell checker to US English and make sure you have taken out any UK references or slang.

- It is hard to know which celebrities are in or out in a foreign market. Intelligence is built up over a lifetime of watching TV and reading pop culture magazines, but when you are working in a foreign country you don't have those frames of reference.

Getting Traction as a Foreign Producer

It can be hard for UK producers to get traction in the US, because, as in the UK, it's all about having a deep understanding of the market and having on-going relationships with the channel executives. "If there was an American company and a British company with a similar idea, our instinct would probably be to go with the American company," admits one US cable channel executive, "because the British production model is different, and the way their shows are cut and paced, all of that is different. I've worked with a number of British producers and if you take them directly from the UK there's always an adjustment period to American TV. We would never do a show with voiceover but every British format has that narrator that is explaining everything that's going on; we're much more interview-heavy. It's not a narrator but it's a person explaining what's going on."

However, British producers do have a certain advantage bestowed by their accent. "As an American you always think if someone has a British accent they are automatically more sophisticated," says one US cable channel exec, "and that's a useful illusion in pitches."

There is also a perception among US channel execs that British programs are generally well made and of high quality. However, British producers can also labor under the misconception that they automatically have a much superior product and this arrogance can mar negotiations. The Americans know their market much better than you do; don't underestimate them.

Cultural Differences in the US Pitch Meeting

Once you've secured your meeting with the channel, think about how you are going to present your pitch: you need to be much more positive in your presentation than you might in the UK. "The Americans pitch big and the British underpitch," says Ben Hall. "Brits say, 'Oh we've got this show, we quite like it …' An international pitch is much more confident."

"Here, it's Hollywood and you sell," agrees Nick Emmerson. "Charisma in the room is almost as important as the idea. It's about timing and confidence—you need to put on a show, and leave them a tape so they can pitch it up. You need to go in and sell it to them hard." John Hesling agrees: "Go in there with a solution and feeling an *über*-confidence that British people don't do very well. You have to say, '*When* we make this' not 'If we make this.' If you are remotely apologetic about an idea you are absolutely buggered. In Britain, people are happy to be pleasantly surprised that something is a success; in LA, people much prefer to believe it's going to be a massive success and then … Bang! It's not a hit. At that point they move on to the next thing. Everyone here wants to believe whereas in Britain everyone wants to say, 'Well, it probably won't work, but let's see.' It's a big difference and you need to know that when you are pitching [in the US]."

And as ever, it all comes down to storytelling. "Build up the story with total confidence, paint a picture with words and take them on a little journey, get them excited," says John Hesling. "You are rarely pitching to the person who can make a decision in the room, so they have to pitch it up to get the money, so give them four or five snippets that will help them pitch it themselves."

On the east coast, the pitches tend to be a little more low-key and Ed Crick thinks that might be changing in LA too: "I think people are much more interested in detail and approach, and that's partly because the commissioning editors who are in place are more often program-makers now, in America, than they used to be. The decision-makers are still businesspeople but businesspeople are much more impressed by the razzamatazz of the pitch than a program-maker who is going to be more interrogative about it."

One last word of advice about pitching in the US: give yourself extra time to get to your meeting, whether you are driving in circles on LA's highways, or negotiating Manhattan's mid-town gridlocked traffic. Also allow time for security checks on arrival. At the channels based in the Rockefeller Center and other skyscrapers you might need to show photo ID and have your photograph taken before they will call upstairs to announce your arrival, and there is a often a queue of people already waiting, which if you haven't factored in enough time, all adds to the stress of your meeting.

Why Do I Need an Agent?

Before you get a meeting with a US channel you'll need to secure the services of an American agent. While agents aren't part of the development landscape in the UK, they are essential when pitching to the networks and cable channels in Los Angeles. "It's a perplexing system as a Brit at first because you have no idea, and I was slightly too embarrassed to ask," says John Hesling. "At first I assumed they were like a lawyer and making sure the idea wasn't being ripped off, but they are this great middle person, so you don't have to have those frustrating conversations about deals, they'll smooth things over, they'll have a quiet word in someone's ear. They are incredibly valuable."

"Agents are there to set up the meetings for you, to sell your idea before and after the meeting and to arrange the best possible deal," says Nick Emmerson. "They allow you to maintain a clean relationship with the network while they do the dirty work." However, you do need to maintain your relationship with your agent, as you would a channel executive, warns Ben Hall: "They do give you a bit of information, but they are so busy, they have so many clients; you get a lot of love if you are successful and you get none at all if you're not, and so you eventually fall off the radar."

From the channel's perspective, the agent acts as a quality control. "We want to make sure the people that are pitching us are coming in having been through a rigorous system of checks and balances," says Tim Duffy, "to ensure: number one, that it's a fresh idea; number two, that it's on brand for the network; and number three, that they are with someone who can execute."

It's not as imperative to have an agent when pitching in New York, but it helps, says one NYC-based channel development executive. "If you have an agent they have relationships with every channel and they can call the five channels that your idea would be appropriate for and get you meetings there. That's part of what you are paying them for, that access." An agent can also help overcome the issue of talent. "If an agent is with a big agency, they'll help you package ideas. So an agent might represent a piece of talent and say well, you should meet this production company, they might have a show for you."

"What we try to do is complete the package so the buyer has no questions," says LA-based agent Seth Lawrence. "When a producer doesn't have a track record of handling millions of US$ from a buyer they are already going in with a number of strikes against them. I don't think that you shouldn't make that attempt; I think you should try and make it foolproof. I'm always trying to think how I can turn a project from a discretionary buy into a must-buy. I might think about partnering them with a big, known production company with a proven track record who can help sell and produce the show and who will be reasonable in the deal-making process."

According to Seth Lawrence, in the alternative [nonfiction] TV space, producers and production company clients will pay an agent 10 percent of their producer fees or production fee (which is 10 percent of the total program budget) if their show is commissioned. Occasionally, if the agent has presented the channel with a strong enough "package," with a strong combination of the following elements—the concept; the talent; and a client with proven production expertise—the channel will agree to pay the agent or agency what's called a "packaging fee," which might range from 1.5 percent to 5 percent of the production budget, depending on genre of program and leverage of the agent. If the agent receives an acceptable packaging fee, the client is commission-free.

CASE STUDY
The Los Angeles Agent
Seth Lawrence, Rebel Entertainment Partners, LA

"I like working with producers and production companies and helping build their business, helping them strategically sell their shows, and position their pitches," says Seth Lawrence.

"I help them figure out what's at the core of the show. Is it just a straight ball and a one-liner sells it? Or do we need to further develop this? What do we need to do to get it so the buyer will pay attention to it?

"I am in constant dialog with my clients; I expect my clients to hit me with good ideas. I have a weekly development call where we go over their entire development and production slate. The goal is to break the production and development slate into what's currently in production, what's in negotiation and which are the new concepts. I also want to know about the old or dead projects too because what is old becomes new again. I don't necessarily think that commissioning editors exactly know what they're looking for all the time until they see it, because a great hit show is a great hit show. And it might take two or three attempts over the months and years, depending on the environment, what's in vogue etc. People forget that the networks originally passed on both *American Idol* and *Survivor*, to name two.

"I have no interest in being a gatekeeper to anybody. When I make introductions from my clients to buyers, I expect them to maintain those relationships.

"We talk to A&E, MTV, VH1, WE tv TLC, etc., on a daily or weekly basis about what they're looking for: what do they need a lead-out for; what do they need a lead-in for; are clip shows working; do they want presenter-led immersive stuff; is the *Dirty Jobs*-type thing still interesting? We blast their briefs out to our clients so they have the cutting-edge intelligence and don't create shows in a vacuum.

"I'll take inspiration from wherever it comes, and I may say, 'Look, based on that idea I think we can sell to two or three places, but if you did it this way … it opens it up and we can maybe pitch it to six outlets instead of three.'

"It's imperative that producers, whether they are first-time producers or seasoned producers, know the channels that they're pitching, know the shows that are on those channels' schedules, and through us or the press have an idea of what will be commissioned in the future, because you don't want to walk in and pitch something they already have or was recently canceled.

"I never like my clients to go into a room and pitch a laundry list of ideas. Buyers want to feel special; they want to feel that you are bringing them your best product. I think the days of pitching five or ten ideas, even if they are one-liners, in the room are over; it's too many. Sometimes less is more: get in, hit them hard, get them excited and get out.

"Sometimes clients will come up with an idea they are passionate about that I don't think they will be able to sell. But I would say to them, 'Look, I've heard many versions of this pitch before and two or three derivatives are currently airing; I don't think that this is a project that you should set up specific meetings for, because I think you will lose credibility; but I would put this in your back pocket as your second or third idea. So when a buyer doesn't connect with a strong piece of talent or tape and asks what else you have, you would at least have something to try.' And occasionally, that kitchen-sink idea does sell."

Post-Pitch Analysis

It is unlikely you will walk out of the office with a commission the first time you pitch an idea, so aim to at least leave with a plan of action. Agree to a further meeting in a month's time to discuss talent or promise to get a budget to them by the end of the week. Having a plan is important, as you need to keep the idea on the channel's agenda. It also helps to focus the team in the aftermath of the pitch. In the US, your agent will deal with follow-up calls and organize further meetings.

The pitching process is intense and concentrated, but when you leave the room it can feel strangely anti-climactic, even if the meeting went well. Take some time out with your team over a coffee, or on the journey back to the office to discuss how things went, work out what could be improved for next time and what needs to be done next. It's important that this time isn't used as a shame and blame session when things didn't go well. Equally, it's good to take time out to celebrate, if only briefly, as other rewards are nonexistent for development staff, unless they are given the opportunity to work on the program just commissioned.

Make a noise about any success back in the office so the production teams feel kept in the loop and the development team and anyone else who was instrumental in the commission get due credit. This is good for morale and keeps everyone's energy high.

Even if you do walk out of the room with a commission, the channel might not be able or prepared to pay the full budget, which means you'll need to pitch further afield to make up the financial shortfall.

Development Master Class 10

Prepare Your Pitch and Make Contact

1. Decide whether you are going to pitch to a production company or a TV channel and research their companies using the resources below.

2. Find out if you need to register with the channel's e-commissioning portal— the details will be on their website.

3. Make an initial approach via email and ask if you can have a meeting to discuss your idea.

4. Polish your:
   a. Written proposal
   b. Verbal pitch
   c. Pitch tape or other visual aids such as a PowerPoint presentation.

5. Practice your pitch to your friends or dinner-party companions and watch to see if they tune out: if so, work on your pitch some more until your audience is rapt.

Explore More

CableReady: US-based representation company that will help you pitch your idea to an appropriate production company or TV network. They work with channels, production companies and individual producers anywhere in the world http://www.cableready.net/.

Hollywood Creative Directory: "the phone book to Hollywood" that lists staff titles, email addresses, telephone numbers, and websites for more than 2,000 production companies, networks, and studios. Updated in January, May, and September. The book is approximately $65 or you can get a monthly subscription to the online site for $19.95 per month http://www.hcdonline.com/.

Hollywood Representation Directory: book and online database that lists the contact details of more than 10,000 US talent agents, entertainment attorneys, and casting directors. Updated twice yearly in April and October. Online subscription is $19.95 per month http://tinyurl.com/hollywoodrep.

PACT: membership site for UK independent producers that has a free directory of production companies, searchable by genre https://www.pact.co.uk.

Writers' & Artists' Yearbook (A&C Black): contact addresses and telephone numbers for UK TV channels. Also lists contact details for UK production companies, including their area of expertise, contact name, telephone number, and website. Updated annually.

Caroline Taggart (ed.): *Writer's Market UK*
Contains useful list of UK TV channels with contact details, an overview of the type of content transmitted, submission details, and staff email formula. Also lists contact details for UK production companies, including websites. Updated annually.

Tom Negrino: *Creating a Presentation in PowerPoint*
An easy-to-follow—and visual—guide to making professional PowerPoint presentations.

Eileen Quinn and Judy Counihan: *The Pitch: The Essential Guide to Selling Stories*
A short, witty, and accessible guide to pitching in the TV or film industry.

TV Mole: research what your target channels have recently commissioned by clicking on the name of the relevant channel in the tag cloud on the front page. If you don't see a channel try searching for it by keyword http://www.tvmole.com.

11

Alternative Sources of Funding

Being good in business is the most fascinating kind of art.

—Andy Warhol

In 2002, Franny Armstrong met her friend, Alex Cooke, at a documentary seminar in Kings Cross, London. "The talk was boring so we sat outside in the foyer with a beer. She said she wanted to make a film about oil. Some time passed. I got up to go to the toilet. As I walked out of the room, mildly pissed [tipsy], the word 'traffic' popped into my head. I didn't know why.

"Walking back in, three minutes later, I realized that we should make a documentary about climate change, pinching the ingenious structure of Steven Soderberg's movie *Traffic*. Five human stories weaving themselves around all sides of a complicated issue. I told Alex. She agreed it was genius and we should have more beers."

Two years later, having finished her previous projects, Armstrong began thinking about the climate change film again. Knowing that she was dealing with a dry subject, but wanting it to have popular appeal, Armstrong decided she needed someone with proven commercial experience, and approached John Battsek, producer of the Oscar-winning *One Day in September*. "I went and gave him the one-minute pitch. 'It's *Traffic*, except it's climate change instead of drugs and documentary instead of fiction.' He said, and I quote: 'Love it. Let's do it.'" Next, Armstrong knew she needed to raise the money to make the film.

Armstrong was forced to learn the art of independent film funding when she was making *McLibel*, a film about a gardener and a postman who took

McDonalds to court and won. She'd been unable to get ITV, Channel 4, or the BBC to commit to the film so she'd adopted the US indie filmmaker fundraising approach, which involved borrowing a thousand pounds from a family friend, maxing out her credit card, moving to a cheap and nasty flat and persuading camera people to work for nothing. *McLibel* was eventually seen by more than 22 million people. It was released theatrically in the UK, USA, and Austria and sold to more than thirty TV channels worldwide, including, eventually, BBC2 in 2005, where it got one million viewers.

By the time Armstrong started working on *The Age of Stupid*, she'd also learned the advantages of keeping complete control of her films. "I realized what a powerful position you are in if you own the rights because then you control the distribution. I ended up getting 22 million viewers for *McLibel* and that's what it's all about for me," she says. "So when we went into this one, it was never an option to get it commissioned. We are not interested in having somebody telling us that we have to water down our message or that some advertising person would not like it. We wanted the film to be completely independent as the overall aim is that it has an effect on climate change and in order to do that you have to maximize the number of viewers." This time her ambition extended to having her film shown in multiplex cinemas around the world, and to reach 250 million viewers.

As *The Age of Stupid* was going to be a much more expensive film than *McLibel*, credit cards weren't an option—so Armstrong came up with a model she called "crowd-funding," in which a large amount of people each invest a small amount of money in exchange for owning a percentage of any profits.

On December 14, 2004, Armstrong nervously pitched her idea to thirty-five people in a room in Soho, London. "It is so, so much harder to explain what a film is going to be, than to answer questions about what a film is." She was shaking as she asked them for an investment of £500 each. "It worked. We sold thirty-three of our one hundred 'shares' on the spot. (Not actually shares, I now know, as that would be illegal without a piece of paper with an official stamp, so they are loans)," she later wrote in her diary. "That's 17,500 quid in the kitty—about half of what [my previous film] *Drowned Out* cost in total—over three years—so we should be able to get pretty far."

In the end, Armstrong would raise the £450,000 production budget (and then the same amount again for the distribution) from no fewer than 228 co-funders, and it was a lot faster than going directly to the TV channel executives. "If you're trying to get funding in a normal way, it normally takes you a year to get it," she points out, "whereas this way it only took us about two months ... and then we had some money, and then we could get going straight away. So there wasn't that horrible gap of despair. And then we just got the rest of the money as we went along, over the years—we didn't get all the money and then start." Investors, who include a women's hockey team and a women's health center, get between 0.05 percent to 1 percent of any profit generated by the film, depending on their level of investment.

Franny Armstrong's model means that she retained all the rights, which allows her to have complete control over—and be creative with—the film's distribution. She hired distributor DogWoof to handle the UK theatrical release on the basis that they would get a cut of the profits, rather than acquire all the rights (i.e. TV, DVD, Internet, nontheatrical, and theatrical) in return for a (usually modest) advance. She also allowed the public to buy a license to show the film via Indie Screenings website, so they could arrange their own events and keep any profits from their screening. This had never been done before in film distribution (imagine your local scout group being allowed to charge for tickets to a screening of *SpiderMan!*). More than 1,100 independent screenings were arranged in the first six months.

In September 2009, the global première of *The Age of Stupid* was held in NYC, but it was no normal première. There was a green carpet leading into a specially erected cinema tent in downtown New York, and the film was beamed by satellite link to more than seven hundred cinemas in more than forty countries; one million people watched it on the day of the global première.

There are a number of types of alternative or international funding open to TV producers and independent filmmakers:

1) Acquisitions

Acquisitions are programs that are bought ready-made, off the shelf, and are sold by distributors who have licensed the exclusive rights to sell the show in their territory. According to the Research Centre, between 10 and 25 percent of finished UK shows have the potential to be sold internationally. They could be one-off documentaries or finished complete series that will be shown "as is."

Programs that are parochial in their content, slow in pace, an awkward length, or have archive or music that is too expensive to clear internationally will not be attractive to acquisitions executives.

Acquisitions are not of specific interest to us, unless your company is specifically interested in building up a catalog of programs they can sell in future, in which case you need be aware of the potential issues.

2) Pre-buy

A pre-buy, or pre-license, is when a buyer commits to buying the finished product by promising money upfront. "That's a lot more valuable to most filmmakers," than someone buying the finished film, says Rudy Buttignol, "because they can usually leverage that into the financing of their project, or if they are from Europe, they can leverage the Media Fund [which provides funding for TV programs that have secured participation from three or more European broadcasters]. A pre-buy is important because it goes directly to the producer for the production budget, whereas a license or a buy of a finished project usually goes to a distributor and then the filmmaker gets their cut somewhere much later. They're often the same amount of money but one goes directly to the producer."

A commissioning editor will pre-buy on average around one in fifty proposals that are pitched, and then only from producer/directors they already know. A channel executive from Denmark, Canada, Australia, or Denmark might spend around 10,000 Euros on a pre-buy; executives in Japan, the UK, USA, France, and Germany might invest a little more.

3) Format Sales

If you are selling a finished format, that is, one that has already been transmitted in your country, an international buyer purchases a format "bible" from you (or more likely, your distributor), which describes in detail how the show can be replicated in their home territory, everything from lighting design to number of participants to plot points and number of crew.

The beauty of a format is that it reduces risk and cost to the format buyers, as all the kinks have already been worked out. "With *Supernanny*, we had the advantage of showing a finished copy of the show," recalls Nick Emmerson. "With a format we can come in and take the risk out of the process. ABC loved the program and Fox loved the idea too. It's now sold around the world."

To sell internationally, a format must deal with internationally recognizable situations and themes. At the entertainment end of the factual spectrum *Supernanny, Wife Swap, Strictly Come Dancing, Changing Rooms, What Not to Wear, How to Look Good Naked, Big Brother, Survivor, 10 Years Younger, Fear Factor, The Apprentice* and *Idol,* are all programs that have done well outside of their home territories.

Usually buyers want to tweak the format a little to suit their own cultural needs. Onscreen talent is often a sticking point when selling ideas abroad: a much-loved host in one country is an unknown in another, although some presenters do cross over. The Brits who have made the transition from presenting UK programs to hosting US shows seem to fall into one of two categories: the rugged, ex-army type, such as Bear Grylls (*Born Survivor*) and Bruce Parry (*Tribe*), or mean and bossy types, such as Simon Cowell (*X-Factor*), Piers Morgan (*America's Got Talent*), Kim and Aggie (*How Clean Is Your House?*) and Jo Frost (*Supernanny*).

4) Fully Funded

A foreign broadcaster might fully fund you to make a program that is unique to them, for example, Shed Media US, the US arm of a UK indie, was commissioned to produce *Real Housewives of New York City* for Bravo (US). If you are pitching programs that you want a foreign broadcaster to fully fund, be aware of their specific needs. For example, consider whether the program you are suggesting can be feasibly produced in the country you are selling it to. For example, what's legal to film in the UK might be illegal in the US or vice versa.

CASE STUDY

Greenlit: *Real Housewives of New York City* (12x60´ Bravo)

Shed Media US

"My brief in the US was to show US buyers that we can do different kinds of shows—in the UK we were making documentaries, docusoaps, and formats," says Nick Emmerson.

"There was a 2x60´ show called *Admission Impossible* made by Ricochet [part of Shed Media plc] in the UK, which was about parents trying to get their children into the school of their choice, with stories of various parents and their kids.

"So we took that idea round the US cable networks in LA and they were interested. We realized we had to set it in LA or NYC and on a whim I thought let's do NYC. Bravo were interested and they gave us some development money to find some women in NYC.

"We hired casting producers and we were trying so hard to break into Manhattan, but it was difficult. We'd find women and then their husbands would forbid them from talking. Then we found Jill Zarin who was at the center of the Upper East Side social set and she had all the connections which gave us an in.

"At this point we were calling it *Manhattan Moms*, because it was about moms and their kids but also about these women trying to maintain and upgrade their status. Bravo loved it but we'd spent a lot more money than they gave us on developing it.

"Then they said, are you OK with it being part of the *Real Housewives* brand? And we said yes.

"It has generated a lot of other business for us directly, and we've been gifted other projects because of that show. *Housewives* upped the ante for us in terms of proving what we could do—it's beautifully shot."

5) Co-production

Ambitious documentaries and drama documentaries, such as *Planet Earth*, *Supervolcano*, *Walking with Dinosaurs* and *Earth: Power of the Planet* are much more expensive to make than entertainment formats; so while a channel may be interested in buying a proposed program, they may not be willing or able to fund the entire budget. In this situation, you must raise the additional funding before your original buyer will formally commit to commissioning your idea. *Planet Earth* was co-produced by the BBC, Discovery (USA), and NHK (Japan); *Space Race* brought together four channels, the BBC, NDR (Germany), Channel One (Russia), and National Geographic (USA); *Walking with Dinosaurs* had five co-funders: BBC, Discovery (USA), Asahi TV (Japan), Pro-Sieben (Germany), and France 3 (France).

In return for funding part of the budget, the international co-producer buys the exclusive right to transmit the finished program in their country. If they are putting money in upfront, as opposed to buying the finished program, they naturally expect to have some control over the content. This means that you must juggle the editorial needs of various buyers, making the life of your production team much more complicated as they must produce various foreign versions, with or without ad breaks, and with or without a presenter or narrator.

International TV Festivals, Markets Forums, and Conferences

If you have pitched your idea in your domestic market with no success, the wider international markets might still hold some opportunities for you. Likewise, if you are an independent producer trying to find out whom you should pitch your program idea to in your home country, the international festivals might, counter-intuitively, hold the key, as many of the commissioning executives you might want to approach will attend.

There are a number of annual television and documentary festivals and conferences each year. Each one, to a greater or lesser degree, provides networking opportunities, workshops, briefings from channel executives, screenings, one-on-one pitching sessions, and the chance for young producers to catch the eye of the channel executives in various pitch competitions. Film festivals are mainly about celebrating the art of film, whereas conferences and forums are more focused on business and building creative and commercial relationships.

The reality is that few deals are actually concluded at these festivals and conferences, so but they are valuable for making contacts and building your network. The Australian Film Commission advise producers that "no one will do business with you unless they know you ... It's not for the faint-hearted or the easily intimidated. You have to be organized, self-confident, focused, and bold. You have to plan and set up as many meetings as you can before you arrive ..."

"Big festivals like Sunny Side of the Docs can work well for the people in power," says filmmaker Dan Edelstyn, "the important people are only there for two days because that's all they can spare, so everyone is falling over themselves to speak to them so [the buyers] can have a nice glass of rosé overlooking the dock while being pitched at by hungry producers. But for the hungry producers who haven't got an international name, your emails won't be looked at by these people, however engaging your project is."

Ed Crick agrees: "It can be quite sad because there are twenty or thirty companies in there who are attracting all the business because they've got on-going relationships with the buyers and then a whole load of mom and pop jobs who have paid their fee and are on cloud cuckoo land if they think they are going to sell a show just because they once made a documentary about skunks in 1987."

Conferences can be daunting and exhausting for the uninitiated. However, if you are realistic, plan ahead, and know what you want to get out of a festival, they can still be worthwhile.

Working the Festival to Your Advantage

It can take a couple of visits to a conference before you begin to do any meaningful business, but they are a great opportunity to educate yourself about global programming trends and meet potential production partners. However, attending conferences isn't cheap, so weigh the cost against the potential benefits. Make sure you make the most of your time by:

* Setting up meetings well in advance. Do this at least six weeks before the conference. Some events work on an application process where you must submit a proposal before the conference and the projects that are chosen will win their producer a pre-arranged meeting with a buyer.

* Making sure you are meeting the right people: some companies send their most junior executives who don't have any power. Check the published list of attendees and their designation before you approach anyone whose name isn't recognizable.

* Being clear about what you want to get out of each meeting—is it a meet and greet? A briefing session? A pitch?

* Scheduling your meetings to start on the hour and keep to schedule.

* Having enough business cards, one-page proposals and DVDs to hand out. Keep your laptop with you at all times in case you get the opportunity to show someone your trailer.

* If you are flying in to a conference in Cannes or Washington DC, try to fly back via London or New York so you can have follow-up meetings on your way home.

"Once you've made a commitment to these markets you have to commit to a long-term relationship," says Rudy Buttignol. "Going on to a market buzzing about it, creating a lot of noise, and then not following through or staying committed is not going to get you anywhere. In my experience it's probably two years from the time you meet people for the first time, to the time that you are working together in some kind of established relationship, so you have to make a commitment and then follow through on it. Stay in touch at relevant times."

Even if you don't have anything to pitch at this stage you can still learn a lot by attending the screenings and talks. "The most important things from any conference are master classes in production," says Ed Crick, "they are always interesting, useful, and valuable. Sometimes the channel head is an interesting and charismatic character so it can be quite good fun to hear what he or she has to say. They're good networking events and meeting people outside of the formal environment can be useful."

As ever, do your research before you attempt to meet the buyers. "The most common problem is that producers don't do their homework," says Iikka Vehkalahti. "If you spend one day checking the websites of channel executives you can find out what kind of films the channel executives are supporting. If someone calls asking what kind of films I am looking for I tell them to look at the website."

CASE STUDY

Greenlit: *Waltz with Bashir* (1x 86′ Theatrical)

Director: Ari Folman

"We were one of the first financers of *Waltz with Bashir*," says Claire Aguilar.

"Ari Folman, an Israeli producer, wasn't selected by the production forum, so his first financer asked if I would hear a pitch from him in a one-on-one meeting. I didn't know him, but I think I'd seen one of his films; he was a fiction maker before.

"He pitched me this idea, which was really complicated. It was basically a biographical film told through animation, about his experience as a soldier in the war. He framed it as a psychological thing, but it's a narrative in a lot of ways. He didn't have any materials, but there was something about it that seemed so new. It was interesting.

"He was cute, charming, and good-looking, and he said he was going to be in the film. And I said as an animated character? And he said, yes, of course. He was going to do his own voiceover, and the interviews would be based on documentary; I thought that was cool. The pitch itself was at a little table and we had cups of coffee and it probably lasted about fifteen minutes. It was very simple, but mind-blowing and so exciting.

"The next month he came back with an animated sample and that was it for us, it was so great. We said, let's do it. And then he came back with a script and we went through the process."

Waltz with Bashir has won sixteen awards, including a Golden Globe, and was nominated for an Oscar and a BAFTA.

There are a number of opportunities for pitching your idea at a festival (in order of desirability): a pre-arranged meeting, as part of an arranged panel or speed pitch, or during networking.

Pre-arranged Meetings

If you are fortunate enough to have been awarded a formal meeting, it is likely to take place in a room away from the hubbub of the festival, but you could find yourself meeting in a bar or café. You have only fifteen to thirty minutes to pitch and discuss your idea, so be prepared with your pitch and your pitch materials such as a one-page proposal and DVD.

Introduce yourself and the title of your project so the buyer can orientate themelves to your pitch (you might be the tenth person they've seen today). "I have met thousands of people during the last twenty years, and most of them expect me to remember their face and their emails when we meet, sometimes after years; remembering all of them is beyond me," says Outi Saarikoski, commissioning editor, YLE co-productions, Finland. "If someone pitches to me they should first introduce themselves and briefly mention the structure of the project; they should be precise about what the film is about." Outi also points out that a buyer might not speak English as their first language, and might not understand everything you say if you are in a noisy bar, or it's at the end of a long day when their concentration is waning. Keep your pitch clear and simple.

Buyers at festivals will want to see a trailer or some footage that you've shot. "You need to be able to show something," says Rudy Buttignol, "unless your last film was an international hit around the world, and by hit I mean winning every film prize at every major film festival and an Oscar, otherwise you need to show something." Just as in a normal TV pitch, seeing the footage first can help the buyer to steer the discussion. "Producers talk and talk and talk instead of showing what has been shot," agrees Iikka Vehkalahti, "if there is a promo tape or DVD be ready to show it. If the producer says, 'Can you wait a minute, I want to get my computer' and then he's running somewhere and two minutes later, he's got his computer and opening it and … it sounds stupid, but five minutes of waiting feels like a long time. But if it's immediate I will absolutely watch it."

Once you've shown them your footage, give them a clearly labeled DVD to take away with them. Outi Saarikoski said that she likes to get one page and a DVD in a plastic folder so they don't get separated and she doesn't lose them as she goes from meeting to meeting.

A trailer/demo for a feature-length documentary film (which is usually what is being pitched at these festivals) should be longer than a TV pitch tape (seven to ten minutes instead of two to three minutes), because the buyer is trying to assess your storytelling skills. As well as a well-edited sequence that showcases your storytelling skills, many of them also want to see ten to fifteen minutes of carefully selected rushes, so they can judge your shooting and directing skills, rather than the skills of your editor.

CASE STUDY

Greenlit: *Intangible Asset Number 82* (1x90′ Theatrical)

Director: Emma Franz

Channel executive: Outi Saarikoski, Commissioning Editor, YLE Co-productions, Finland

When Australian musician Emma Franz came across a great music story that she wanted to make into a documentary she decided to try to find a funding partner at the Australian International Documentary Festival.

"I looked through the list of channel executives on the AIDC site and Outi Saarikoski's profile indicated she was interested in commissioning cultural documentaries," says Franz.

"I sent her a fairly standard short pitch, which included a one-paragraph synopsis, a sentence or two about why I felt my film fit within her mission statement, and a request for a meeting. She didn't respond to me immediately, but at the conference she called, which is unusual because most replies you receive are by email.

"When we met, my first impression was that Outi works intuitively. She was such an attentive listener. Often, when you are pitching to people they seem like they'd rather be somewhere else. Outi watched my eyes, smiled, and listened and responded to everything that I said. A lot of our conversation was about other music or films that we liked, which made me feel comfortable. I think that's also testament to Outi's affability, it doesn't often happen that way. She asked me why I wanted to make the film, and I sensed that that was the most important thing for her.

"Later, of course, I sent more material including a written treatment and a trailer, and not long after I received a letter of commitment."

Outi Saarikoski remembers Emma's initial approach. "Her project was not in the forum and she didn't have a pitch fest meeting arranged with me but she asked would I still like to meet her in the bar of the hotel. By intuition, I thought yes, I will meet her. I want to stress that this is an exception!

"We met and it was all so easy and we just chatted. I had such a good feeling about her. I trusted in her, even though she had done nothing on film; she was a jazz musician. Usually I like to be with producers and filmmakers, who are quite well known, and Emma was directing and producing her own film. We kept in contact, then Sunny Side of the Doc asked if I had any potential projects in an early development stage, so I gave Emma's project: *Intangible Asset Number 82*.

"She sent the proposal to Sunny Side of the Doc and they called me immediately and said they wanted to add this project to their catalog, so Emma was invited to La Rochelle in France to pitch it and we met again.

"I suggested that she should submit an application for her project to be considered for the IDFA forum in Amsterdam and her project was accepted and she pitched it there.

> "Once the film was finished—it took a couple of years—the film was invited to Brazil. This year the film has been to SXSW and then the film was invited to HotDocs in Toronto."
>
> *Intangible Asset Number 82* won Best Documentary at Durban Film Festival and has been an official selection at several others.

Panel Pitching

While the stakes are high during all pitching sessions, the public festival pitches can be more stressful than normal. The "pitch competition" is a common event at conferences and festivals. A couple of hours before the planned event a small number of producers are chosen from a list of applicants and told they will be pitching to a panel of channel executives in front of several hundred conference delegates. Sometimes, there is real funding to be won, but not always, so check before subjecting yourself to this gladiatorial-style arena.

So what are the advantages of subjecting yourself to the panel pitch? "For fifteen minutes you are going to get everybody's undivided attention," points out Rudy Buttignol, from "people representing the world's market in your genre, who might never have heard of you before, and not know what your film is, but they will quietly sit there and actually listen—which is a miracle in itself, considering that most people in our business have ADHD. And they usually ask some intelligent questions. That's pretty good marketing for your idea."

It can also be excellent pitching practice, says Buttignol. "Most people start off pitching the research or pitching the background, pitching the context, everything except the story. That's why workshops and pitching forums are so good, because it forces people to articulate it and when you get all the feedback you'll see they often point to the same difficulties." Claire Aguilar agrees: "A lot of people get freaked out, trying to get through the pitch. It's an intimidating process; but there's no reason to be afraid, and it's like public speaking, the more you do it the better you get at it."

Remember to practice answering the questions you might be asked, says Emily Renshaw-Smith. "Typical questions are: 'What will we see in this film? Does this fit into our programming? Have you got access to your characters secured yet?' Write down the five most likely questions that you will get asked and make sure you answer them in your pitch or you have answers prepared for the Q&A session."

Speed Pitching

Another popular, and more intimate, format for pitching sessions is the "speed pitch." Prior to the event, you must register for the session and if you are lucky enough to be accepted, you will get three minutes of a channel executive's undivided attention. But this pitch format brings a different kind of pressure.

Chris White, director of programming and production for PBS's POV, described a RealScreen speed pitch he attended as a buyer:

"So, here's the drill. The clock starts. There are brief introductions, and I slide my card across the table and encourage producers to feel free to follow up if they have any questions after their time is up. Looking slightly relieved, but knowing that twenty seconds have already passed, the pitch begins. Fifteen or twenty sentences later we hear, 'One minute left!' Eyes widen and they start to talk faster, trying to wrap things up, say what they want to say, and get a little feedback. 'Fifteen seconds!' A look of sheer panic overcomes them as they shove DVDs, business cards, and one-sheets into my hands and try to sputter out a few last words. Time is up. Producers who continue to talk are politely tapped on the shoulder. If their lips continue to move the Commandant grabs them by the scruff of the neck and hurls them back into the pen. And so, we begin again."

The moral is to be prepared, and practice your pitch so you are confident you can deliver what the buyer needs to know. You can't possibly give a full pitch in three minutes but the buyer should be able to tell within that time whether your idea has potential for their channel. Concentrate on telling them the essentials. What's the headline idea? Who is telling the story? What's their point of view? Who are the characters? How many episodes? Is it funny, revelatory, serious or does it have unique access? If the idea you're pitching fits the channel brief it is likely that the commissioning executive will invite you to a follow-up meeting.

Networking

If you weren't able to secure a formally arranged meeting with a channel executive you still might be able to make contact after a panel session, for instance. Introduce yourself, ask an intelligent question (not a question they've just answered) and ask for their card.

If you spot them around the festival campus, take a moment to read their body language. "A commissioning editor can easily read if someone wants to approach," says Iikka Vehkalahti, "but you should see if they have time to concentrate on you. If I have time and space in my brain, then I will talk to you. If my mind is totally occupied or exhausted after two days of having discussions every ten minutes, and I feel I cannot take more in or I cannot concentrate, then you should understand, it's nothing personal. There is no point having a discussion with someone if your mind is somewhere else."

"How should you approach a buyer at a festival? Civilly," says Rudy Buttignol. "Approach the person as a person, as a human being as opposed to a funding sex object. You can't start pitching in someone's face: 'Did you ever hear about this famous author in 1833, in Austria?' to which the answer is inevitably, 'I haven't.' Being pestered for your encyclopedic knowledge of all humankind's history is boring. The buyers and commissioning editors who are hounded are actually pretty interesting ordinary human beings if you engage them in a conversation, and most people are glad to participate as opposed to being stopped and being pitched."

Emily Renshaw-Smith suggests you take a casual approach. "Try to make friends with everyone and don't necessarily think of it as networking, just think that you're going to meet a bunch of interesting people and something might come out of it later."

How Not to Pitch at a Festival (or Anywhere)

Buyers at festivals hear dozens of pre-arranged pitches every day, and are aware that they are likely to be approached by producers outside of the formal meetings. How you make that approach is important. "There's a scary look that you see when you look round and see someone and you think, oh god, I'm going to get stuck with them for ages," says Emily Renshaw-Smith.

Don't attempt to pitch to a buyer when they are in the middle of a meeting. "A lot of people come up and say I just want five minutes with you to tell you about my project," says Claire Aguilar, "and sometimes they do that when you are in a meeting with somebody. It's kind of insane, and horrible and it's rude; you're in a meeting."

However, buyers said that they were, in principle, open to impromptu pitches.

"It happens to be where the oddball idea comes to you every once in a while that you might say yes to; you've always got to be open to the unexpected," says Rudy Buttignol. "You just don't know: here comes a producer with a pitch and it could be wonderful," agrees Claire Aguilar. But it can also be overwhelming, she says: "Sometimes I want to put a bag over my head and run away."

Even if buyers feel like running there might be nowhere to hide. "The first time at IDFA it was like a crazy circus, even if I went to pee someone was trying to pitch me," recalls Iikka Vehkalahti. Astonishingly, he's not the only one. "I have been pitched in the toilet," says Claire Aguilar. "I had this eye contact with somebody in the bathroom, and I could tell she wanted to talk to me, but I went in the stall and all of a sudden I saw this piece of paper being jutted through from the stall next to me, and she said, 'Please can you read my pitch?' I said, 'This is not a good time—take your paper or I will do something with it you wouldn't want me to do.' That person actually posted her flyer on the bathroom stall, which was interesting … but a lot better than thrusting it between the stalls. Some producers will do anything to get attention."

You could find yourself standing next to a buyer in the crush of the bar. Resist the urge to pitch. You might have only one chance and you don't want to do it under the influence of gin, nor do they want to be cornered when all they want to do is get a drink at the end of a long day. "If someone is having a beer in the bar there's a strong likelihood they don't want to talk about your idea right at that moment," advises Emily Renshaw-Smith, "just have a chat so they know who you are and then you can email them afterwards and say, 'Hey, we met and I'd love to talk to you about my idea.'"

Counter-intuitively, if you don't pitch to a buyer it will make you stand out and lure them into asking you to pitch. "A cold pitch is pointless," says Rudy Buttignol. "The most interesting projects I've ever gotten involved with were with people who I sat and shot the breeze with; we talked about everything under the sun and had a great conversation and at the end of an hour, it was like, 'Well, hey, what project are you doing?' The great pitches are the ones where the buyer actually asks you what you are doing and they keep asking, 'And then what else? And how are you going to do that? Who else is involved and how much is it going to cost? When are you going to do it?' It's the art of conversation more than anything else."

Competition, even in the "relaxed" atmosphere of the social events, is fierce. "At the parties it can be like a meat market stampede," says Dan Edelstyn. "It's hard to make eye contact. I've met some interesting people for about five minutes, but it's hard not to feel like you've wasted your time."

Unfortunately, if you want to build your contacts you need to persevere. "I would say be as visible as you possibly can," says Barry Gibb. "When you are freelance, Sheffield Documentary Festival feels like a fortune, but it is the best money you will ever spend. Just be visible, have cards, have a showreel, go and talk to people. The whole industry is driven by faces, by the people you know and whom you met last night and had a drink with. You don't know you are having a drink with the head of commissioning for Channel 4 or the BBC, you are just having a laugh and that is valuable. If there are competitions go for them; you have nothing to lose. Put yourself out there, be seen as a filmmaker, be associated with things."

Alternative Funding Sources

If you have had no luck with the TV channel executives, and you are still determined to make your film, you need to up the ante. Some people go to extreme lengths to get their films made. Robert Rodriguez raised $7,000 to make his feature film *El Mariachi* by subjecting himself to medical experimentation. It is to be hoped you won't need to go to those lengths, but there are one or two things you could try:

1) Grant Foundations and Funding Agencies

In the UK, three national screen agencies (Scottish Screen, Film Agency Wales, and Northern Ireland Screen), along with the various English regional screen agencies, provide funding for projects that originate in, or contribute value to their region.

Other foundations have special areas of interest. For example, the Wellcome Trust will help fund the development of TV programs or films that will help the public understand and engage with the biomedical sciences.

The Good Pitch is a roving pitching forum run by Channel 4's BRITDOC Foundation, which offers filmmakers the chance to pitch their social-justice project to an invited audience of NGOs, ad agencies, brands, and foundations.

MEDIA is a European funding body that helps producers with development and production funding for programs that have European broadcasters attached.

Check their websites to find out what funding is currently available, and the deadline for applications. You have to fill in a grant application form and ensure that your bid conforms to all their requirements in order to be in with a chance of success.

The End of the Line was funded by the UK's Channel 4 BRITDOC foundation, and a range of UK and US not-for-profit organizations including WWF, the Marine Conservation Society, and Oceana. Its UK theatrical release was funded by Waitrose supermarket.

2) Ad Funded Programming (AFP)

Ad funding is an increasingly important source of funding for program-makers. Advertisers looking for new ways to reach their target audience have started funding whole series rather than just the thirty-second ad spots. In 2003 Duracell fully funded a thirteen-part science and technology series called *Explorations*, which was made by Zig Zag (and 'powered by Duracell'), Kraft Food funded *Simon Rimmer's Dinners* on Good Food and Specsavers funded *The Book Club* on More4. "There will be more advertiser funded programming," predicts Ben Hall.

Specialist AFP sales agents, such as Krempelwood, will help you find brands who might be interested in funding your program.

3) Crowd Funding

Alternatively, you could ask your audience to pay for your film, as Franny Armstrong did with *Age of Stupid*.

Robert Greenwald's *Iraq for Sale: The War Profiteers* was funded by Greenwald's fans, who responded to an email plea for donations of $50 in return for an end credit. Of 170,000 people on the mailing list, 3,000 responded with donations totaling $185,000. With a few large donors giving between $82,000 and $100,000, the total amount raised was $267,892. In ten days. Greenwald was, it was reported, "stunned." (Jim Gilliam, Greenwald's twenty-eight-year-old producer, wrote the crucial email while lying gasping in his sick bed as he waited for a double lung transplant.)

There are a number of websites springing up, such as IndieGoGo, that aim to help you engage with your potential audience via trailers and blogs before pitching your funding needs to them. The Tipping Point Film Fund is another "crowd-funding" site, sponsored by the Co-operative.

Blast!, a documentary about cosmology, was funded through ArtistShare, which allowed people to donate money in return for different levels of access to the film: $19.95 bought newsletters during the production period, photographs, and access to deleted scenes; $75,000 bought an executive producer credit, dinner with the filmmakers, a personal cosmology lecture, signed copies of the director's journal, and emails to scientists during the production, access to "personal or controversial" footage, signed DVDs, and VIP tickets to screenings, among other benefits.

You might be wondering what all this independent filmmaking and distribution has to do with getting your idea on TV? Once you have built your audience online, channels are more likely to take notice of you. Granted you might have done all the hard work already, but at least you might be able to license your film to them and get it in front of more viewers.

Web Channels

Putting your work up online is also a good way to hone your production skills. "What I'm always astonished by is that there is editing equipment sitting around totally underused and nobody is coming in at the weekends to cut their own material," says Adam Curtis. "It's now so cheap to go out and film stuff and put stuff up, making little mini-dramas with reality; why not? You can add them to your own websites and ask channel controllers to look at them."

Another route you could take, if you lack experience, is to approach a web channel dedicated to developing new talent, such as Current.tv, which is on web, satellite, and cable. "We are not expecting those filmmakers to be with a production company or have anyone else helping them," says Emily Renshaw-Smith. "We can't afford a big budget, so we make up for that by being accessible, providing an opportunity and support normally offered by a production company; we are open to people contacting us and pitching ideas. I'm surprised at how few people do considering how easy it is to pitch in to us."

Being a smaller channel means that Current TV is hungry for publicity and they actively seek opportunities, such as the *Facebook vs. Twitter* stunt, that will attract the press. "The stunts work well for getting a lot of noise around our programming. What I love is that the films are being made by first-time filmmakers and then they'll suddenly find themselves with a double-page spread in *Now*

Magazine because we've pushed it through with a whole lot of other stuff; we punch above our weight in terms of PR."

And once you've had a couple of shorts transmitted on a web channel, you can use it as a calling card. One Current TV filmmaker landed a job with the BBC's natural history unit; another got development money from BBC3 and has done some presenting for *Unreported World* on Channel 4.

So, by now, you may have got interest from a broadcaster and located top-up funding; the final step is to make sure your project doesn't stall at the last minute.

Development Master Class 11

Meet the Money People

1. Sign up to the newsletter at tvmole.com to get a list of upcoming TV conferences: aim to go to at least one in the next year.

2. Read TRC Media's *Inside the Distributors* report for a good introduction to selling in the international market http://tinyurl.com/trcdistributors.

3. Several months before the conference sign up for any "meet market" sessions so you can pitch your ideas to several buyers over the course of a couple of days.

4. If you are getting started in the business sign up for one of the entry-level pitching sessions, such as the Mini Meet Market at Sheffield Doc/Fest.

5. Explore alternative ways of funding your idea:
   a. *Crowd Funding*
      The Age of Stupid—an independent documentary about climate change that was funded by more than 600 ordinary people who donated money or invested in the project http://www.ageofstupid.net/money.
   b. *Grant Funding*
      The End of the Line—funded by grants from a number of US and UK not-for-profit organizations such as WWF, the Marine Conservation Society, the Waitt Family Foundation, and Britdoc http://endoftheline.com/film/.
   c. *Fan Funding*
      Blast!—an independent documentary about a group of scientists who

travel to the Antarctic to launch a high-altitude telescope, funded via ArtistShare http://tinyurl.com/blastdoc.

d. *Advertiser Funded Programming* (AFP)
   The TV Book Club (10x30')—Specsavers opticians fund More4's new book club.

Explore More

Alabama Film Organization: has a useful list of US film foundations and grants http://tinyurl.com/afogrants.

ArtistShare: primarily a site for musicians where fans can help fund a project in exchange for "access to the creative process" http://www.artistshare.com/home/about.aspx.

Channel 4 BRITDOC Foundation: UK foundation that offers funding to socially aware documentaries that wouldn't be funded by a UK broadcaster. Also runs the Good Pitch, which brokers "relationships between third sector and filmmakers" for social-justice films. The Good Pitch tours the UK and North America http://britdoc.org/.

Indiegogo: provides online resources for "fundraising, promotion and discovery," where filmmakers can upload their pitch and ask for funding http://www.indiegogo.com/.

Nicol Wistreich, Adam P. Davies: *Film Finance Handbook 2007/2008: How to Fund Your Film*
Aimed at feature (narrative) film producers but has an extensive global directory of 1,000 funding awards, some of which fund documentaries.

Morrie Warshawski: *Shaking the Money Tree: How to Get Grants and Donations for Film and Television*
A guide to planning your fundraising strategy and how to apply for grants from corporations, individuals, and foundations.

Carole Lee Dean: *The Art of Film Funding*
US-focused book written by a TV producer who founded the Roy W. Dean Grant Foundation, which has granted more than $2milllion to filmmakers. Visit her website to find out more about the grant guidelines http://www.fromtheheartproductions.com/howto.shtml.

UK Film Council: funds documentaries that are intended for theatrical (cinema) release http://www.ukfilmcouncil.org.uk/featuredocs.

Selected TV Conferences and Markets

Listed in chronological order January–December—visit their websites for more details.

NATPE (National Association of Television Program Executives)
Scheduled to be held in Miami in 2011 and 2012 (previously held in Las Vegas).

Realscreen Summit, Washington DC, USA

Berlinale European Film Market, Berlin, Germany

Filmart, Hong Kong

MIPTV, Cannes, France

Durban Wild Talk Africa, South Africa

Hot Docs, Toronto, Canada

Realscreen's Factual Entertainment Forum: The Real Deal, Santa Monica, USA

Banff World TV Festival, Canada

Sunny Side of the Doc, La Rochelle, France

Media Guardian Edinburgh International TV Festival, Scotland

WestDoc: The West Coast Documentary and Reality Conference, Santa Monica, USA

MIPCOM, Cannes, France

Sheffield Doc/Fest, UK

World Congress of Science and Factual Producers (WCSFP), roving

12 Getting the Greenlight

When R. J. Cutler, an Emmy-winning LA-based producer, read an article about the annual Metropolitan Museum Costume Institute Ball in New York City he was intrigued by the glamor of a fundraising event that encompassed the cream of the fashion, art, society, and entertainment worlds. Presided over by Anna Wintour, editor-in-chief of *American Vogue*, it is an event run like a military operation; albeit a military operation with Chanel and diamonds.

R. J. contacted Vogue's Director of Communications, Patrick O'Connell, to discuss the possibility of making a documentary series about the Costume Institute Ball. They had a number of discussions, but it became clear that it wasn't going to work out, as there were too many logistical problems associated with filming at the Met. But R. J. still had a feeling that something would come of the discussions.

Then it happened: one Thursday he was summoned to a meeting with Anna Wintour the following Tuesday. R. J. promptly flew from Los Angeles to New York City and subjected himself to a manicure in preparation for his meeting with the queen of fashion.

Her icy reputation earns Anna Wintour as much press as the clothes featured on the glossy pages of her magazine. She is variously described as distant or shy; her staff are said to have to intuit what she is thinking as she uses silence and a well-aimed glance to communicate; her economy of speech gives little away and she brooks no questions.

However, she had an intriguing suggestion for R. J.: he should film the preparations in the run-up to the publication of the biggest *Vogue* edition of the year: the September issue. R. J.'s immediate thought was that it would make a fantastic television series, so he set out to pitch it. Having access to Anna Wintour was an obvious coup and he soon had a development deal with US cable channel Oxygen.

And that's when things started to unravel. "We got them everything that they wanted in the development deal," says R. J., "but they somehow convinced themselves that, although we had complete access, Anna Wintour wouldn't give the access that I had been saying we had.

"Then we sold it to Lifetime, but in the middle of negotiating a deal they became convinced that Anna wouldn't do it. And then we got Bravo on board, who very quickly decided that it wasn't possible to get the access.

"It was a fascinating thing, because we had caught lightning in a bottle with the access we had been granted by Anna, but nobody believed us. They weren't skeptical of my agreement with her; they were skeptical about her willingness to be revealing, they were intimidated by her reputation."

R. J. had secured unprecedented access and a lot of keen interest from the channels, but all his potential buyers had taken fright at the last moment. He had reached an impasse.

Over dinner with a friend, R. J. complained how he hadn't been able to get the Anna Wintour project off the ground, and how he was hankering to return to making feature documentaries (such as his Oscar-nominated *The War Room*). "My friend said, 'Why can't the Anna Wintour project be a film? Why wouldn't that work, why does it have to be a television show?'" he recalls. "This is why you have friends: they ask silly questions that you forget to ask yourself.

"Maybe all these people in the television environment who wanted in and then got cold feet, maybe there was a reason they got cold feet. Maybe the story of Anna Wintour shouldn't be told in a television environment with act-outs and the kind of overt conflict and lack of subtlety that reality television requires. Maybe a film environment would be right for her: it was instantly clear to me that that was the right way to go."

Once R. J. had had the realization that he needed to change the medium, the project picked up. "It took me maybe three days to sell that show to A&E IndieFilms, who agreed to come on board as executive producers and finance the film. They were willing to take the risk."

The September Issue premièred in NYC in August 2009, having won the Excellence in Cinematography Award: US Documentary at Sundance.

If you have done all your research, secured your access, found your host and agreed finer details of the format with a channel, you should have everything that the channel needs to progress to the next stage but, as R. J. Cutler's experience shows, things aren't that simple. Successfully steering your idea though the greenlighting process can be as time-consuming and much more frustrating than originating, developing, and pitching your ideas. It's a process that requires tact, tenacity, and patience, as well as the ability to maneuver around potential potholes.

Once you have pitched your idea to a channel executive or other buyer for the first time, there are a number of outcomes. In order of likeliness: you will get a pass, a maybe, or a yes. Rarely will you get a yes "in the room," and when you do there are still a number of hurdles before the final greenlight. Some programs can languish in apparent limbo for months, if not years, before the final details are agreed.

This delay can be due to the convoluted chains of command in channel commissioning. It is likely that once your channel executive has expressed an interest in the project, they must pitch it up to their channel head for approval. Then you must negotiate and agree the contract, budget, and delivery schedule with the channel's business affairs department, before it is finally signed off by the channel's Program Finance Committee. Inevitably, this all takes time.

Your speed of response to the channel's initial reaction is vital. The longer your idea sits on the channel development slate the riskier it is; as the more time that passes the more opportunities are there for your idea to start sounding less appealing (or for the channel controller to move to a job at a different channel, leaving your idea orphaned, as happened with *Robot Wars*), so drive it through to commission by providing a more detailed treatment, budget, and agreeing talent as soon as you can. This stage of the process will be handled by you or an executive producer in conjunction with your company's head of production.

But whatever happens during the pitch, you can't afford to relax yet.

Getting a No

No is the most likely word you will hear after your pitch. Don't take it personally. Conservative estimates suggest that only one in ten ideas pitched are commissioned, and the actual number could be fewer. "You might have a very good proposal and a great taster tape with good access, but they still don't commission it," says one development producer, "maybe because the schedule's been jiggled or a new sports contract is going take up the schedule and they no longer have a slot for your documentary."

If the channel isn't interested, they will, at best, tell you so immediately. All producers prefer to be told no, rather than be strung along in the hope of a commission. If you know that the channel doesn't like the idea, you can stop working on it, take it elsewhere, or find out if you can tweak it to better suit the channel. "I think they are doing you a disservice if they are misleading you," says Chuck Braverman. "I would much rather get a no than be dragged on for six months with a maybe. If they tell you no, you can ask why, and the answer is important." It could be because they have already commissioned a similar program or that it doesn't fit with their channel's brand.

"I try as much as possible to say no in the room," says Nick Shearman. "Someone warned me that unless you absolutely believe in an idea, say no, because if you are not immediately sure of the idea then the likelihood is that you never will be. I think that was a good piece of advice."

Sometimes they just aren't sure. Being a good channel executive "is about being able to say no in the room when you know it's not right," says one US cable exec, but "it takes a long time to get to that point where you just know, it sounds pretty simple but it takes a long time." In order to save wasted time, it may be necessary to make a judgment about whether an inexperienced or indecisive channel executive is merely feigning interest to get you out of the room.

Another US channel executive said that the circumstances of the pitch might make it uncomfortable for them to say no. "If they are a top-level producer and their agent is in the room, I'm not going to pass in the room, unless it's someone I have a longstanding relationship with and I have that comfort level."

Simon Dickson points out that channel executives might have another reason for not saying no straight away. "You might want to think about it in the bath tub for a couple of nights. Or you might want to wait a week or two to see if a comparable idea that is coming from another company is better or worse than the one that you've just been pitched. Every company rightfully wants as quick an answer as you can give them in respect of their unique ideas, but I work for the broadcaster, and it's my responsibility to achieve the best overall output that I can for our audience. So I'm balancing the needs of my audience with the needs of them as a company."

If there's a rigid silence after your pitch, or they pronounce your idea to be "interesting," give up and go home, as they're not actually interested. They hope that producers will get the hint from a lack of further correspondence from the channel.

But "no doesn't mean the end of the line," says R. J. Cutler. "Sometimes you get a no and the person who is saying no to you just wants to understand the project differently, so that they can say yes. Or you need to adjust the project. I always say a 'no' is a pathway to 'yes,' and sometimes it's going to be a different project entirely. With the Anna Wintour project, I tried to sell it as a TV series, but it was only when I tried to sell it as a film that I was able to sell it easily."

So it's not the no that counts, it's how you choose to deal with it. When a channel executive says no to your pitch, you can do one of four things: accept their decision, try to change their mind, change your proposal, or kill the idea.

1) Accept Their Decision
You can simply choose to accept that they don't like the idea and move on to pitch it to another channel. Before you do that, check that the basic idea is sound and that you have tweaked the format to fit the next potential buyer.

2) Try to Change Their Mind
If the channel executive has said no but you are convinced that the idea is a good one for them, ask them for feedback, if a reason isn't forthcoming. It might be that they misunderstood your pitch, and you can get things back on track with a brief explanation. But don't push it, if the channel executive seems adamant. "There has to be a point when you accept no," says Martin Trickey. "It doesn't mean you can't push a bit, but don't keep coming back and back and back, you aren't doing yourself any favors."

Ben Hall agrees: "If they don't like it, they don't like it. Don't argue with them. If they express doubt, you can say, yes but what about this ... But if they say, no, it's not for me, or they are sitting back and arms are crossed, don't argue. Say fine, we'll come back with something else."

Not everyone is so polite. "I had one guy who pitched into a season we were doing," remembers Emily Renshaw-Smith, "and I said, 'I'm sorry, you've missed the deadline for this season, and we probably wouldn't have picked it for this reason ...' and gave him a bit of feedback on the idea and then I said, 'Don't be discouraged, because we've got more seasons coming up.' He then replied and said he thought they were all crap and wasn't interested in anything else we were doing!"

If you are rude during or after a pitch it is likely you will never get another chance. "The number-one outcome of a pitch is that they will buy the show," observes Ben Hall. "The second best outcome is that they will see you again. The worst outcome is that they will never see you again. During my first pitching trip to America, I was with a big agent and so we saw all the top people out in LA. Afterwards the agent said: 'That was brilliant: they're not going to buy anything but they want to see you again.'"

3) Change Your Proposal

> *If one cannot catch the bird of paradise, better take a wet hen.*
>
> —Nikita Khrushchev

You might have a sense that the channel executive might reconsider if you changed the proposal or attached different talent. It's up to you to decide whether you want to make your idea as it stands. "If we think it's got meat but won't work for us we will tell them what will work for us," says Martin Morgan, "but sometimes they decide not to go forward with us on that basis."

If, on the other hand, you want or need to get the business, then go back and rework your proposal in a way that will appeal to the buyer. "There are a lot of different roads that lead to Rome," says Seth Lawrence, "and as long as Rome is where the commission is I don't care how clients get there as long as we do." Some producers find this hard. "You start to realize that you are not just pleasing yourself," says Barry Gibb, "there's a producer, there's the channel and it's a royal pain in the arse, actually." Many channel executives expect some kind of creative input. "The producers that you tend to get a bit of traction with are very flexible," says Lucy Pilkington. "So if you say, oh, I'm not sure; rather than being all deflated they can have a collaborative discussion with you. When the idea is being formed is when you need the greatest dialog, because we need to work out what exactly the show is and how it works for us, and the producers need to know that the broadcaster understands the show that they're making."

However, these painful creative conversations are a necessary and useful part of the process. "The people pitching get to hear from the channel controller themselves why an idea is slightly or wholly not right," says Tom Archer, and that benefits "everyone by getting that dialog opened up and then maybe next time they'll be spot on." A UK producer/director agrees, "It is nice to have that immediate feedback, because you think, OK I can do something with this, I can turn it into a positive experience because I can go back and rework this. You get the germ of an idea that you can actually turn into something from a passing comment. Those little things are so vital but don't always get fed back, and great opportunities are lost."

CASE STUDY
Greenlit: *1900 House* (4x60′ Channel 4)
Wall to Wall

"*1900 House* was the product of a two-and-a-half-year conversation between me and Sara Ramsden at Channel 4," says Alex Graham. "It took two-and-a-half years to persuade her to make that show, and for most of those two-and-a-half years I was pitching completely the wrong show.

"The show I was pitching was a bit crap, and Sara's brilliance was in understanding that there was something in what I was pitching, but she was robust enough not to commission it, she was tough enough to hold out.

"I think that the best, and most innovative ideas come out of dialog."

4) Kill Your Idea

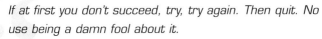

If at first you don't succeed, try, try again. Then quit. No use being a damn fool about it.

—W. C. Fields, attributed

If you have pitched the same idea a number of times, and are still hitting a brick wall, analyze why that might be the case. Are you targeting the right ideas to the wrong channel? Is your idea essentially flawed? Or is the wrong person pitching? Work out what's wrong, and then take Harry Beckwith's advice to "fix your messengers, fix your message."

Otherwise, accept that some ideas just don't work out. Keep the relationship with the channel on a good footing and try again with something else.

Development producers are used to repeated rejection, accepting it as an inevitable part of the production process. However, other people who have invested time and energy in an idea they originated or have come to think of as their own can take a rejection badly and may need to be supported as they deal with feelings of anger, denial, and despondency. If you've been working closely with them on their proposal, explain that many things can make or break a proposal, many of them having nothing to do with the idea itself.

Getting a Maybe

Maybe is the most difficult response to deal with.

Sometimes you will get an expression of interest, and a request to provide a format breakdown, casting tape, or a detailed treatment. Channel needs fluctuate on a daily basis, so sometimes channel executives want to keep hold of a proposal in case it's needed to plug a looming gap in the schedule, but they don't want to commit formally to something they might not actually need.

So an expression of interest might be a way of buying some more thinking time, says Simon Dickson. "You might be contemplating having another conversation in a few days' time, where you might be saying yes to them about something else; on other occasions, you want to have a conversation with someone else on the team to confirm your instinct is right."

Other channel executives feel powerless to make a decision themselves, and keep the indie producer on side while they get their boss to take a look at it, which can take weeks or even months. They might also be obliged to run an idea past other departments such as multiplatform commissioning or marketing.

"It's important to follow up and figure out if there's anything that needs to be done beyond what's already in place—but the commissioning editor may say, 'I like it. It's got everything, it's clean, but I need to have the right environment or the right opportunity to bring this up,'" says Seth Lawrence. "This is a business of people and these are decisions that are not generally made by one person any more, they're made by committees, and so you need to give your commissioning editor the right amount of latitude to bring it up."

If the channel are interested in your idea, but aren't yet convinced enough to commission it, they might be willing to fund some secondary development. Secondary development money might be used to work up a full treatment, do some casting, find talent or do a recce. "We do several phases of development," says Tim Duffy. "I might give you some money to flesh out the idea on paper or put together a casting reel. I might give you money to produce a bible for a big formatted reality show that you can't pilot." It's a cost-effective way of the channel reducing their risk of commissioning something that might not work out, but channels are increasingly reluctant to pay for secondary development.

Yes

If the channel executives do genuinely like the idea they will let you know about it, although they might not actually tell you they love it as they still might not, at this early stage, want to commit themselves. If they are keen, they will ask for more details.

First, it is likely that they will want to see a fuller proposal. It is in your interest to get the revised document back to the channel as soon as you can, while they still have their enthusiasm for the idea. If you let it drag on and don't deliver until months later you may have missed your moment.

If you are proposing a content-rich documentary series, this will be a three- to five-page treatment with a detailed outline of the series narrative, with an episode breakdown of what each week's program will contain, the names of key interviewees, details of any special archive or filming techniques and so on. The development team could write this document, but it can be beneficial at this stage to ask the person who will act as executive producer on the series to write the treatment, so they have ownership of the editorial content and are involved in the early-stage discussions with the channel.

Alternatively, you could bring in a series producer for a couple of weeks to flesh out the proposal. Again, if the program is greenlit, they will be working on it, so they have an emotional investment in getting the idea through. It is preferable to have one senior producer working on the idea from the early stages, as it is difficult to keep track of conversations and the reasons for the program's evolution if it is handed on to different people. They can also begin building relationships with important academic experts and consultants and concentrate on developing a strong narrative.

If you are proposing a more entertainment-focused format, the channel will want to see a format breakdown and running order, which means describing in great detail each format point: what happens and when. A running order is a timed breakdown of an episode, including any ad breaks, showing when each format point occurs and how long each part of the narrative lasts. Formats are specialized, so get someone who is an expert format producer to help you refine the proposal and write the running order, if you don't have the experience.

If your format requires onscreen talent, the channel has to approve your choice. Ideally, if you have produced a persuasive talent reel, they will buy your program on the strength of that. If not, find a host and fast. Many promising proposals have died because it proved too difficult to cast the host, so if you haven't already found them you are at a disadvantage, racing against the clock. The longer it takes to find someone, the more opportunity you give the channel to change their mind about commissioning your idea. Casting is notoriously difficult and labor-intensive and the channel will have strong views on whom they like and don't like. If you can, it is advisable to invest in a specialist casting director (especially in the US) as they have ready-made contacts and a good understanding of channel tastes. Again, the channel may be willing to fund several weeks of casting effort.

Piloting

Ideally you want a commission that goes "straight to series," that is, once the editorial, talent, and budget issues are agreed, you can hand the idea off to the production team and it goes into production. This is most likely when you are pitching a narrative-driven documentary series or an observational documentary-type reality series.

If you are proposing a format there is an extra step of production that can delay the commission of a full series: the pilot episode. This happens when the channel want to see exactly how the format would play out on screen. In this instance, they might commission you to make a single show, which may or may not be transmitted on the channel.

Some channel executives favor an incremental approach. "I'll put steps into my deal," says Tim Duffy. "I'll give them the $25K to get me to the point where I can extrapolate off of that to put the money into a single air-able pilot. Then we'll trigger that pilot, and spend $350K. If we love it, we'll spend $4 million on ten episodes of television. But that's the game, you're always hedging your bets." While a pilot commission is better than nothing, it is by no means certain that you will get the greenlight for a series.

You must put as much work into the treatment, budget, and casting for a pilot as you would for a series. The pilot needs to be made by an experienced producer who understands the format and the channel needs. The pilot is the hardest show to make, as it is the program where things are still being worked out by trial and error, but with a tight time constraint and under intense channel scrutiny. The producer must be a skilled negotiator and diplomat to keep the channel happy while staying true to the original format.

Once the pilot has been delivered to the channel they review it to see whether the format works satisfactorily. Sometimes, this is enough to persuade them to order a full series, but it is more likely that they will want to get some audience reaction. They will schedule to transmit it (as is usual in the UK), or will arrange special non-broadcast audience screening (more usual in the US).

Depending on the audience reaction to the pilot, the channel will order a full series, or reject it. In the US, if the channel like the pilot show and it tested well in front of an audience, it is likely that they will order a full series and transmit the pilot as part of that series. If they are disappointed with the pilot show, they will transmit the single episode, but bury it somewhere in the schedule. This way, they still fill a gap in the schedule, so the pilot hasn't been a complete waste of money, but they aren't hoping or expecting to attract an audience. Unfortunately, the production company can wait anxiously for the results of the pilot screening, with a production team on standby ready to leap into production once the pilot has aired, without realizing that the channel has already made their decision, but not formally communicated it to the production company. If the pilot goes well, and the audience figures are encouraging, you can look forward to the greenlight for a full series.

Money Matters

Budgeting

Once you have agreed the editorial content of your pilot, film, or series, you must come to an agreement about the budget. At this stage you'll have to turn your one-page proposal into a more detailed treatment from which you can work out how many filming days you'll need, how much international travel you'll need to do, the size of the production team you'll need etc. Submit a budget that details all your staff costs, number of filming and editing days, location costs, equipment hire, consultants' fees, music and archive rights, and everything else that you will need. A sample budget template is provided in the Appendix.

The budget needs to be prepared by an experienced production manager, who has a good understanding of the channel budget, scheduling and production costs.

Don't submit a budget that is higher than the channel average without good reason. You might need to tweak the format a little to make it more affordable, but you should discuss this with the channel editorial team. If you can't get the budget into the ballpark, or have to change the editorial too much you may lose your commission.

There's always a tension between the channel, who want the cheapest programs they can get, and the producer, who wants the highest budget they can negotiate. "Part of my job is to question that price and negotiate," says channel executive Nick Shearman. But there is a risk to a hard negotiation. "What happens is that people put on a cheap price and you agree a commission and then they come back to you a month or two later and they say they can't deliver it for that: that's pointless and it leaves us all looking stupid."

If your production is justifiably expensive—such as a groundbreaking landmark specialist factual show—stand your ground. "If you are going to be ambitious and are realistic about the price, then fight for it," advises Keith Scholey. "If you can't get the money for that level of ambition don't do it, stick to your guns. You've got to have a lot of courage to go for that position but that's how the great things are made; the investment has to be right. If you fall below that price you may well find you can't deliver what you sold, and the whole thing disintegrates during the process, often a couple of years down the line and then no one's happy." You could, of course, look for co-production partners, particularly if you are making a high-end, content-rich documentary series, but this takes time during which the channel has the opportunity to change its mind.

Know the Deal

If you are a producer pitching to an independent production company and they like your idea, you should always seek an option fee (these fees vary wildly). If they manage to get some secondary development money from a channel to work up the idea in more detail, or decide to develop the idea further themselves, the production company should bring you on to the team to do that, for which you should be paid a salary.

If your idea is commissioned, there is no guarantee that you will be able to produce/direct the project, as channels often want an established name; however you might be able to negotiate another paid role on the production, such as consultant.

You might also be able to negotiate a cut of the production fee if the idea is sold. The production fee (a kind of service charge paid by the channel to the production company for making the program) is typically 10 percent of the program budget. Depending on the quality of your idea, format detail and/or the level of exclusive access to a desirable person, archive, or organization you're bringing to the project, you could expect to negotiate a payment of 15 to 60 percent of the production fee. In other words:

If the total program budget is $100,000
Production fee = $10,000
20 percent = $2,000
60 percent = $6,000

The more the project is dependent on you, i.e. you have secured exclusive behind-the-scenes access to Barack Obama or the Queen, the greater financial cut you can expect to be able to negotiate. If your idea is still only a subject area or relies heavily on a slight twist to a familiar format, you will not get anything at all.

If you invent a hot new format that attracts international sales, you could benefit from a cut of the format fee, which is generally 5 percent of the production budget.

So if a program costs $100,000 per episode
Format fee = $5,000 per episode
If you had negotiated a cut of 50 percent of the format fee you would get $2,500 per episode.

If your idea is commissioned, there may be scope for DVD sales and books; income from these sales is known as "back end" and you could negotiate for a percentage of this revenue too (somewhere between 15 and 50 percent, but you could negotiate different percentages for different media, e.g. books and toys).

It can be hard, especially when you are starting out, as being seen as pushy could mean that a production company chooses not to deal with you at all. "The first deals that you do will probably be shit deals," says Ben Hall, but "it's about creating your calling card, it then becomes much easier to go to see the next production company."

If a production company or a channel expresses interest, the best advice is to talk to one of the specialist companies who will advise and negotiate any deal on your behalf; a selection are listed at the end of this chapter.

Things That Go Wrong

Sometimes it seems like you have the deal in the bag, and then something happens to make it all fall through. Remember, channel executives have hundreds of ideas passing through their hands. If yours is limping along, and another arrives that fits the brief and is ready to go, yours might get bumped.

The biggest risk to your almost-commissioned idea is that the channel undergoes a change of personnel or a rebranding just as your idea is making its way through the labyrinthine system of budget, talent, and schedule negotiations. Many an idea has been in the latest stages of development or pre-production when a channel chief has left their job or been fired, and the idea has suddenly stalled as the channel regroups (such as happened in the case of *Robot Wars*). Decisions are delayed until the new incumbent is at their desk, and invariably they look at the development slate and take a vigorous broom to it, sweeping out anything that their predecessor liked and completely change the brief. Unfortunately, it can take a few months for them to decide what the new direction will be, so in the meantime development producers are left to second-guess the situation.

Sometimes the fact that you've been efficient in securing your onscreen talent can trip you up. "Often producers will bring us talent and will have already negotiated a deal with that talent that makes the cost of the show prohibitive," warns one US cable channel exec. Or they might have "negotiated a deal that violates every kind of precedent we've tried to set. So we'll be interested in the project, and then when we talk to the agent and find out what deals they have in place we realize that makes it impossible. So it's always preferable, if you have a piece of talent, to negotiate a holding deal or a deal that says it can be renegotiated by the channel that picks it up."

CASE STUDY

Greenlit: *Falklands: The Islanders' War* (2x60′ History Channel)

Point of View Production Company

"The pilot was made in April or May, and we took it to the History Channel in June," says producer Mike Ford. "They loved it immediately because it had a fresh angle, but we then had to try to get a co-producer on board.

"Channel Five agreed to co-produce and everything seemed to be going well. We planned to go to the Falklands in November to film. In late September, we went on a recce, which was co-funded by Channel Five and the History Channel, to get the main characters on tape so the commissioners could see them. We presented that tape, which was just two or three minutes long, featuring five or six interviews to the commissioners in October.

"Just as we were about to begin principal photography in November, the head of History at Channel Five left and all commissioning was frozen, which was a real setback and left the filming hanging by a thread.

"We got around the problem by increasing the running time from a one-hour documentary to a two-hour documentary totally funded by the History Channel. It was a very tight budget for a two-hour film but we knew we could do it. Principal photography was completed on the islands in March, with the interviews already completed. We didn't start viewing rushes and digitizing tapes until April 4 and had to deliver to the History Channel in mid-May for the anniversary in June. So the workload was intense and we didn't sleep much for those six weeks!

"The week before transmission the History Channel arranged a screening in Soho, London, for the media. Channel Five came and congratulated me on the film and said they wished they'd had the courage to go through with it."

Handing Over to the Production Team

Victory has a hundred fathers, but no one wants to recognize defeat as his own.

—Count Galeazz Ciano

Once you get the greenlight you can celebrate and move on to the next idea that needs attention. But before you do, make sure that you thoroughly brief the production team about the agreed program and any discussions you've had with the channel that have shaped the program along with any on-going issues that need to be addressed. It is likely that you will have to initiate this meeting as production have no idea where the idea came from or who has been developing it (if they even realize it has had a long and eventful life before it got to this stage).

A number of things can happen once your idea goes into production. It could go on to be a massive hit and win awards because your instinct and vision were clear and everything was set up well and because it had a great production team working on it. It could become a sleeper hit for seemingly random reasons. Or it could be a failure, because your vision was unclear or unrealistic, the wrong production team was hired to work on it, or it suffered an unfortunate scheduling clash, against the *X-Factor* finale, or *Superbowl* for example. Whatever the outcome, give credit where it's due, take responsibility where appropriate, and apply what you learned in future.

What Next?

As for you, the development producer, you too might need to move on. Development is relentless and generally thankless, so most people find it hard to sustain their freshness and enthusiasm over a long period. "It's very easy to get into a rut in development and you can go for a long, long time without selling an idea," says Nick Emmerson. "It's easy to get burned out in development." Some deal with this by periodically taking a production job and then returning when they feel refreshed. "I think if you are in development too long you can start to develop ideas for commissioners and not the audience and you have got to be careful of that," says Dan Hall.

It helps if you know how to make shows as well as develop them, so that you aren't suggesting the impossible. "You have to have been responsible for delivery at some level," says Ed Crick. "To be a good development assistant producer [AP] you should have been an AP on a show; to be a good development producer you should have taken something through the edit; to be a good development executive you should have series produced; to be a good head of development you need to have been in a position where you felt the burn when the buck stopped with you."

When Emma Swain was invited to work in commissioning, she felt she needed some executive producing experience. "I remember insisting that I should be allowed to executive produce because I feel that the minimum level you should be at in order to commission effectively is to be an executive producer, because you need to know what it's like to drive a project rather than be just one of the production team."

Development as a Career

If you are one of the small band of people who are dedicated to development and have no desire to work on a production, you should move jobs periodically so you can get experience of developing different types of shows and get exposure to and experience of different channels. People like to pigeonhole others and it's easy to be labeled as a format developer or a history specialist, but development skills are transferable and therefore so are you. Build your relationships, develop a strong portfolio and remember to keep taking creative risks.

Although development can be an intensely frustrating and thankless task, it also has much to recommend it. "I know that most people think that working on production is much more interesting than working in development, but I don't. I like working on lots of different things at once, from serious access documentaries to frivolous entertainment formats, I find that stimulating," says one development producer. "I once spent six weeks working on a program casting hundreds of people for a show and I had the same conversation twenty times a day for six weeks: that's not interesting."

Development is creatively and intellectually invigorating. What other job offers the chance to research anything from the efficacy of grandma's cleaning methods (*How Clean Is Your House?*) to the best way to survive in a desert (*Born Survivor*) or extreme fishing in Alaskan waters (*Deadliest Catch*)? "If you think that development is boring you're not doing it right," says an experienced UK development producer. This variety is exhilarating, as is the thrill of the chase.

If you specialize in development and prove yourself creative, responsive, and able to deliver to deadlines, your skills will be highly sought after and your ascent can be fast. Indeed some producers go into development solely because they want promotion to a senior management role: if they have proven success at selling ideas they are in a much better position than other candidates. While some program-makers never see the whites of a channel executive's eyes, you'll have access to some of the most senior and influential people in the industry, probably some ten years before the jobbing producer/director/executive producer ever meets an elusive channel executive. I have a vivid memory of sitting in the sixth-floor boardroom at BBC's Television Centre when we were pitching ideas to the controller of BBC1—ideas that I'd originated, developed, and/or written—when I had a sudden shock of realization. I was still a junior researcher, but here I was sitting in the same room as, arguably, the most powerful and important woman in television, in a building I'd seen every week as a child on one of my favorite after-school TV programs, *Blue Peter*. It seemed inconceivable.

Once you've fallen in love with the drama of development you might choose to follow a career as a commissioning editor, then you'll be in a position to directly influence what people watch on television.

The Benefits of Working in Development—Even if You'd Rather Not

If you are a committed program-maker, there are still plenty of benefits to spending some time learning the craft of development. Spending time in development is a good opportunity to make long-lasting connections; it's never a bad thing to know people who know channel executives. You'll be one step closer to the decision-maker if you ever want to pitch your own ideas, and will be first to know when there are new production jobs coming up.

Arrive at an interview with an independent production company or broadcaster with proof that you know how to develop ideas and you'll stand out. "If you've not got any credits but lots of ideas you can pitch your idea to the company's managing director or CEO and say, 'Look, I've got access to this particular community or story,' and then you and that idea come together, as a package," says an experienced development producer. If the company likes your idea they will probably want to bring you into their development team to work it up more until it's pitch ready. Once you've got your first commission under your belt you become much more valuable: if you've had one good idea it's likely you'll have more, so any sane employer will want to hire you and hold on to you.

So, whether you are a fair-weather or dedicated developer, you now know how the system works as well as anyone and better than most. Keep your eyes open for new ideas, watch TV, cultivate your contacts, write like a copywriter, and pitch with passion. Do all that and you'll need only one more thing: good luck!

Master Class 12

Get the Greenlight

1. If your pitch went well, celebrate! Then make sure you are in a good position to negotiate a good deal by exploring the resources below.

2. If the channel showed some interest but was non-committal, respond to their suggestions, address their concerns, rework your proposal, and get it back to them fast. Don't give them time to go cold on the idea.

3. If they passed on the idea, take a step back and ask yourself whether you still believe in the idea: if not, kill it and move on to something else.

4. If you believe your idea has legs, work out if there is somewhere else you could take it and start the whole process again.

5. Repeat.

Explore More

The Age of Stupid website provides a budget breakdown of their £485K feature documentary http://www.ageofstupid.net/budgets.

Scribd provides a downloadable documentary budget template http://www.scribd.com/doc/8710684/Documentary-Budget-Format.

CableReady: US-based development, distribution, and representation company that will broker deals between you and a production company or TV channel. They work with channels, production companies, and individual producers anywhere in the world http://www.cableready.net/.

cmbusinessaffairs.tv: UK-based business affairs consultancy that works on a pre-agreed hourly rate. Advises on development and production including drafting and vetting of contracts http://www.cmbusinessaffairs.tv/index.html.

Rights TV: UK consultancy offering business affairs advice to people in the TV industry, including guidance on development deals, co-production agreements, writer's rights, and licensing deals. They provide a free initial consultation and a flexible fee structure http://www.rights.tv/index.html.

Mark Litwak: *Dealmaking in the Film and Television Industry: From Negotiation to Final Contracts*
Written by a US entertainment attorney and professor of entertainment and copyright law but aimed at professional and aspiring film and TV producers.

Linda Stradling: *Production Management for TV and Film*
An experienced production manager's guide to running a production, including budgeting and scheduling. Contains handy website references to sample budgets and other paperwork.

Reality Check—Idea Tick List

Work through this checklist to check if your idea is ready to pitch:

1. Can it be pitched in a sentence? ☐

2. Is there a clear story? ☐

3. Can you describe your characters? ☐

4. Can it be cast? ☐

5. Do you have exclusive access? ☐

6. Is there an authentic narrative? ☐

7. Is there a clear format? ☐

8. Who is the onscreen talent? ☐

9. Is there scope for multiplatform content? ☐

10. Is there potential for international format sales? ☐

11. Does it avoid being style over substance? ☐

12. Does it reveal something new? ☐

13. Is it timely and relevant? ☐

14. Does it avoid cliché? ☐

15. Can it be visualized from a paper proposal or do you need a pitch tape? ☐

16 Can the program be made in the necessary time frame? ☐

17. Does it fit the channel's brief? ☐

18. What's the budget? ☐

Sample Budget Template*

This template covers the main categories you might need to include in your budget. Budgets are referred to in terms of "per hour" or "per 30'" rather than total series budget. For example a 13x60' series that costs £1 million in total will have a budget of approximately £77K per hour.

Title	
Program Code	Episodes x Duration
CORE PROJECT COSTS	**0.00**
Core Team Salaries	0.00
Contingencies	0.00
Production Fee	0.00
Completion Guarantees	0.00
FILM PRODUCTION COSTS	**0.00**
Development – Rights/Options Payments – Writer's Fee – Research 	 0.00
Producer/Director – Executive Producer – Series Producer – Producer/Director 1 – Producer/Director 2 – Edit Producer – Assistant Producer 	 0.00

*Based on a UK production budget.

Artists – Artists – Overseas Artists/Extras etc. – Stand-ins, Doubles, Stuntmen – Footsteps and Effects – Tutor/Chaperones	0.00
Presenters/Interviewees – Presenters – Interviewees – Voiceover Artists	0.00
Production Unit Salaries – Production Executive – Production Manager – Production Co-ordinator 1 – Runner – Production Accountant – Accounts Assistant – Researcher – Loggers	0.00
Crew—Camera – Lighting Director – Lighting Cameraman – Camera Operator – Assistant Camera – Vision Mixer	0.00
Crew—Sound – Sound Recordist – Boom Operator – Sound Assitant – Sound Supervisor – Sound Engineer	0.00

Crew—Lighting – Gaffer – Electrician – Generator Operator	0.00
Art Department – Set Designer – Model Maker	0.00
Crew—Wardrobe/Make-up/Hair	0.00
Crew—Editing – Offline Editor – Online Editor – Dubbing Editor – Assistants	0.00
Crew—Second Unit	0.00
Salary and Wage-related Overheads – Holiday Credits – Employers National Insurance—Crew – Employers National Insurance—Artists	0.00
Materials—Art Department – Sets – Construction Materials – Props—Hired – Props—Purchased – Action Props – Consumables	0.00

Materials—Wardrobe/Make-up/Hair – Wardrobe Costumes—Hired – Wardrobe Costumes—Purchased – Repair and Cleaning Costs – Wardrobe Storage – Make-up Materials – Hair Materials – Hair Consumables – Wigs	0.00
Production Equipment – Camera Equipment – Consumables – Grip Equipment – Sound Equipment – Lighting Equipment – Editing Equipment – Autocue	0.00
Facility Package – Camera Crew/Equipment – Sound Crew/Equipment – Lighting Crew/Equipment – Editing Facilities – Design Package	0.00
Studios/Outside Broadcasts – Studios Fee – Recording Studios – OB Unit – Sound Mobile – Portable Single Camera – Studio Crew Costs	0.00

Other Production Facilities – Rehearsal Room – Location Offices – Location Fees – Gratuities – Security and Police – Location Equipment	
	0.00
Film/Tape Stock – Film Stock – Shooting Tapes – Offline Tapes – Online Tapes – Viewing Copies – Sound Stock – Dubbing – Effects Stock – Masters—Vision – Masters—Sound – Safety/Delivery Copies	
	0.00
Post-production—Tape – Tape Transfers – Offline Editing – Online Editing – Caption Generator – Special Effects – Lay Off – Audio Dubbing incl. Sound Mix – Lay Back – Telecine – Autoconform	
	0.00
Archive Material – Viewing Costs – Search Fees	

– Processing and Transfer – Royalties—Film and Tape Archive – Stills Archive – Sound Archive	
	0.00
Rostrum/Graphics – Rostrum – Graphics – Titles and Credits	
	0.00
Music (Copyright/Performance) – Composer – Musicians – Musical Director – Hire of Music – Music Remixing and Editing	
	0.00
OVERHEADS	**0.00**
Travel/Transport – Recce/Pre-production Costs – Production Costs – Artists – Equipment – Freight – Carnets and Agent Fees – Excess Baggage – Visas – Inoculations – Petrol and Parking – Courier Bikes and Cabs – Set Storage/Disposal – Set Transport	
	0.00
Hotel/Living – Pre-production and Recce Costs – Crew Accommodation	

– Artists' Accommodation – Location Catering – Living Allowances – Meal Allowances—Crew – Meal Allowances—Artists – Gratuities – Hospitality – Laundry	0.00
Other Production Costs – Transcription – Post-production Scripts – Publicity Stills	0.00
Insurance/Finance/Legal	0.00
Production Overheads – Office Rent – Rates – Power/Lighting/Heating – Printing and Stationery – Postage – Photocopying and Computers	0.00
Total	**0.00**

Channel Budget Guide

A channel's program budgets vary depending on program genre and timeslot; and each proposal is assessed according to its scale and ambition, so these figures are only a rough guide to ballpark budgets. Check with individual channel executives to find out what they are currently paying.

Selected UK Channels

Channel	Genre	Cost
BBC1	Entertainment	£200K–£280K per hour
BBC2/BBC4	Arts	£80K–£250K per 60'
BBC3	Factual	£130K–£180K per 60'
BBC Multiplatform	Science and Natural History; History, Current Affairs, BBC3 Factual, Religion; Factual, Documentaries, and Arts	£15K–350K depending on scope of project £20K–£200K £10K–£250K
ITV1	Daytime Factual	£30K–£50K per 60' Up to £250K per 60'
ITV2/ITV3/ITV4	Factual/Entertainment	£10K–£200K per 60'
Channel 4	Daytime Science Documentaries *Cutting Edge* strand	£50K per 60' £150K–£160K per 60' £100K–£200K per 60' £75K–£200K per 60'
Five	Factual Factual Entertainment	£80K–£90K per 60' £30K–£100K
National Geographic UK	Factual/Specialist Factual	£35K–65K per 60'

History	History	£30K–£35K per 60'
Virgin 1	Factual Entertainment	£110K per 60'
Sky 1	Factual; Features	£70K–£150K per 60' £70K–£130K per 60'
Sky Arts	Arts	Up to £50K per 60'
Home	Features and Formats	Up to £50K per 60'
Current.tv	Documentary	£300–£1K per 8' £5K per 30' £8K per 60'

Selected US Channels

Channel	Genre	Cost
Broadcast Networks – ABC – CBS – NBC – FOX	Entertainment Reality	Low-cost programming $250K–$500K per 60' Primetime programming $500K+ per 60'
Cable Channels – Bravo – TLC – Oxygen – Discovery	Documentary Reality Formats	$100K–$250K per 30' $250K–$500K per 60'
Small Cable Channels – Fox Reality – DIY Channel – HGTV	Formats	$65K–$100K per 30' $100K–$250K per 60'

Glossary

All definitions related to their common use in relation to development and commissioning; some words have different meanings in other contexts. Some terms are specific to the UK or the US (as indicated), others are used interchangeably and American usage is gradually creeping into the vocabulary of UK channel executives. To avoid misunderstandings ask for clarification during any business dealings.

Term	Main Use	Meaning
360-degree Content		Shorthand for program content that can be accessed via a number of devices e.g. TV, online, mobile phone etc.
AFP		Advertiser-funded programming (as opposed to channel-funded).
A.I. (Appreciation Index)		A way of measuring how much the audience enjoyed a program measured on scale of 1–100 (the higher the number, the greater the enjoyment).
Alternative Programming	USA	Nonscripted/factual programming. Often used interchangeably with Original and Reality Programming.
Audience Ratings		Measurement of how many people watch a program, measured in millions and broken down into different demographics e.g. 18–34 yrs or 25–54 yrs. Also measured in increments of fifteen minutes throughout the program so producers know if/when viewers switch over.
Back End		Refers to the potential income from selling a format globally, and related books, DVDs, games, toys etc.

Term	Main Use	Meaning
BBC Red Button	UK	An interactive application that allows digital TV viewers to choose a different view or extra content than that shown in the main program. For example, viewers of Wimbledon Tennis Championships can choose which court to watch.
Broadcaster		Large channel that caters to a broad demographic e.g. ABC, NBC, CBS, and Fox in the US and BBC1, BBC2, ITV1, Channel 4, and Five in the UK. *See also*: Terrestrial.
Cable Channel		Small, niche channel that caters to a specific demographic or interest group. *See also*: Digital Channel and Satellite Channel.
Channel Brief		A channel's wishlist of the kind of programs they want to commission over the coming year.
Channel Controller	UK	The executive in ultimate charge of a TV channel; usually has the final say on which programs are commissioned. *See also*: GM.
Codec		Software that compresses and decompresses digital video and/or audio, which allows you to upload material to video sharing sites.
Commercial Broadcaster		A TV channel that relies on income from advertisers for its income and program budgets.
Commission		When a channel agrees to the editorial content and budget of a proposed program and formally agrees that production can begin, the program is said to be commissioned. *See also*: Greenlight.

Term	Main Use	Meaning
Commissioner/ Commissioning Executive	UK	The person responsible for taking pitches from producers and deciding which ideas to take forward, and ultimately buy.
Content		New word for programming: usually used to mean multiplatform material but is increasingly used in relation to TV.
Co-production		When two or more channels contribute part of a larger program budget, usually in return for exclusive rights to show the program in their country.
Cross-platform		Content that can be accessed via different platforms e.g. TV, radio, online, iPod etc.
Daytime		Programming broadcast between the hours of 9AM–6PM.
Demo		A 2–3-minute sequence designed to sell a program concept. *See also*: Tape, Sizzle Reel, Reel, Taster, *and* Teaser.
Development Executive	UK	Senior development producer at a TV production company; usually supervises a development team.
Development Executive	USA	Channel executive who issues briefs, receives pitches, and decides which ideas to progress. May also supervise the making of commissioned programs. *See also*: Director/ VP/SVP/EVP Development.
Development Producer		Person who originates and develops and pitches new TV ideas. *See also*: Producer.
Digital Agency		A production company specializing in generating, developing, and making

Term	Main Use	Meaning
		content intended to be viewed online or via mobile devices such as mobile phone or MP3 player such as the iPod.
Digital Channel		Shorthand for smaller, niche channel that caters to a specific demographic or subject area, e.g. food or history. (Digital also refers to programming received via a digital rather than analog signal.) *See also*: Cable Channel *and* Satellite Channel.
Digital Producer		A content producer specializing in generating, developing, and making online/mobile content.
Director		Person who decides on the look of a program, plans the shoot and, on location, directs the cameraperson to get the necessary shots.
Director/ Development	USA	Junior channel executive, who receives pitches and decides which ideas to progress.
Early Peak		A scheduling term for early evening, usually 6PM–8PM. *See also*: Shoulder Peak.
EPG (electronic program guide)		The onscreen TV guide that viewers scroll through using their remote control.
Episodic Narrative		A story line that starts and finishes in one single episode.
EVP/Development USA		Executive Vice President. Channel executive who issues briefs, receives pitches, and decides which ideas to progress. May also supervise the making of commissioned programs. *See also*: Director/VP/SVP/EVP Development.

Term	Main Use	Meaning
Executive Producers		Senior producers who supervise the production of a program or series; usually oversee several projects at once.
Factual	UK	Nonscripted TV programming, that favors information over entertainment although there is often an overlap.
Factual Entertainment	UK	Nonscripted, but often formatted, programming with entertainment at its heart. Programs take place in the real world and tackle universal topics—fashion, food, property—but casting and/or time are controlled by the production team in order to produce the greatest human drama or transformation within the shortest time possible.
Features and Formats	UK	Genre of programs that includes formats, magazine programs, and entertainment-heavy factual programs.
First Look		A deal whereby a producer agrees to show his ideas to a production company, channel, or distributor to give them first refusal.
Format Bible		A detailed production manual for a formatted program that allows it to be sold around the world and dictates how it can be faithfully reproduced in different countries without losing its integrity and brand values.
Formats		Programs that are constructed in such a way that the same thing happens from week to week. The format rather than the content drives the narrative.

Term	Main Use	Meaning
Fringe		Early evening in the TV schedule. *See also*: Shoulder Peak and Early Peak.
GM	USA	General Manager—the executive in ultimate charge of a TV channel; usually has the final say on which programs are commissioned. *See also*: Channel Controller.
Greenlight		When a channel agrees to the editorial content and budget of a proposed program and formally agrees that production can begin. *See also*: Commission.
HD		High-definition footage (transmitted on an HD TV) gives a crystal-clear image. Many channels now require producers to deliver their programs in HD.
Host	USA	Person who presents a program, introduces and interviews guests, takes the viewer on a journey, or shares their expertise. *See also*: Presenter and Talent.
Independent Filmmaker		Producer/directors who produce "authored" one-off documentary films, raising the money from various grants and foundations; as opposed to the jobbing director/producer who works as a gun for hire, making programs for independent production companies or in-house channel production departments.
Independent Production Company		A company that makes content for several clients, including TV channels and corporate clients. Some are one-man bands, others

Term	Main Use	Meaning
		multi-million-pound businesses with offices around the world (known as super-indies).
In the Room	USA	Anything that happens in a pitch meeting with a channel executive happens "in the room."
Leave Behind	USA	A one-page proposal that a producer might leave with channel executives following a pitch meeting. *See also*: One Sheet.
Logline		A one-line explanation of the idea. *See also*: Strapline *and* Tagline.
MD		Managing Director—the person in charge of an independent production company.
NDA		Non-disclosure agreement—a contract that specifies that a production company cannot discuss an idea with any third party without the consent of the originator of that idea. *See also*: Submission Release.
One Sheet	USA	A one-page proposal that a producer might leave with channel executives following a pitch meeting. *See also*: Leave Behind.
Original Programming	USA	Nonscripted/factual programming. Often used interchangeably with Alternative and Reality Programming.
Overnights		Audience viewing figures from the previous day, expressed in millions of viewers.
Paper Format		A written proposal outlining the details of a TV format that has not yet been made.
Peak	UK	The evening schedule from roughly 8PM onward. *See also* Primetime.

Term	Main Use	Meaning
Pilot		A test program commissioned by a channel to reassure themselves that a format works before they commit to a full series. The pilot might be a non-transmission pilot (for internal channel viewing only) or a transmission pilot, which is broadcast and viewer response scrutinized.
Platform		The place where content can be viewed or accessed e.g. TV, online, MP3 player.
Presenter	UK	Person who presents a program, introduces and interviews guests, takes the viewer on a journey, or shares their expertise. *See also*: Host *and* Talent.
Primetime	USA	The evening schedule from roughly 8PM onward. *See also* Peak.
Producer		Person who manages a production, decides on the look and narrative of program, and hires directors and researchers to fulfill that vision. Producers are often directors too. *See also*: Development Producer.
Production execs		Catch-all term for executive producers who oversee the making of TV programs, usually several at once. They might be based at an independent production company or work for a channel.
Proposal		A one-page description of the content, look, and feel of a proposed TV program.
PSB		Public service broadcaster—a TV channel that doesn't operate on purely commercial basis, receives public funds, and is required to

Term	Main Use	Meaning
		transmit a certain quota of programming that informs rather than entertains e.g. news, current affairs, science etc. For example, BBC and Channel 4 in the UK and PBS in the USA.
Quarter		TV channels split the year into four quarters when thinking about scheduling (and commissioning) programs: Winter, Spring, Summer, Autumn/Fall. Also known as 1st Q, 2nd Q, 3rd Q, and 4th Q.
Reach		The percentage of potential viewers who actually watched a program.
Reality	UK	Highly formatted entertainment shows that include ordinary people, often in extraordinary situations.
Reality	USA	An umbrella term for everything that isn't scripted or documentary programming.
Reel		A 2–3-minute sequence designed to sell a program concept. *See also*: Tape, Sizzle Reel, Demo, Taster, and Teaser.
Rights		The person, or company, who owns the rights to a program (intellectual property) has the right to exploit (sell) it around the world. When a channel commission a program they retain the exclusive rights to transmit that program for a number or times/years in a specified country or territory. A distributor buys the rights to a program in order to sell it around the world.
Rushes		Raw footage shot on location from which finished programs are edited.

Term	Main Use	Meaning
Satellite Channel		Small niche channel that caters to a specific demographic or interest group. *See also*: Cable Channel *and* Digital Channel.
Season	UK	A series of separate programs around a similar subject grouped together to make more impact in the schedule. E.g. BBC4 runs regular seasons such as: Japan Season, SciFi Season, and Fatherhood Season.
Season	USA	Series, e.g. *Deadliest Catch* Season 1 and *Wife Swap* Season 9.
Secondary Development		If a channel is interested in an idea but it will be expensive to do the necessary research in order to turn it into a commissionable proposition the channel might agree to fund some secondary development. This money might be used to fund a recce or to find talent.
Shoulder Peak		A scheduling term for early evening, usually 6PM–8PM. *See also*: Early Peak.
Showrunner	USA	The person in overall charge of a production—responsible for the look of the show, the budget, and hiring and firing staff.
Sizzle Reel	USA	A 2–3-minute sequence designed to sell a program concept. *See also*: Tape, Reel, Demo, Taster, *and* Teaser.
Specialist Factual	UK	Programming that falls into one of the following categories: Science, History, Art, Religion, Natural History (and sometimes Business).

Term	Main Use	Meaning
Strapline		A one-line explanation of the idea. *See also*: Logline *and* Tagline.
Stripped		A scheduling term that means a program will be transmitted on consecutive nights instead of consecutive weeks.
Submission Release		A contract that a channel or independent production company usually requires the unknown originator of an idea to sign before they will accept an unsolicited idea for consideration. *See also*: NDA.
SVP/ Development	USA	Senior Vice President. Channel executive who issues briefs, receives pitches, and decides which ideas to progress. *See also*: Director/ VP/EVP Development.
Tagline		A one-line explanation of the idea. *See also*: Strapline *and* Logline.
Talent		General term for people who appear onscreen in a major and recurrent role. *See also*: Presenter *and* Host.
Tape		As in: "Do you have anything on tape?" A 2–3-minute sequence designed to sell a program concept. *See also*: Reel, Sizzle Reel, Demo, Taster, *and* Teaser.
Taster		A 2–3-minute sequence designed to sell a program concept. *See also*: Tape, Sizzle Reel, Demo, Reel, *and* Teaser.
Teaser		A 2–3-minute sequence designed to sell a program concept. *See also*: Tape, Sizzle Reel, Demo, Taster, *and* Reel.

Term	Main Use	Meaning
Terrestrial	UK	The term used for the big five UK channels: BBC1, BBC2, ITV1, Channel 4, and Five. *See also*: Broadcaster.
Treatment		A 5–10-page detailed outline of a proposed TV program or series, including the narrative arc or format points. Sometimes used interchangeably with Proposal.
Twin Tick		System whereby two channel executives have to agree to commission a program before it is given the greenlight, usually a commissioning/development executive and the head of the channel.
TX		Transmission.
Voiceover		A scripted narration that describes what's happening onscreen or gives additional essential information in order to move the story along. Usually recorded after the program has been edited.
VP/Development	USA	Vice President. Channel executive who receives pitches and decides which ideas to progress. *See also*: Director/SVP/EVP Development.
Watershed	UK	The time—9PM—before which content containing sex, violence, or profanity may not be broadcast.

End Notes

Introduction

1   "fewer than one in one hundred": TRC Media, "Inside the Commissioners," Full Report, 2003, p. 27.

2: Do You Have What It Takes?

17   "When Mark Burnett": Biography constructed from accounts in Burnett, Mark, *Dare to Succeed*, Hyperion, 2001; Burnett, Mark, *Jump In!*, Ballantine Books, 2005; Bazalgette, Peter, *Billion Dollar Game*, Time Warner Books, 2005, pp. 91–2; Interview with Katie Couric, Today, NBC, January 25, 2005 http://www.bing.com/videos/watch/video/mark-burnett-on-jump-in/6dhs67i.

24   "New ideas are usually": Bazalgette, Peter, *Billion Dollar Game*, Time Warner Books, 2005, p. 1.

27   "Programs such as *Survivor*": Littleton, Cynthia, "Dialogue: Producer Mark Burnett," *The Hollywood Reporter*, May 26, 2004 http://www.hollywoodreporter.com/hr/search/article_display.jsp?vnu_content_id=1000 518943.

28   "One commissioner received": "Inside the Commissioners: Full Report," Research Centre for TV and Interactivity, 2002, p. 23.

3: Understanding the TV Landscape

34   "*Why isn't there anything*": Allman, Kevin, *TV Turkeys*, Perigree Books, 1987, p. 15.

34   "In 1982": Narrative constructed from telephone interview with David Pritchard and Pritchard, David, *Shooting the Cook*, Fourth Estate, 2009.

35   "Commissioning used to be": "Inside the Commissioners: Executive Summary," Research Centre for TV and Interactivity, 2002, p. 6.

35   "The whole point of the television industry": Allman, Kevin, *TV Turkeys*, Perigree Books, 1987, p. 15.

35   "Fifty years ago": Bianco, Anthony, "The Vanishing Mass Market," *Businessweek*, July 12, 2004, p. 62, cited in Jenkins, Henry, *Convergence Culture*, New York University Press, 2006, p. 66.

36   "In 1992 MTV": Bazalgette, Peter, *Billion Dollar Game*, Time Warner Books, 2005, p. 41.

37   "spend millions of dollars": Allman, Kevin, *TV Turkeys*, Perigree Books, 1987, p. 16.

37   "this is a culture": Julian Bellamy, Head of Programmes, Channel 4, Keynote Speech, Televisual Intelligent Factual Festival, July 14, 2009.

38   "relative costs": Brown, Maggie, *A Licence to Be Different: The Story of Channel 4*, BFI, 2007, p. 254.

39   "not looking for": Beckwith, Harry, *Selling the Invisible*, Warner Books, 1997, p. 97.

43   "David Broome": Malcom, Shawna, "Audiences Relate to NBC's 'Loser,'" *Variety*, February 9, 2009 http://www.variety.com/article/VR1117999883.html?categoryid=3547&cs=1.

43   "In the simplest": Bayles, David and Orland, Ted, *Art & Fear*, Image Continuum, 2009, pp. 40–1.

46   "It's best not to": Carter, Bill, *Desperate Networks*, Doubleday, 2006, p. 95.

46   "The only feedback": TRC Media, "Inside the Commissioners," Executive Summary, 2003, p. 4.

49   "You talk to the commissioners": Ridley, Beth, "The Art of Television," Nouse, May 12, 2009 http://www.nouse.co.uk/2009/05/12/the-art-of-television/.

49   "Programs tend to be": TRC Media, "Inside the Commissioners," Executive Summary, 2003, p. 6.

50   "mocking up the front covers": "Voyeur TV," *Time* cover, June 26, 2000 http://www.time.com/time/covers/0,16641,1101000626,00.html.

52   "getting people to think": Julian Bellamy, Head of Programs, Channel 4, Keynote Speech, Intelligent Factual Festival, 14 July, 2009.

4: Generating Ideas

57 "In 2000, ex-advertising": Video interview with Bertram van Munster, Buddy TV, October 28, 2007 http://www.buddytv.com/articles/the-amazing-race/exclusive-interview-bertram-va-13082.aspx, retrieved August 2009.

57 "Stephen Lambert's wife": Flett, Kathryn, "The Great Pretender," *Observer,* January 25, 2004.

58 "she had an insight": Wieners, Brad, "Adventure Travel 2006: Amazing Travel Tips," *National Geographic* http://www.nationalgeographic.com/adventure/0511/whats_new/amazing_race.html.

58 "Good story ideas": King, Stephen, *On Writing,* Hodder & Stoughton, 2001, p. 29.

58 "in a survey compiled by the Research Centre": TRC Media, "Risky Business: Inside the Indies," Executive Summary, 2002, p. 6.

73 "*Wife Swap* was originally": Leonard, Tom, "TV Wife Swap Creator Is Staying Loyal," *Telegraph,* November 27, 2003 http://www.telegraph.co.uk/news/uknews/1447857/TV-Wife-Swap-creator-is-staying-loyal.html.

73 "Your imagination": Osborn, Alex F., *Applied Imagination,* Charles Scribner's Sons, 1957, p. 62.

77 "The ceramics teacher": Bayles, David and Orland, Ted, *Art & Fear,* Image Continuum, 2009, p. 29.

78 "The first third": Tharp, Twyla, *The Creative Habit,* Simon & Schuster, 2003, p. 191.

80 "Likewise, *Rock School*": Sharp, Elsa, *How to Get a Job in Television,* A&C Black, 2009, p. 43.

81 "said that they thought": TRC Media, "Inside the Commissioners," Full Report, 2003, p. 18.

84 "Twyla Tharp collects": Tharp, Twyla, *The Creative Habit,* Simon & Schuster, 2003, p. 80.

5: Developing an Idea

90   "On a drizzly Thursday": narrative constructed from account in Bazalgette, Peter, *Billion Dollar Game*, Time Warner Books, 2005, pp. 73-7, 92-4, 98-101, 110-17, 125-9.

92   "totally isolated": Bazalgette, Peter, *Billion Dollar Game*, Time Warner Books, 2005, pp. 99-100.

92   "Big Brother is watching": Bazalgette, Peter, *Billion Dollar Game*, Time Warner Books, 2005, pp. 99-100.

92   "the rats-in-a-cage": Bazalgette, Peter, *Billion Dollar Game*, Time Warner Books, 2005, p. 101.

93   "Elvis": Lewis, Jane, Profile: Peter Bazalgette, *MoneyWeek*, January 27, 2007 http://www.moneyweek.com/news-and-charts/profile-peter-bazalgette. aspx.

94   "When Andrew Jerecki": from *"Capturing the Friedmans*—Director Andrew Jarecki Interview" at Sundance 2004 http://www.spike.com/video/ capturing-friedmans/2532437.

95   "I like to twist": Carter, Bill, *Desperate Networks*, Doubleday, 2006, p. 100.

95   "Some of his ideas": Carter, Bill, *Desperate Networks*, Doubleday, 2006, p. 100.

96   "*Broadcast* announced that": Parker, Robin, "C4 to Stage Plane Crash," *Broadcast*, November 12, 2009 http://www.broadcastnow.co.uk/ 5008105.article.

107   "In his book *Applied Imagination*": Osborn, Alex F., *Applied Imagination*, Charles Scribner's Sons, 1957, pp. 261-317.

110   "fantastic ideas should drive": Burns, Michael, "Impossible Picture," *Broadcast*, August 29, 2008, p. 23.

112   "Robert Thirkell's lead": Thirkell, Robert, Chapter 1—Character, Trouble-shooter TV http://www.robertthirkell.com/C%20%0haracter.html.

120 "There is a very fine line": Fey, Christoph, *Trading TV Formats*, European Broadcasting Union, p. 61.

120 "Caution may demand": Fey, Christoph, *Trading TV Formats*, European Broadcasting Union, p. 61.

120 "In principle, one": Fey, Christoph, *Trading TV Formats*, European Broadcasting Union, p. 12.

120 "the original combination": *Barris/Fraser Enterprises v Goodson-Todman Enterprises*, 1988, quoted in Fey, Christoph, *Trading TV Formats*, European Broadcasting Union, p. 52.

120 "ideas themselves cannot": Fey, Christoph, *Trading TV Formats*, European Broadcasting Union, p. 53.

120 "originality can be expressed in": Fey, Christoph, *Trading TV Formats*, European Broadcasting Union, p. 73.

121 "Castaway TV": Fey, Christoph, *Trading TV Formats*, European Broadcasting Union, pp. 93–5.

121 "Endemol, the producers": Fey, Christoph, *Trading TV Formats*, European Broadcasting Union, p. 106.

121 "CBS, the channel": Fey, Christoph, *Trading TV Formats*, European Broadcasting Union, p. 111.

121 "CBS took Fox": Fey, Christoph, *Trading TV Formats*, European Broadcasting Union, p. 117.

121 "RDF Media took": Fey, Christoph, *Trading TV Formats*, European Broadcasting Union, pp. 142–3.

121 "the court determined": Fey, Christoph, *Trading TV Formats*, European Broadcasting Union, p. 113.

125 "a Texan man": Fey, Christoph, *Trading TV Formats*, European Broadcasting Union, pp. 146–8.

125   "there are some basic things": list collated from Fey, Christoph, *Trading TV Formats*, European Broadcasting Union, p. 17; Alliance for the Protection of Copyright, *The APC Code of Practice*, 2009; and email correspondence with Iain Walmsley, Consultant, Rights TV, January 13, 2010.

127   "Here is a paragraph": email correspondence with Iain Walmsley, Consultant, Rights TV, January 13, 2010.

128   "Don't worry": Weiss, Eric A., *A Computer Science Reader: Selections from Abacus*, Springer, 1988, p. 404.

6: Considering Multiplatform Content

133   "A Californian supply": narrative constructed from Jenkins, Henry, *Convergence Culture*, New York University Press, 2006, pp. 25–58.

135   "SurvivorSucks.com": Quantcast: SurvivorSucks http://www.quantcast.com/survivorsucks.com.

136   "Elsa Sharp says that": Sharp, Elsa, *How to Get a Job in Television*, A&C Black, 2009, pp. 254–5.

151   "Matt Locke": Kiss, Jemima, "Channel 4 Plans 'Jackass' Sex Education," *Guardian*, April 29, 2008.

7: Writing a Killer Proposal

161   "Daisy Goodwin": Ben Frow Interview, *Media Guardian*, March 31, 2003.

161   "Producers spent six months": Clarke, Steve, "How to Pitch," RTS Futures, November 26, 2007 http://www.rtsfutures.org.uk/show_news_stories/45.

162   "a list of 'signature titles'": Kennedy, Reess, "Deadliest Blog Entry," July 27, 2009 http://www.cableu.tv/cuconfidential/.

164   "Following two feuding": quote from proposal courtesy of Libby Overton.

164   "How can we account": Cialdini, Robert B., "What's the Best Secret Device for Engaging Student Interest? The Answer Is in the Title," *Journal of Social and Clinical Psychology* 24 (2005): 22–9, quoted in Heath, Chip and Heath, Dan, *Made to Stick*, Random House, 2007, p. 81. *Drugged Culture* proposal courtesy of Barry J. Gibb.

167 "*Writing is easy*": Fowler, Gene, quoted in Bayles, David and Orland, Ted, *Art & Fear*, Image Continuum, 2009, Preface.

168 "If it's this hard": Beckwith, Harry, *Selling the Invisible*, Warner Books, 1997, p. 13.

8: Finding and Keeping Talent

178 "In February, 2003": narrative constructed from accounts in Burnett, Mark, *Jump In!*, Ballantine Books, 2005, pp. 189–96; and Carter, Bill, *Desperate Networks*, Doubleday, 2006, pp. 199–200.

178 "need a hit of oxygen": McIver, Meredith, "Mr. Trump's Office," The Trump Blog, August 9, 2007 http://www.trumpuniversity.com/blog/post/2007/08/mr-trumps-office.cfm.

180 "The minute I viewed": Burnett, Mark, *Dare to Succeed*, Hyperion, 2001, p. 140.

183 "He must kowtow": Sewell, Brian, "Anguish of the TV Presenter," *Evening Standard*, July 1, 2003 http://www.thisislondon.co.uk/news/article-5548341-details/Anguish+of+the+TV+presenter/article.do.

183 "I said no to TV": Grylls, Bear, "This Much I Know," *Observer Magazine*, November 30, 2008, p. 10.

195 "Acquired Situational Narcissism": Kirwan-Taylor, "I Love Me," *The Times*, October 6, 2005.

9: The Pitch Tape

204 "an indoor sports hall": Directors: Henry Alex Rubin, Dana Adam Shapiro, *Murderball*, 2005.

207 "Delissa had taken": Lipscomb, Georgina, "A Pitch Is Worth 1000 Words," *Broadcast*, April 29, 2006 http://www.broadcastnow.co.uk/news/multi-platform/news/indie-business-a-pitch-is-worth-1000-words/1190352.article.

210 "taster tapes where": Clarke, Steve, "How to Pitch," RTS Futures, November 26, 2007 http://www.rtsfutures.org.uk/show_news_stories/45.

220 "I told them that": Lipscomb, Georgina, "A Pitch Is Worth 1000 Words," *Broadcast*, April 29, 2006 http://www.broadcastnow.co.uk/news/multi-platform/news/indie-business-a-pitch-is-worth-1000-words/1190352. article.

221 "is a short [film] without an ending": Dean, Carole Lee, *The Art of Film Funding*, Michael Wiese Productions, 2007, p. 123.

222 "The scenes need to show": Dean, Carole Lee, *The Art of Film Funding*, Michael Wiese Productions, 2007, p. 124.

222 "It is obligatory": Dean, Carole Lee, *The Art of Film Funding*, Michael Wiese Productions, 2007, p. 124.

222 "If a scene was that good": Dean, Carole Lee, *The Art of Film Funding*, Michael Wiese Productions, 2007, p. 122.

222 "Fernanda Rossi outlines": Rossi, Fernada, *Trailer Mechanics*, Magafilms, 2005, p. 109.

10: The Pitch

234 "We get so many ideas": Harrison, Cassian, specialist factual commissioning executive, BBC, Televisual Intelligent Factual Festival, July 14, 2009.

237 "According to a study": Brown, Paul B. and Davis, Alison, *Your Attention Please*, Adams Media, 2006, p. 125.

237 "He always carried": Heath, Chip and Heath, Dan, *Made to Stick*, Random House, 2007, p. 142.

238 "he persuaded a Russian admiral": "Obituary: Philip Jones," *The Times*, July 31, 2009, p. 60.

239 "A production company pitching": "The Art of Pitching—Perfect Pitch," *Broadcast*, May 10, 2002 http://www.broadcastnow.co.uk/news/multi-platform/news/the-art-of-pitching-perfect-pitch/1142880.article.

239 "Lorraine Heggessey": Clarke, Steve, "How to Pitch," RTS Futures, November 26, 2007 http://www.rtsfutures.org.uk/show_news_stories/45.

240 "One death": "U.S. Annual Average of Animal-Related Fatalities During the 1990s," Florida Museum of Natural History http://www.flmnh.ufl.edu/fish/sharks/attacks/relariskanimal.htm.

242 *"Don't use jargon"*: Hauge, Michael, *Selling Your Story in 60 Seconds*, Michael Wiese Productions, 2006, p. 27.

242 *"Avoid hype"*: Hauge, Michael, *Selling Your Story in 60 Seconds*, Michael Wiese Productions, 2006, p. 28.

11: Alternative Sources of Funding

258 "In 2002, Franny Armstrong": narrative constructed from *The Making of The Age of Stupid*, *Age of Stupid*: A Masterclass with Franny Armstrong at Sheffield Doc/Fest November 7, 2009, blog entries on http://www.ageofstupid.net/making_of_doc and email correspondence dated January 27, 2010.

258 "The talk was boring": Armstrong, Franny, "A Film About Oil," June 26, 2002 http://www.ageofstupid.net/diaries/a_film_about_oil.

258 "I went and gave him": Armstrong, Franny, "Signed Up John Battsek Today," May 20, 2004 http://www.ageofstupid.net/diaries/signed_up_john_battsek_today.

259 "I realized what a powerful": Kuc, Kamila and Vickova, Kate, "Franny Armstrong Interview," London International Documentary Festival, 2009 http://www.lidf.co.uk/lidf09/conversations/franny-armstrong-interview/.

259 "It is so, so much harder": Armstrong, Franny, "17,500 Quid in the Kitty," December 14, 2004 http://www.ageofstupid.net/diaries/signed_up_john_battsek_today.

260 "If you're trying to get": Ivan, Sophie, "Birds Eye View: Franny Armstrong," Little White Lies http://www.littlewhitelies.co.uk/interviews/birds-eye-view-franny-armstrong.

264 "no one will do business": "Tips for Filmmakers: MIPTV & MIPCOM," Australian Film Commission, December 2003 http://www.afc.gov.au/downloads/fmo/mipcommiptv.pdf\.

271   "So, here's the drill": White, Chris, "Speed Pitching at the Realscreen Summit," January 31, 2008 http://www.pbs.org/pov/blog/2008/01/speed_pitching_at_the_realscre_1.html.

12: Getting the Greenlight
287   "fix your messengers": Beckwith, Harry, *Selling the Invisible*, Warner Books, 1997, p. 237.

292   "you should always seek": Iain Walmsley, Consultant, Rights TV, email correspondence, January 13, 2010.

292   "negotiate a cut of the production fee": Iain Walmsley, Consultant, Rights TV, email correspondence, January 13, 2010.

Appendix: Channel Budget Guide
308   "BBC1": Fry, Andy, "How to Be Lean on Screen," *Broadcast*, June 12, 2009, p. 29.

308   "BBC2/BBC4": Rushton, Katherine, "Mark Bell," *Broadcast*, October 2, 2009, p. 13.

308   "BBC3": Parker, Robin, "Harry Lansdown," *Broadcast*, July 31, 2009, p. 13.

308   "BBC Multiplatform Science and Natural History": "The Commissioners," *Broadcast*, November 20, 2009, p. 17.

308   "BBC Multiplatform": "The Commissioners," *Broadcast*, November 20, 2009, p. 17.

308   "ITV1 Daytime": Fry, Andy, "How to Be Lean on Screen," *Broadcast*, June 12, 2009, p. 29.

308   "ITV1 Factual": Brech, Poppy, "Alison Sharman," *Broadcast*, July 10, 2009, p. 11.

308   "ITV2/ITV3/ITV4": McMahon, Kate, "Zai Bennett," *Broadcast*, September 4, 2009, p. 13.

308   "Channel 4 Daytime": Warner, Helen, "Come Pitch to Me," *Broadcast*, December 11, 2009, p. 17.

308 "Channel 4 Science": Parker, Robin, "David Glover," *Broadcast*, August 21, 2009, p. 13.

308 "Channel 4 Documentaries": Parker, Robin, "Making Docs Outside the Box," *Broadcast*, October 30, 2009, p. 15.

308 "Channel 4 *Cutting Edge*": Brech, Poppy, "Mark Raphael," *Broadcast*, July 17, 2009, p. 13.

308 "Five Factual": Andrew O'Connell, Commissioning Editor, Factual, Commissioning Index http://tci.bradcastnow.co.uk/commissioning-editors/72.

308 "Five Factual Entertainment": Steve Gowans, Head of Factual Entertainment and Acting Head of Features, Commissioning Index http://tci.broadcastnow.co.uk/commissioning-editors/36.

308 "National Geographic UK": Shepherd, Robert, "Simon Bohrsmann, National Geographic UK," *Broadcast*, October 23, 2009, p. 12.

309 "History": Shepherd, Robert, "Richard Melman," *Broadcast*, October 16, 2009, p. 13.

309 "Virgin 1": Shepherd, Robert, "Mark Sammon," *Broadcast*, July 24, 2009, p. 13.

309 "Sky 1": Shepherd, Robert, "Stuart Murphy," *Broadcast*, August 28, 2009, p. 13.

309 "Sky Arts": Rouse, Lucy, "The Art of a Good Channel," *Broadcast*, November 13, 2009, p. 15.

309 "Home": Shepherd, Robert, "Establishing a Secure Home," *Broadcast*, November 6, 2009, p. 15.

309 "Selected US Channels": Anderson, Donna Michelle, *The Show Starter*, Movie in a Box Books, 2006, pp. 90–2.

Select Bibliography

Alliance for the Protection of Copyright, the, *The APC Code of Practice*, 2009

Allman, Kevin, *TV Turkeys* (New York: Perigree Books, 1987)

Anderson, Donna Michelle, *The Show Starter* (Sherman Oaks, CA: Movie in a Box Books, 2006)

Arden, Paul, *It's Not How Good You Are, It's How Good You Want to Be* (London: Phaidon, 2007)

—, *Whatever You Think, Think the Opposite* (London: Penguin, 2006)

Bayles, David and Orland, Ted, *Art & Fear* (Santa Cruz, CA: Image Continuum, 2009)

Bazalgette, Peter, *Billion Dollar Game* (London: Time Warner Books, 2005)

Beckwith, Harry, *Selling the Invisible* (New York: Warner Books, 1997)

Bodycome, D., *How to Devise a Game Show*, Version 5 (Adobe), May 2003 www.ukgameshows.com 2002-3

Brown, Paul B. and Davis, Alison, *Your Attention Please* (Avon, MA: Adams Media, 2006)

Brown, Maggie, *A Licence to Be Different: The Story of Channel 4* (London: BFI, 2007)

Burnett, Mark, *Dare to Succeed* (New York: Hyperion, 2001)

—, *Jump In!* (New York: Ballantine Books, 2005)

Campbell, Joseph, *The Hero with a Thousand Faces* (London: Fontana Press, 1993)

Campbell, Joseph and Moyers, Bill D., *The Power of Myth* (New York: Doubleday, 1998)

Carter, Bill, *Desperate Networks* (New York: Doubleday, 2006)

ChillOne, *The Spoiler* (Bloomington, IN: iUniverse, 2003)

Csikszentmihalyi, Mihaly, *Creativity*, (New York: HarperPerennial, 1997)

Davies, Adam P. and Wistreich, N., *The Film Finance Handbook—How to Fund Your Film* (London: Netribution, 2008)

Dean, Carole Lee, *The Art of Film Funding* (Studio City, CA: Michael Wiese Productions, 2007)

Essany, Michael, *Reality Check* (Burlington, MA: Focal Press, 2008)

Fey, Christoph, *Trading TV Formats*: The EBU Guide to the International Television Format Trade (Geneva: European Broadcasting Union, 2007)

Glynne, Andy, *Documentaries: And How to Make Them* (Harpenden: Creative Essentials, 2007)

Hauge, Michael, *Selling Your Story in 60 Seconds* (Studio City, CA: Michael Wiese Productions, 2006)

Heath, Chip and Heath, Dan, *Made to Stick* (New York: Random House, 2007)

Jenkins, Henry, *Convergence Culture* (New York: New York University Press, 2006)

Litwak, M., *Dealmaking in the Film and Television Industry: From Negotiation to Final Contracts* (Los Angeles, CA: Silman-James Press, 2009)

McKee, Robert, *Story* (London: Methuen, 1999)

Marsh, David and Marshall, Nikki, *The Guardian Stylebook* (London: Guardian Books, 2004)

Murray, Susan and Ouellette, Laurie, *Reality TV* (New York: New York University Press, 2009)

Negrino, Tom, *Creating a Presentation in PowerPoint* (Berkeley, CA: Peachpit Press, 2005)

Osborn, Alex F., *Applied Imagination* (New York: Charles Scribner's Sons, 1957)

Potter, Ian, *The Rise and Rise of the Independents* (Isleworth: Guerilla Books, 2008)

Pritchard, David, *Shooting the Cook* (London: Fourth Estate, 2009)

Quinn, Eileen and Counihan, Judy, *The Pitch* (London: Faber & Faber, 2006)

Rossi, Fernada, *Trailer Mechanics* (New York: Magafilms, 2005)

Sharp, Elsa, *How to Get a Job in Television* (London: A&C Black, 2009)

Stradling, Linda, *Production Management for TV and Film* (London: Methuen Drama, 2010)

Strunk, William, Jr. and White, E. B., *The Elements of Style* (New York: Penguin Press, 2005)

Taggart, Caroline (ed.), *Writer's Market UK 2009* (Cincinnati, OH: David & Charles, 2008)

Tharp, Twyla, *The Creative Habit* (London: Simon & Schuster, 2003)

TRC Media, "Inside the Commissioners," Full Report, 2003

—, "Inside the Distributors," Full Report, 2005

—, "Risky Business: Inside the Indies," Full Report, 2002

Trout, Jack, *The Power of Simplicity* (New York: McGraw-Hill, 1999)

Truby, John, *The Anatomy of Story* (London: Faber & Faber, 2008)

Truss, Lynne, *Eats, Shoots & Leaves* (London: Profile Books, 2003)

Vehkalahti, Iikka and Edkins, Don, *Steps by Steps* (Johannesburg: Fanele, 2008)

Vogler, Christopher, *Writer's Journey* (Studio City, CA: Michael Wiese Productions, 3rd edition, 2007)

Von Oech, Roger, *A Whack on the Side of the Head* (Menlo Park, CA: Creative Think, 1992)

Warshawkski, Morrie, *Shaking the Money Tree: How to Get Grants and Donations for Film and Television* (Studio City, CA: Michael Wiese Productions, 2010)

Writers' & Artists' Yearbook 2008 (London: A&C Black, 2007)

Index

ROBERT THIRKELL

PROFESSIONAL MEDIA PRACTICE

C.O.N.F.L.I.C.T.

AN INSIDER'S GUIDE TO STORYTELLING
IN FACTUAL/REALITY TV AND FILM

*" The recipe book of great
television from one of the
best TV makers in the world"*

Jamie Oliver

**£14.99
paperback
9781408129098**

Story structure is a huge weakness for many factual or reality filmmakers
and TV producers, who often concentrate on subject areas and
issues rather than dramatic and memorable narrative. Consequently
programmes fail to attract the audience or win any awards.

In this book, Robert Thirkell, the international consultant known as
'The TV Troubleshooter' and renowned television producer, sets out
a professional toolkit for developing a compelling storyline in factual
and reality programmes and films. Based on his popular international
C.O.N.F.L.I.C.T seminars, it lifts the lids on the making of leading series
such as *Kitchen Nightmares*, *Wife Swap*, *The Apprentice*, *Coastguards*,
Firefighters, *Oprah's Big Give Fat March*, *Jamie's School Dinners* and
When Big Chef Met Little Chef as well as offering insight and advice from
leading filmmakers and TV producers worldwide.

The tips and tools go right the way through the filmmaking process from
finding stories and characters, to structuring scripts and filming, editing,
through to delivery, titles and getting people to watch.